THE SOCIAL PHILOSOPHY OF ADAM SMITH

ARCHIVES INTERNATIONALES D'HISTOIRE DES IDEES

INTERNATIONAL ARCHIVES OF THE HISTORY OF IDEAS

Series minor

8

J. RALPH LINDGREN

THE SOCIAL PHILOSOPHY OF ADAM SMITH

THE SOCIAL PHILOSOPHY
OF ADAM SMITH

by

J. RALPH LINDGREN

MARTINUS NIJHOFF / THE HAGUE / 1973

PRINTED IN THE NETHERLANDS

For Shirley, Thomas, Michael, David,
Timothy and Kathryn

TABLE OF CONTENTS

Preface   IX

Chronology   XV

Table of Abbreviations   XVI

   I. INQUIRY   1

  II. MORAL JUDGMENT   20

 III. PSYCHOLOGY   39

 IV. GOVERNMENT   60

  V. COMMERCE   84

 VI. COMMERCIAL POLICY   110

VII. RELIGION   133

Works Cited   153

Index   159

PREFACE

Adam Smith was one of the most important seminal social philosophers of modern times. Although his great masterpiece – the *Wealth of Nations* – is most frequently associated with the field of economics, it has exercised a profound and abiding influence not only in that but in all areas of social theory and practice as well. In view of this it is not a little puzzling that after nearly two centuries there does not exist a single reliable account of the full range of his social philosophy.

The circumstances which have contributed to this void in the literature are easily identified. All who are at all familiar with Smith's life and writings recognize that he was a philosopher by profession and that all his writings were conceived and executed as works of philosophy. During his lifetime his work was viewed in that perspective. At about the time of his death in 1790, however, Smith's work was eclipsed in the field of philosophy by Hume and Reid in Great Britain and Kant on the continent. Thereafter the interpretation of his writings was taken up by those who were profoundly interested in only one aspect of his work, viz., his political economy. In the process of explicating that feature of his thought the social philosophy upon which his political economy was based and of which it was but one application was at first ignored and then represented as rather simplistic. His supposed advocacy of " 'bourgeois economics,' that is the economics of those economists who look with favour on working and trading and investing for personal gain" (Cannan 1926, p. 129) is generally believed to have derived from a perspective which is strongly reminiscent of the one so eloquently expressed by Alexander Pope in his *Essay on Man*. Smith is said not only to have believed that "whatever in the long run is, is right" (Campbell 1971, p. 53), but to have based his entire *Wealth of Nations* on another of Pope's theses.

Thus God and Nature linked the gen'ral frame, and bade Self-love and Social be the same.

Over the past half-century these and other popular caricatures of Smith's views have been shown to be distortions of the historical record (see, for example, Viner 1927; Ginzberg 1934; Bittermann 1940). Recently William Grampp found existing commentaries to be so unreliable that he simply ignored them: "There is not space enough, nor have I the inclination to contend with [Smith's] major critics. . . . I do wish to make it clear that my objection to the commentaries is that they are mistaken" (1965, vol. II, p. 4). This was certainly an over-reaction. It has been largely due to the work of a few careful scholars that we now know how misleading the popular image of Smith's social philosophy is.

Before proceeding it is essential to recognize if not understand how and why so much distortion has crept into this particular chapter of intellectual history. Unless the repeated strategic mistakes of previous students of Smith are recognized they are apt to be repeated. Fortunately these can be identified without launching into an essay on the methodology of historical research in the field of philosophy. The principal obstacles to achieving a reliable understanding of Smith's social philosophy have been clear for some time. On the one hand, his aims have typically been neglected.

Adam Smith undoubtedly started with the purpose of giving to the world a complete social philosophy. He accomplished the greater part of his design, and yet is seldom remembered except for his economical work and only for part of that. (Bonar 1893, p. 149)

The tendency of Smith's commentators to ignore or at least neglect his overall objectives and instead to be satisfied with piecemeal interpretations may be explained in a variety of ways. Certainly one explanation is the difficulty of the task. In this connection Alexander Gray was certainly right to observe that "Adam Smith is difficult to apprehend in his totality for the perverse reason that he is in parts so regrettably well known" (1931, pp. 123-4). This, however, does not explain why his aims are neglected even when interpreting those parts of his work which are well known to every schoolboy.

On the other hand Smith's interpreters frequently proceed by accommodating his views to their interests, categories and paradigms. In this connection V. W. Bladen complained of "The self-centered expectation that other economists must be striving to answer the question we ask: When the answer fails to satisfy we treat it as one more error on the part of our predecessors . . ." (1960, p. 625). What Bladen does not seem to appreciate is that this tendency to interpret the expressed views of an ancestor by attempting to show how those views fit into our perspectives, answer our questions, further our objectives, has its roots in the habit of what Thomas Kuhn calls "normal science" and not in some "self-centered" eccentricity. Kuhn observed that those who are convinced that they have the right answers or at least are asking the right questions and are on the right track to those answers come to perceive the earlier classics in their field "as leading in a straight line to the discipline's present perspective" (1962, p. 166). This tendency is evident as early as Aristotle and as recently as Schumpeter. This, of course, does not vindicate such practices as any less parochial than Bladen suggested. Still, such scientists ought not to be faulted because they organized their scientific research in strict compliance with current canons of scientific practice. Their mistake lies in presuming that the canons currently appropriate to the practice of scientific research are likewise the canons appropriate to the practice of historical research into earlier work in the same field. Wesley Mitchell recognized this and suggested that the history of economic theory "may fairly be said to be outside the field of economics, in the field of intellectual history" (1967, vol. I, p. 7). Be that as it may, it seems clear that the only reliable bases for interpreting the writings of any man, especially a philosopher, are his own interests, categories, and paradigms.

My primary purpose in this volume is to present a more reliable and comprehensive account of the social philosophy of Adam Smith than is presently available. In pursuing this objective every effort is made to avoid the difficulties experienced by previous students of Smith by undertaking the interpretation of his thought from his own perspective. A sympathetic understanding of the views of a Scottish social philosopher whose active years spanned the third quarter of the eighteenth century, before western civilization had been transformed by the combined impact of the American, French, and Industrial revolutions, is not as easily attained as is commonly believed. In undertaking this project I have tried to preserve the balance and doctrinal dependencies which Smith espoused. Since the most reliable evidence of what Smith thought is what he said and especially what he wrote and published or permitted to be published under his own name, I have concentrated my efforts on his *Essays on Philosophical Subjects, Theory of Moral Sentiments,* "Considerations Concerning the First Formation of Languages" and *Wealth of Nations.* Lesser attention is given to his two sets of "lectures" and biographical data is used sparingly. Throughout I have tried to take full advantage of the sound contributions of previous students of Smith while at the same time avoiding those procedures which have proven to be sources of distortion. Finally, all speculation as to alleged influences on or by Smith as well as his rightful place in the history of philosophy, economics, sociology, etc. is avoided. Insofar as my findings are valid these relationships appear to be in need of thorough reconsideration.

Throughout this volume I have insisted that we accommodate our interpretation of Smith's work to his interests, methods and objectives. I know of no alternative seeing that our aim is to understand him. Still, this approach places severe strain upon the imagination of readers – especially those who are in the habit of regarding his work as an episode in the development of a currently fashionable scientific theory or political attitude. Several stylistic devices have been employed in order to ease this burden. Hopefully these will also minimize the occasions of misunderstanding to which this study is susceptible because its sympathetic approach to Smith's writings differs so sharply from the one we have grown accustomed to expect.

First, I have treated what I take to be the essential core of any adequate account of Smith's social philosophy in six largely independent units each, with the exception of chapters five and six, in a separate chapter. In this way I hope to gradually introduce the reader who is acquainted with only one aspect of Smith's work to the full range of his thought. The integrity of his total philosophical position as well as the final cogency of each of its aspects will become apparent by following out the cross-references within the text of each chapter. This is especially important in the case of chapters five and six which in many ways form the climax of this study.

Second, I have, wherever considerations of accuracy permit, approached each unit within the context of the present state of the literature. In this way I have tried to maintain maximum continuity with the work of previous Smithian commentators. It was possible to follow this approach in every case except that of chapters five and six. There I preferred, for reasons already indicated, to approach the *Wealth of Nations* from within the context of Smith's own moral philosophy and according to his own method of inquiry. To have done otherwise would have resulted in devoting an unacceptably extended portion of those chapters to purely academic polemics. Those interested in my views on the major alternatives to my interpretation will not find them difficult to locate in the text and footnotes of those chapters.

Third, I have suggested contemporary theorists whose work in certain respects parallel positions I attribute to Smith. In doing so I do not mean either to imply an "influence" or to defend the positions cited, but only to provide an additional vantage point from which readers who are acquainted with contemporary theorists might be better able to understand Smith. In addition these references may tend to allay the suspicions of some that by denying that Smith stood foursquare behind the liberalism of John Stuart Mill I have in effect shown that his views are for that reason obsolete. Fourth, I have avoided issuing critical evaluations of Smith's philosophy either in whole or in part. Until there is general agreement on something approaching a definitive account of Smith's social philosophy, such exercises are premature and not a little distracting.

Finally, I have made every effort to be concise. In this way I hope to entice a wide range of readers to consider the central core of Smith's social philosophy. In this connection it should be observed that this study does not pretend to exhaust all dimensions of Smith's work. It stops short of treating his theories of economic growth and of history. These and other topics were omitted because they are not, on my reading of Smith, part of the central core of his social philosophy. These judgments are of course subject to debate. In an important sense this study constitutes an invitation to such debates provided they are conducted with the intention of understanding Smith's thought on the basis of sound textual evidence rather than ideological exercises intent upon enlisting Smith's support in someone else's cause.

This is a study in the history of social thought, but like all such studies its value is not restricted to historians. Notwithstanding the aversion of some to reading old books and books about long dead authors, it is a matter of importance if not urgency that we understand our intellectual forebears, especially those who have influenced the course of our own history. The reasons for this being the case are many. Two of these deserve explicit mention here. One was proclaimed by John Maynard Keynes. "A study of the history of opinion is a necessary preliminary to the emancipation of the mind" (1926, p. 16). The other was set down by Sheldon Wolin. "An historical perspective is more effective than any other in exposing the nature of our present predicaments; if it is not the source of political wisdom, it is at least the precondition" (1960, p. v).

A more accurate and complete understanding of Smith's social philosophy is valuable not only to historians of social thought but also to social theorists as well – whether their fields are philosophy, economics, sociology, anthropology, political science or psychology – for both of the reasons mentioned above. It will serve the emancipating function because, as will become apparent in the course of this study, Smith dealt with many of the same problems which vex and many of the same issues which divide contemporary social theorists. While Smith's solutions may not be directly applicable to our own times, serious social theorists can certainly attain a firmer grasp of these problems and issues by appreciating how and why Smith resolved them as he did. At the very least those whose disciplines are fast becoming dominated by mathematical models and game theory will find Smith's approach refreshing.

A better understanding of Smith's social philosophy also illuminates what Wolin called "our present predicaments" in a variety of ways. I will mention only one here, the one which might otherwise escape notice. Smith set an example which few social theorists since Marx have followed. He asked what if any effect the commercial practices of his day had upon the tone and quality of the moral life of his community. He found that they had a corrupting influence upon the morals of even the common people. Having recognized that, Smith went to enormous lengths to achieve a reliable understanding of those practices, mounted a stinging philosophical critique of the then orthodox theory which was accepted as justifying those practices, developed a concrete and feasible organizational strategy for preserving the integrity of the moral community without substantial sacrifice of economic efficiency and took one monumental step in the direction of persuading those in power to support that strategy. The accuracy of this description will be established in the course of this study. My point here is that an important part of our present predicament is the glaring deficiency in the number of social theorists committed to following Smith's example. This line of inquiry is ordinarily avoided because it is associated exclusively with the memory of Karl Marx. But one need not subscribe to Marxism to engage in a critique of political economy. Smith engaged in precisely that but did so from within a tradition and consistently with moral values which most men find congenial. This realization may itself be sufficient to counter-act the reticence of social theorists and enable us to initiate what is plainly needed – a careful, informed, cooperative, sustained, multi-disciplinary critique of the commercial practices of our own society.

The primary objective of this study is to present a more reliable, sympathetic and complete account of the social philosophy of Adam Smith than is presently available. It is on that basis that this study should be judged. Its subsidiary but by no means unimportant objective is to call attention to the character and quality of his work in the hope that the vision of his genius will inspire us to rise to the enormous challenge of the advanced industrial society of our day as well as and perhaps better than he rose to the challenge of the commercial society of his age.

Finally, I should like to express my appreciation to the National Science Foundation whose generous financial support (Grant Number

GS-27371) enabled me to gain sufficient leisure to finish this manuscript and to the editors of the University of Chicago Press for permission to reproduce in somewhat altered form the article which is the basis of Chapter One. ("Adam Smith's Theory of Inquiry," *The Journal of Political Economy*, vol. 77, no. 6, Nov./Dec., 1969, pp. 897-915). I should also like to acknowledge my indebtedness to the present and past curators of Harvard University's Kress Library of Business and Economics under whose care the Vanderblue Collection of Smithiana has flourished and with whose kind permission I have had the opportunity of benefiting from the work of so many previous students of Adam Smith.

I regret that Samuel Hollander's *The Economics of Adam Smith*, (Toronto: Univ. of Toronto Press, 1973) arrived too late for inclusion in this study. I would have welcomed the opportunity of both profiting from certain of his findings and of showing the relevance of this study for his work.

CHRONOLOGY OF THE LIFE AND WRITINGS OF ADAM SMITH

April or May 1723	– Born, Kirkcaldy, Scotland
1737-40	– Student of Hutcheson, University of Glasgow
1740-46	– Snell Exhibitioner, Oxford University
1748-49	– Lectured on Rhetoric and Belles Lettres, University of Edinburgh
1751-52	– Professor of Logic, University of Glasgow
1751-64	– Professor of Moral Philosophy, University of Glasgow
1755	– Two anonymous articles in *Edinburgh Review*
1759	– *Theory of Moral Sentiments*
1760-62	– Dean of Faculty
1761	– "Considerations Concerning the First Formation of Languages"
1762-64	– Vice Rector of University
1764-66	– Tour of France as tutor to the Duke of Buccleugh
1766-76	– Solitary work at Kirkcaldy
March 9, 1776	– *Wealth of Nations*
November, 1776	– Eulogy to David Hume
1778-90	– Commissioner of Customs, Edinburgh
July 17, 1790	– Died, buried Cannongate Churchyard
1795	– *Essays on Philosophical Subjects* – composed prior to 1759.

TABLE OF ABBREVIATIONS

"Letter"   "A Letter to the Authors of the Edinburgh Review," in *The Early Writings of Adam Smith*, J. R. Lindgren, Editor. New York: Kelley, 1966.

"Astron."   "The Principles Which Lead And Direct Philosophical Enquiries: Illustrated by the History of Astronomy," in *Ibid*.

"Physics"   "The Principles ... : Illustrated by the History of the Ancient Physics," in *Ibid*.

"Logics"   "The Principles ... : Illustrated by the History of the Ancient Logics and Metaphysics," in *Ibid*.

"Imit. Arts"   "Of the Nature of that Imitation Which Takes Place in What Are Called the Imitative Arts," in *Ibid*.

"Ext. Senses"   "Of the External Senses," in *Ibid*.

"Lang."   "Considerations Concerning the First Formation of Languages and the Different Genius of Original and Compounded Languages," in *Ibid*.

MS   *The Theory of Moral Sentiments*. New York: Kelley, 1966. (Reprint of Bohn Library Edition).

WN   *An Inquiry into the Nature and Causes of the Wealth of Nations*. E. Cannan, Editor. New York: Modern Library, 1937.

LJ   *Lectures on Justice, Police, Revenue and Arms*. E. Cannan, Editor. Oxford: Clarendon, 1896.

LR   *Lectures on Rhetoric and Belles Lettres*. J. M. Lothian, Editor. London: Nelson, 1963.

CHAPTER I

INQUIRY

The work of Adam Smith is generally regarded as a clear example of the Enlightenment practice of adapting beliefs in natural law, benevolent Providence and Newtonian mechanics to the study of society. Likewise, originality and humanitarian concern are seldom among the qualities associated with his memory. The *Wealth of Nations* is held in high regard, even as a milestone in the history of thought, mainly because it managed to systematize an unwieldy mass of economic opinion according to those popular beliefs of Smith's day. In point of method, his work is typically viewed as wholly eclectic. Joseph Schumpeter expressed this view forcefully: ". . . [T]he fact is that the *Wealth of Nations* does not contain a single analytic idea, principle, or method that was entirely new in 1776" (1954, p. 184).

This general estimate of the nature and value of Smith's work was first expressed by Cliffe Leslie, Leslie Stephen and Wilhelm Hasbach and is still widely allowed today. Alexander Gray's statement of this view is representative: "Herein lies the *a priori* element in Adam Smith; there is a natural order, appointed by a wise Providence in which self-interest will supply the necessary drive to make the machine go, and will also act to produce equilibrium between contending forces" (1931, p. 125).[1] The plausibility of this interpretation derives principally from certain of Smith's more general remarks on method. It is, for example, the same as the procedure which he attributed to early theistic philosophers ("Physics," pp. 117-18).

Although still very much the fashion this interpretation of Smith's method has not gone unchallenged. Whenever serious attempt has been made to verify its accuracy significant difficulties have arisen. Jacob Viner (1927) found that this method was not employed in the *Wealth of Nations*. He went on to conclude that while beliefs in natural law and benevolent Providence did play an important part in the *Moral Senti-*

---

[1] The most extreme proponent of this view (Cropsey 1957) rightly contended that it reduces in its essentials to the mechanistic rationalism of Thomas Hobbes.

ments they were abandoned in the later work. The lesson gathered by others from Viner's essay was that comparative studies of the two works raise more problems than they solve and so ought in prudence to be avoided.

Once the study of Smith's method was restricted to the *Wealth of Nations* it fell into neglect. Although Viner's implicit caveat is still generally honored, there has arisen an undercurrent of discontent. Henry Bittermann (1940) working in Smith's early writings and *Moral Sentiments*, argued at length against Viner's conclusion. Not only was the *Wealth of Nations* not predicated on beliefs in natural law and benevolent Providence, but neither was the *Moral Sentiments*. Smith employed the same method in both of these works, viz., that of Newtonian mechanics. This opened the door once again to comparative studies of Smith's writings. A few recent studies have attempted to develop a more accurate interpretation of Smith's method (Taylor 1960; Becker 1961; Thompson 1965; Campbell 1971). These proposed to show how a careful analysis of Smith's early work throws considerable light on the *Moral Sentiments* and the *Wealth of Nations*. The results of these researches, while suggestive, are neither entirely clear nor convincing.[2]

Few would dispute the contention that an accurate grasp of Smith's method of inquiry is essential to an adequate understanding of his principal doctrines. The dominant view is that Smith was basically eclectic; that he employed the model of mechanics in moral as well as natural philosophy and that his confidence in this procedure was founded upon his belief in natural law and benevolent Providence. The poor showing of this interpretation when compared to Smith's practice suggests that it may be basically misleading.

A complete statement of Smith's method would take his own theory of inquiry as its point of departure and terminate in detailed discussions of his practice in the *Moral Sentiments* and the *Wealth of Nations*. Only in this way can bias be avoided and strict verification provided. The purpose of this chapter is more limited in scope. It proposes to develop a trustworthy and accurate statement of Smith's theory of inquiry. The current view of Smith's method will be clarified, criticized and revised.

---

[2] The most extensive of these (Campbell 1971) was predicated upon the remarkable hypothesis that not only the *Wealth of Nations* and the *Lectures on Justice*, but also the *Moral Sentiments* were "works of science rather than of philosophy" (p. 19). Indeed, they were supposedly intended by Smith to conform to the principal canons of Popper's hypothetico-deductive model (p. 32). Curiously, Campbell's analysis led him to recognize that Smith's performance did not measure up to those standards (p. 236). Ordinarily such discoveries are viewed as disconfirmatory of interpretative hypotheses.

In the process a number of specific points will be argued. Smith did not entertain realistic epistemological views, but one more accurately described as conventionalistic; he adopted language not mechanics as the model of inquiry; and drew a fundamental distinction between the methods of inquiry in natural and moral philosophy.

I

Early in his discussion of inquiry Smith indicated that it is occasioned by wonder and aims at diminishing if not eliminating wonder ("Astron.," pp. 45, 50). This statement however profound is quite ambiguous. What did Smith mean by "wonder?" Any interpretation of Smith's theory of inquiry turns on the answer to this question.

Men attempt to anticipate the future in order to prepare themselves emotionally for whatever it brings, thereby maintaining a degree of calm and tranquility. When an object excites an emotion for which one is not prepared, it occasions that sharp change in disposition known as surprise ("Astron.," p. 33). That same object which excites surprise also occasions wonder. Men prepare themselves for the future by constructing an image of the object which is anticipated and exciting thereby that passion which the object is expected to excite. They are able to forecast which object is apt to occur by accustoming themselves to certain arrangements of objects and sequences of events. This complex of arrangements and sequences serves to guide the imagination in constructing the image of the expected object. I shall call this complex one's *outlook*.

When an object confronts us in other than its expected context or order, that object excites not only the shock of surprise, but also raises doubt as to the adequacy of our outlook. "We start and are surprised at seeing it there, and then wonder how it came there" ("Astron.," p. 39). The object constitutes a challenge to somehow accommodate our outlook and what appears to be an exception. At first we attempt to locate the object among our accustomed assortments or within established sequences ("Astron.," pp. 37-8, 41). Failing this we may be tempted to dismiss it as a result of chance ("Astron.," p. 38). If these measures fail to relieve the situation, pathological symptoms will begin to appear unless the outlook itself is revised. Such a revision is accomplished by forging new assortments of objects or new links between events. To the extent that this effort is successful, confidence that our outlook will enable us to face the future with calm and tranquility is reestablished and wonder is diminished if not eliminated.

This analysis seems to have suggested to Becker and Campbell that wonder is a species of anxiety and that inquiry is a coping device the aim of which is to so recast one's outlook as to avoid the shock of surprise.[3] This view of inquiry appears to be confirmed by Smith's description of philosophy.

> Philosophy is the science of the connecting principles of nature ... Philosophy, by representing the invisible chains which bind together all these disjointed objects, endeavours to introduce order into this chaos of jarring and discordant appearances, to allay this tumult of the imagination, and to restore it, when it surveys the great revolutions of the universe, to that tone of tranquility and composure which is both most agreeable in itself, and most suitable to its nature. Philosophy, therefore, may be regarded as one of those arts which address themselves to the imagination ... ("Astron.," p. 45)

Smith's illustrations drawn from the history of astronomy reinforce the plausibility of this interpretation of wonder and inquiry. Over the centuries various theories of the heavens have gained in popularity and then declined according as they were more or less comprehensive, coherent and familiar.[4] A received outlook is considered to be in need of revision when, confronted by a genuinely new object or singular event, it is found to lack comprehensiveness.[5] Alternative outlooks which comprehend the full range of objects and events of interest are compared in terms of both

---

[3] "He sees the terminus of successful inquiry in the conquest of wonder and surprise occasioned by the unexplained ..." (Becker 1961, p. 14). "The function of an explanation is to restore the imagination to its usual smooth and tranquil state" (Campbell 1971, p. 33).

[4] "... [T]he basic test of a theory is whether or not it connects as large as possible a number of observed events in the simplest and most familiar way" (Campbell 1971, p. 39). Simplicity was not one of the final tests of an outlook for Smith. Indeed he was highly critical of "men of system" who, like Epicurus, indulged "the propensity to account for all appearances from as few principles as possible" (MS, p. 438).

[5] On the one hand, we find that new objects and singular events initiated revision of received outlooks. The more magnificent irregularities of the heavens excited the wonder of primitive men ("Astron.," p. 47); the lesser irregularities came to the attention of the more observant (p. 49); the erratic movement of the planets perplexed astronomers from earliest times (p. 54) through Copernicus (p. 71) to Kepler who finally rendered those movements regular (pp. 90-91); the irregularity of the distances of the planets from the Sun excited Kepler's wonder (p. 91); Galileo's discovery that a ball dropped from the mast of a moving ship falls to the base of the mast had a considerable impact on the climate of opinion as did his telescopic observations of the satellites of Jupiter, the phases shown by Venus and Mercury and the "mountains and seas" on the moon (pp. 84-5). On the other hand we find that confirmation of predictions based upon an outlook regularly enhanced its acceptance – as happened with the predictions of Hipparchus (pp. 64-5), Rheinholdus (pp. 76-7), Cassini (pp. 91-2), and Newton (pp. 101-7) – and the failure of such confirmation regularly occasioned revision – which accounts in part for the final decline of the Ptolemic (pp. 69-70) and Cartesian systems (p. 99) and also the resistance to the Copernician view, – which Smith termed "the prejudice of the senses." (pp. 75-81)

the degree of coherence they introduce into appearances and the extent to which the patterns of association they employ are familiar both to astronomers and the general public.[6]

Wonder, then, is currently understood as a type of anxiety or tension which results from the recognition that one's outlook is not a reliable basis for preparing oneself emotionally for the future. This anxiety or tension is reduced when, by recasting one's outlook to take account of what has proved recalcitrant from an earlier perspective, confidence is restored in one's ability to forecast the future and so to avoid the shock of surprise. That confidence is restored, according to the current interpretation, when by the process of inquiry "the real claims which Nature makes use of to bind together her operations" ("Astron.," p. 108) are recognized. Differing claims about the character of these "real chains" are evaluated according to the criteria of comprehensiveness, coherence and familiarity. According to this interpretation Smith held that the function of philosophical inquiry was to enable men to confidently forecast the future by providing them with an outlook the rules of which are believed to correspond more or less exactly with the causal laws which in fact govern the occurrence of objects and events.

Although possessed of initial plausibility this account of Smith's notions of wonder and inquiry is ultimately misleading. This becomes evident when his view of the factors which govern the formulation of any outlook is taken into account. It has appeared to many that Smith understood the process of formulating an outlook to take either of two forms. On the one hand, there is classification of objects according to the resemblance they are observed to bear to one another. On the other, is the connection of events which are observed to be constantly conjoined in time. This reading led many to the conclusion that Smith adopted a fundamentally realistic epistemology, that is, the belief that objects and events are related independently of our knowledge by causal laws or "real chains" and that men can recognize these relations or at least

_____

[6] Systems of the heavens are often appraised in terms of coherence – the system of concentric spheres ("Astron.," pp. 57-8) and that of Ptolemy (pp. 69-70) were finally given up because they lacked coherence: Eudoxus (p. 57). Copernicus (p. 71) and Kepler criticized the received systems because they lacked in regularity. Familiarity became a particularly difficult condition to satisfy once the mathematicians had distinguished between the real and the apparent motions of the heavenly bodies (p. 59) and had proceeded to neglect the latter (p. 69). The equalizing circle was invented to satisfy this demand (pp. 60-61) as was Kepler's immaterial virtue (p. 93), but to no avail. It was only when Newton suggested that gravity (which is clearly familiar) produces the motions which describe the courses of the heavenly bodies at the velocities and distances suggested by Kepler that a satisfactory alternative to ancient superstition was at last developed (p. 100).

confirm the correspondence of their hypotheses to them. None of these estimates are accurate.

When two objects, however unlike, have often been observed to follow each other, and have constantly presented themselves to the senses in that order, they come to be so connected in the fancy, that the idea of the one seems, of its own accord, to call up and introduce that of the other. ("Astron.," p. 39; also see "Astron.," p. 36 and "Lang.," pp. 227-34)

The primary feature of observation as Smith understood it is not recognition but recollection. When one observes that two objects resemble one another or that two events are constantly conjoined in time, what he observes is that the one excites or "calls up" the image of the other. The rules according to which forecasts are developed, when those rules are reduced to statements, describe the ways in which the images of these objects and events are already associated "in the fancy." Accordingly, observation presupposes that an outlook is already established. Observational procedures, therefore, are not formative of an outlook but merely apply one which is already established.

The way in which an outlook is formulated depends on how these associations come about. The suggestion that many of these result from habit and custom is not a particularly novel one. Smith's interpreters however have not acknowledged the extent to which he held that human knowledge is governed by convention.[7] Smith insisted that very few of the distinctions which men draw between objects and events may reasonably be regarded as corresponding to the way in which the extramental is in fact divided. Only the distinctions between one's own self and something else, between the solid parts of an external object and between the sentient parts of one's own body are real and not merely conventional distinctions. Beyond these, however, no such claim is warranted ("Ext. Senses," pp. 185-8, 191, 197).

Two of the consequences of this predominantly conventionalist epistemological position are of interest here. First, the way in which things and people are or may be related to one another, independently of our conventional schemes, does not fall within the range of human knowledge. Smith's insistence on this is consistently borne out, especially in his essay on the history of astronomy.[8] Accordingly, the laws which

---

[7] Although Thompson acknowledged this briefly (1965, p. 222), Becker expressed the far more common conviction that Smith espoused empirical realism (1961, pp. 16-17) as did Bittermann, (1940, pp. 499-502) and Campbell (1971, pp. 41-5).

[8] See his remarks on the equalizing circles ("Astron.," p. 61); systems as imaginary machines, (p. 66); Kepler's hypothesis when confirmed by the observations of Cassini, (p. 92); and the concluding remarks of the essay regarding the system of Newton, (p. 108).

govern events in the extra-mental order – if indeed there are any – can never be known by men [9] nor can any hypothesis purporting to represent that order ever be verified.[10]

Second, the initiation of inquiry, i.e., the attempt to revise a received outlook, presupposes that the way in which ideas are associated is recognized as a product of custom or convention and so is a fit subject for possible revision. Campbell correctly observed that Smith did not use the word "natural" and its variants with notable consistency (1971, pp. 236-7). Nevertheless, he ordinarily referred to judgments, actions and patterns of association as "natural" where these resulted from habits which men did not explicitly recognize as such. This lack of appreciation on the part of most men of the conventional character of the greater part of their knowledge deprives them of the awareness that their outlooks and so their practices can by revised. So long as anyone regards the order of appearances to be by "nature" in the sense that their order is given in experience as fixed and beyond his control, he will not be able to entertain the suggestion of revising his outlook. Thus, the custombound artisan maintained: "It is their nature . . . to follow one another in that order, and accordingly they always do" ("Astron.," p. 44). The philosophical inquirer, by contrast, has a more discerning eye. Knowing that his habitual perspective is merely a product of custom and convention, the prospect of revising it is always a live possibility to him.

II

Reconsideration of the received interpretation of Smith's theory of inquiry leads to the discovery that it has been based upon a mistaken interpretation of the nature of wonder. Wonder is excited by new and

---

[9] "The harmony and beneficence to be perceived in the matter-of-fact processes of nature are the results of the designs and intervention of a benevolent God" (Viner 1927, p. 202). Such an interpretation, as Bittermann contended, is in direct although by no means obvious violation of Smith's epistemological position. It is likely that Smith entertained a belief in the existence of a benevolent deity, but that belief was not and could not have been, based as Campbell contended (1971, pp. 60-2, 230-3) on observation of the order, harmony and beneficent tendency of extra-mental events whether external or internal to man.

[10] ". . . [T]o gain acceptance, such hypotheses *not only* must be verified or be successful in that sense *but also* must be subjectively satisfying to the human mind" (Taylor 1960, p. 51; also see Campbell 1971, pp. 41-5). As will be shown shortly, the confirmation of predictions evident in the essay on the history of astronomy does not serve to verify the claim that an hypothesis represents the order of extra-mental events. It is, on the contrary, merely one of the procedures required to render a hypothesis, in Taylor's words, subjectively satisfying.

singular objects or events not because they were unforeseen or even un-foreseeable, but because they are unusual.

We wonder at all extraordinary and uncommon objects, at all the rarer phaeno-mena of nature, of meteors, comets, eclipses, at singular plants and animals, and at every thing, in short, with which we have before been either little or not at all acquainted; and we still wonder, though forewarned of what we are to see. ("As-tron.," p. 30)

Frequently men are moved to philosophical inquiry because they feel very insecure when confronted by an unforeseen object or event. Still, according to Smith, wonder is evoked by unusual objects or events "though forewarned of what we are to see." Thus, it may be that Smith experienced wonder when the comets appeared in 1758 as had been previously predicted ("Astron.," p. 106). Such objects are wondrous in spite of our ability to forcast their occurrence. The new and singular seem to occasion inquiry not so much because they raise doubts about the reliability of one's forecasting models as because they raise doubts about one's ability to order and harmonize appearances. The unusual excites inquiry because it is regarded as humiliating.

If this suggestion is correct, inquiry is an effort to introduce order and harmony into appearances and to do so in such a way as to confirm one's own capabilities for doing so. This does appear to have been Smith's view. Inquiry does strive "to render the theatre of nature a more co-herent, and therefore a more magnificent spectacle, than otherwise it would have appeared to be" ("Astron.," pp. 45-6). Indeed, philosophy

... never triumphs so much, as when, in order to connect together a few, in themselves, perhaps, inconsiderable objects, she has, if I may say so, created another constitution of things, more natural indeed, and such as the imagina-tion can more easily attend to, but more new, more contrary to common opinion and expectation, than any of these appearances themselves. ("Astron.," pp. 75-6)

The satisfaction which attends the successful execution of inquiry ap-pears to be a type of delight in accomplishment, a celebration of that independence and a renewal of that self-confidence which, as much as leisure and the establishment of civil government, separates civilized man from his cowardly and superstitious ancestors ("Astron.," pp. 49-50). Those who execute inquiry with exceptional "acuteness and compre-hensiveness" are applauded because their accounts are themselves sources of wonder and admiration (MS, p. 20). Smith was interested in inquiry generally and astronomy in particular as one of the humanities. What attracted him to these studies was the fact that what we call science represents with exceptional clarity the creative ingenuity of men. That same pleasure occurs similarly in what Smith called the imitative arts.

That pleasure is founded altogether upon our wonder at seeing an object of one kind represent so well an object of a very different kind, and upon our admiration of the art which surmounts so happily that disparity which Nature had established between them. ("Imit. Arts," p. 146)

This similarity suggests that the nature of inquiry lies not so much in its being "the science of the connecting principles of nature," as "one of those arts which address themselves to the imagination" ("Astron.," p. 45).

The arts address themselves to the production of beautiful objects, of objects which excite the sentiment of admiration ("Astron.," p. 30). Although every beautiful object involves imitation, not every sort of imitation excites admiration. Mere duplication, for example, the most exact imitation, is not productive of beauty. Those productions of art which seem to be most capable of exciting our admiration are the ones which incorporate an element of tension within the correspondence presented.

But though a production of art seldom derives any merit from its resemblance to another object of the same kind, it frequently derives a great deal from its resemblance to an object of a different kind, whether that object be a production of art or of nature. ("Imit. Arts," p. 138)

Painting, for example, produces a two-dimensional object which resembles another in three dimensions. Smith emphasized, however, that admiration is intensified as the disparity between the imitating and the imitated objects increases, provided only that they "should resemble at least so far, that the one should always readily suggest the other" ("Imit. Arts," p. 159).

The satisfaction excited by such objects is composed of wonder at seeing an object of one kind represent another of a very different sort, and of admiration of the genius of the artist who has succeeded in surmounting that disparity. This, as was mentioned above, is the same pleasure which attends the successful execution of inquiry in which much the same feat is performed in imagination. Smith, however, did not reduce inquiry to imaginary portraiture. Although both the experience of objects of art and that of harmonious natural phenomena evoke wonder and admiration, there is one important difference.

The nobler works of Statuary and Painting appear to us a sort of wonderful phaenomena, differing in this respect from the wonderful phaenomena of Nature, that they carry, as it were, their own explication along with them, and demonstrate, even to the eye, the way and manner in which they are produced. ("Imit. Arts," p. 146)

Admirable objects of art openly display the technique employed to produce the resemblance, whereas those of nature do not reveal to the observer "how this wonderful effect is produced." The "theatre of nature" must be rendered an admirable spectacle by inquiry into the ways in which these appearances have come to be associated with one another.

This analysis suggests a revised account of the nature of inquiry. Inquiry aims to recast our outlook so as to render the spectacle of nature more admirable. According to this definition an adequate outlook must not only meet the standards of comprehensiveness, coherence and familiarity, but also that of beauty. Taken together these four may be regarded as the necessary and sufficient conditions of the successful completion of inquiry in natural philosophy. In order to show how these conditions are satisfied by such inquiry we need to appreciate how they are satisfied by the arts.

The arts have to do with the production of beautiful objects, objects which excite admiration. Apparently each does this in approximately the same way. The parts of the artifact are arranged according to certain rules. In painting areas of color are ordered according to rules of perspective ("Ext. Senses," p. 203), a dance is a succession of gestures regulated by time and measure, a tune is a sequence of sounds also ordered according to time and measure ("Imit. Arts," p. 149). It is by virtue of these rules of composition that the artifact achieves that correspondence with the imitated object which excites admiration.

There are, of course, many differences between the various arts. One of these differences is of particular importance to the discussion of the method of inquiry. The imitative arts, as opposed to instrumental music for example ("Imit. Arts," pp. 159-60, 164), excite admiration only indirectly through the mediation of imagination. A painting directly suggests to the observer the image of an object which is quite distinct from itself. This image is the imitated object, the meaning or the expression of the painting. The observer, by an act of sympathy, presents this image to his own passions and excites thereby the feelings which he takes to be the same sort of sentiment as the artist felt when he composed the painting ("Imit. Arts," p. 161). In the case of the imitative arts the correspondence which excites admiration holds between these three terms, viz., the artifact, the image and the sympathetic sentiment.

Smith listed inquiry among those arts which address the imagination – as one of the imitative arts. Inquiry is an effort to invent a rule of composition according to which an idea of one object is made to correspond with an image which will, by an act of sympathy, dispose the observer to the experience of quite a different object. It is in this way that men anticipate the future. Considered in point of logical procedure, inquiry appears to be an attempt to supply the missing premise of an enthymeme.[11] Logical analysis, however, does not seem to afford a very penetrating approach to Smith's theory of inquiry. One which is more in keeping with his own preferences is available through a consideration of language (*MS*, p. 495; Stewart 1858, pp. 11, 37).

In that inquiry is a species of the imitative arts, its procedure may be regarded as fundamentally the same as that of these arts.[12] Turning to the technique of the imitative arts, language is again found to be of central importance. The thesis which will be defended here is that Smith regarded language as the prototype of the imitative arts and so also of inquiry.

That language is an imitative art is clear. Just as a painting suggests to the spectator the image of an object quite different from the two-dimensional patchwork of colors, so also does a linguistic utterance suggest to the hearer the image of an object quite different from the complex of sound. That language is the prototype of the imitative arts is a more difficult point to establish. To do so it is necessary to show first that all the imitative arts are engaged in the formation of systems of signs and second, that these are systems of conventional signs, the paradigm of which is language.

A review of all that has been discussed up to this point will convince even the most cautious reader that the sign-signified relation has been under consideration in one form or another all along and so that the arts and inquiry as well are engaged in the formation of systems of signs. Whether speaking of resemblance, correspondence or meaning, whether showing how one maintains his tranquil disposition by foreseeing what the future is apt to bring or the ways images come to be associated with one another or discussing the expression of painting, Smith was everywhere employing variants of the sign-signified relation.

As was shown above, Smith was committed to a fundamentally conventionalistic epistemological position. All associations which are mediated through imagination are governed by habit and custom. We must

[11] Thompson proposed that the search for supposed connecting links was in fact a search for "fruitful analogies" (1965, p. 233). This does not seem to have been Smith's intention. Analogies have four terms whereas Smith's connecting links were third terms. These links function in much the same way as do middle terms in standard Aristotelian syllogisms, uniting the major and minor terms.

[12] Thompson remarked: "Yet it is a striking feature of Smith's system of science that he more frequently refers to his own standards of judgment as *aesthetic* than as strictly *rational*, and that as his final criterion of truth he is willing to accept neither the rational test of consistency nor the empirical standard of correspondence with the observed facts." (1965, p. 219).

conclude then that the systems of signs developed by the imitative arts are one and all governed by convention. It may be safely concluded that all the imitative arts, and among them inquiry, are efforts to formulate systems of conventional signs. Thus, Smith's *Wealth of Nations* was largely devoted to explicating the customary rules which govern the assignment of value to money – which is certainly an excellent example of a conventional sign. Accordingly, as language is the prototype of systems of conventional signs, an investigation of the formulation of a language may be expected to reveal how inquiry functions.

III

Language first comes into existence when it becomes possible "to express our opinion" and that was certainly possible long before the invention of even the impersonal verb. A song or a dance, for example, may be made to represent something quite distinct from motion and sound ("Imit. Arts," p. 148). In Smith's view language as well as all the imitative arts were initiated by an act which made one object stand for another distinct particular object. Each took its beginning with marks ("Lang.," pp. 225, 239).

Before moving on to the more sophisticated types of signification several important features of this type of assignment require emphasis. First, the object signified is selected from all available objects on the basis of the interest of the speaker. Second, the object selected as a sign is selected on the basis of two criteria both of which have to do with the aesthetic preferences of the language community. Smith called them "the love of analogy" and "a certain regularity of sound" ("Lang.," pp. 231, 234, 238). Finally, as was seen to be the case with painting, the mark indirectly signifies an imitated object by directly signifying the image of that object. When this type of assignment has been accepted within a group, the mark will evoke the image of its unique correlate in the minds of the hearers.

More sophisticated systems result when, due to the growing burden of marks, general signs are substituted for marks. This is accomplished in a variety of ways all of which reduce to association of ideas ("Lang.," pp. 227-34). The introduction of general terms into a language has a profound effect upon the sign-signified relation. In the case of marks, the sign, the image it evokes and the event it signifies are each simple unities. With the introduction of general terms, the sign and the image evoked are transformed into complex unities, while the event signified retains its simplicity. The precise role of inquiry as an art which addresses the imagination is embedded in this set of consequences.

The introduction of general terms into a language renders every utterance which employs them a complex unity. The reason for this is that a general term signifies indeterminately. The general term "tree," which may once have marked a particular tree, is later used to denote any tree. Such terms cannot stand alone. The speaker who intends to communicate his opinion by using general terms must supplement these with other auxiliary parts of speech the function of which is to specify or determine which of the possible objects falling under the signification of the general term is the one which interests the speaker.

The unity of the complex utterance was viewed by Smith in two ways roughly corresponding to the contemporary distinction between grammar and semantics. An utterance may be regarded as a number of sounds grouped together into an acceptable set. Here the rules which govern the groupings of the parts of an utterance in a language, the grammatical rules, are dependent upon the aesthetic preferences of the community. On the other hand, an utterance may be viewed as a set of signs the unity of which is the image it evokes or is intended to evoke in the mind of the hearer. The grammatical parts of the utterance then will compose the semantic formula according to which the hearer constructs the image of the object signified. Further since the utterance contains at least one general term and an auxiliary part of speech, the hearer must construct that image in several steps – as many in fact as there are grammatical parts to the utterance. The image evoked by the utterance "the green tree by the cave," therefore, is an image composed of three elements – substance, quality and relation. The change undergone by the image evoked by a sign with the introduction of general terms into it is termed by Smith a "metaphysical division" ("Lang.," p. 239-49). He described it in this way in order to emphasize his contention that there can be no warrant for even wondering whether the structure of our ideas corresponds to that of the objective states they represent. These latter objects are regarded as simple unities, i.e., without structure ("Lang.," p. 240). Rather, the structure of our ideas "seems to have arisen more from the nature of language, than from the nature of things" ("Logics," p. 130). There can be no correspondence test of a semantic formula. The criteria by which these sets of associations are evaluated are comprehension, coherence, familiarity and beauty. Both the semantic and grammatical rules reflect the aesthetic preferences of the community.

It is in this matrix that Smith's theory of inquiry must ultimately be located und understood. Any object or event may be regarded by an observer as a sign. All that needs be satisfied for this to occur is that he associates that object or event with the image of another one in accordance with the semantic rules of correspondence currently accepted in his community. When these associations become in the least degree abstract the possibility of an inadequate semantic formula is opened up. When a semantic formula falters – usually on account of failure of comprehensiveness – the observer feels as though he were confronted with a gap. That gap is the one which divides the simple unity of the signified event from the complex unity of the sign object and image. Through a semantic failure in the attempt to bridge that gap by what Smith called a "grammatical circumlocution" ("Lang.," p. 240), the imperfection of all human artifice is revealed; that indeed is a staggering and humiliating realization.

Inquiry is an attempt to bridge this gap by revising the semantic formula ordinarily associated with the sign-object. It recommends altering these associations in whatever aesthetically acceptable ways are necessary to assure that the image of the signified-object is evoked. To the extent that inquiry succeeds it restores the faith of men in their own capacity to master their environment by articulating it according to shared interests and aesthetic preferences. The image of nature so ordered by man is at once an object of admiration and the terminus of inquiry.

Drawing attention to one of the consequences of this conclusion may serve to emphasize its importance to those whose interest in Smith's work is confined to the *Wealth of Nations*. One of the most persistent contentions of historians of economic theory has been, as was indicated above, that Smith held the same sort of mechanistic views as he attributed to early theistic philosophers. That Smith's epistemology precluded his ever having shared this view was rightly argued by Bittermann, but apparently to no avail. What appears to be called for here is an alternate reading of those passages in which Smith noted the similarity between machines and systems.

Careful consideration of the *locus classicus* ("Systems in many respects resemble machines" "Astron.," p. 66) reveals two points of interest. On the one hand, while noting that machines and systems are similar Smith did not here or any place else suggest that systems imitate machines or vice versa. On the other hand, the similarity he emphasized pertains to the pattern of their development. The condition of expanding the application of both is the simplification of their internal principles. The same pattern was observed to be operative in systems of written and spoken languages ("Lang.," pp. 241-2) and accordingly Smith compared languages and machines in this same respect ("Lang.," pp. 248-9). This pattern was laid down by Smith, however, not as a principle of mechanics, nor even as a logical principle, but as a maxim of grammar.

In general it may be laid down for a maxim, that the more simple any language is in its composition, the more complex it must be in its declensions and conjugations; and on the contrary, the more simple it is in its declensions and conjugations, the more complex it must be in its compositions. ("Lang.," p. 246)

Accordingly, it may be concluded that language is the prototype not only of the imitative arts but also of the productive arts. This pattern of development obtains in the case of every object of human art as a formal consequence of its being a product of the efforts of men to comprehend their environment by articulating it according to shared interests and aesthetic preferences. It can be detected wherever human effort is expended – from theoretical systems and machines to civil and moral society where the division of labor (*WN*, pp. 3-12) and the mutual encroachment of the rules of justice and those of the other virtues (*MS*, pp. 250, 303-4) are discernible.

IV

In the above analysis I have attempted to present an accurate interpretation of Smith's understanding of the nature and principles of inquiry in natural philosophy. This analysis was undertaken in the expectation that it would enable us to come to a better understanding of Smith's method of inquiry in his two major works in moral philosophy – the *Moral Sentiments* and the *Wealth of Nations*. Before Smith's practice in these works can be fairly examined in the light of his theory of inquiry one last theoretical issue requires examination.

One of the assumptions of previous students of Smith's methodology has been that he recognized no essential difference between the methods of inquiry in natural and moral philosophy. "Since it may be safely assumed that Smith did not hold to a logical dichotomy of *Naturwissenschaft* and *Geisteswissenschaft*, the ethical and economic works might be expected to imitate the Newtonian method" (Bittermann 1940, p. 502; also see Campbell 1971, p. 60). Our concern here is with accuracy of the contention that Smith regarded the method of inquiry appropriate to natural philosophy to be interchangeable with the method appropriate to moral philosophy. Campbell, who supports this view, represented Smith's moral theory as presented in the *Moral Sentiments* as an attempt to explain moral behavior by deducing typical instances from descriptive laws (1971, p. 59-60).

He is not concerned to analyse moral judgments as they actually occur in order to present an accurate phenomenological description of them. He aims to explain their existence and content by presenting an analytical model from which the facts to be explained can be deduced; in this it partakes of the nature of a genetic explanation, outlining the various features of human nature so far as is necessary to explain how men could have developed a system of moral judgments. (Campbell 1971, p. 120)

This approach to social studies has long been popular among social theorists. The question before us here is not whether it is reasonable for us to employ it, but whether Adam Smith subscribed to it. I shall contend that he did not. While there is no textual evidence on this matter one way or another in Smith's early writings, the *Moral Sentiments* presents ample evidence in support of this contention. There Smith described the moral philosophy of David Hume as predicated on this same methodological assumption. His critique of Hume indicates what Smith took to be the principal shortcomings of the procedure which is, ironically, ordinarily attributed to him.

Hume held that praise and blame are rooted in the perception of utility. Smith understood Hume's usage of the term "utility" quite different than have later utilitarians and economists (see Chap. IV). This difference resulted from different analyses of why utility pleases. For Hume, an object which is fitted to produce another object pleases, not because it actually produces or is expected to produce the other object, but because it evokes the image of that object in the mind of the beholder.

The utility of any object, according to him, pleases the master by perpetually suggesting to him the pleasure or convenience which it is fitted to promote. Every time he looks at it, he is put in mind of this pleasure; and the object in this manner becomes a source of perpetual satisfaction and enjoyment. (*MS*, p. 257)

Smith's reception of what he took to be Hume's notion of utility was mixed. On the one hand he recognized its value in analyzing the pursuits of wealth and power. Both types of ambition exhibit the same phenomenon.

... [T]hat the exact adjustment of the means for attaining any convenience or pleasure should frequently be more regarded than that very convenience or pleasure in the attainment of which their whole merit would seem to consist, has not, so far as I know, been yet taken notice of by anybody. (*MS*, p. 258)

This displacement of values comes about when men consider human affairs from a distance, abstracting from the preferences and aversions of those whose interests are actually at stake. Once such an abstraction occurs the spectacle can only be appraised on the basis of purely aesthetic principles and so reduces to a matter of taste (MS, pp. 270, 277). The motive to consider human affairs in this way and to act in accordance with such a view, however, is not the love of virtue, but the love of system (*MS*, pp. 342-3).

Although Smith found Hume's notion of utility to be of great analytic value, he took exception to Hume's resolution of "our whole approbation of virtue into a perception of this species of beauty which results from the appearance of utility" (*MS*, p. 270). Such a reduction presupposes that the subject matter of moral philosophy is in no way distinct from "all the general subjects of science and taste. . . ." (*MS*, p. 19). Smith raised two objections to this view.

For, first of all, it seems impossible that the approbation of virtue should be a sentiment of the same kind with that by which we approve of a convenient and well-contrived building; or, that we should have no other reason for praising a man than that for which we commend a chest of drawers.

And, secondly, it will be found upon examination, that the usefulness of any disposition of mind is seldom the first ground of our approbation; and that the sentiment of approbation always involves in it a sense of propriety quite distinct from the perception of utility. (*MS*, 271)

Smith held that the correctness of any theory, opinion or judgment whatever is decided on the basis of its consistency with the customary interests and preferences of the relevant community as judged by any competent member of that community *(MS,* p. 16). In the case of theories about objects the practical consequences of which may be ignored, i.e., "all the general subjects of science and taste," only aesthetic interests and preferences are relevant. Theories relating to such matters are judged on the basis of comprehensiveness, coherence, familiarity and beauty alone. In the case of theories about the actions of men and especially those which are of practical consequence to anyone, both the aesthetic and the moral preferences of the community must be considered to be relevant. Thus, any theory which purports to describe why men act and react as they do must satisfy not only those criteria appropriate to natural philosophy, but must also be consistent with the moral values actually supported by men in that particular community. This fifth criterion for judging a theory, peculiar to theories of human action, is propriety (*MS*, pp. 21-5).

In his two major works Smith was indeed intent upon showing why men acted as they did. He was aware, however, as Gunnar Myrdal is in our day (1958, p. 157-8; 1969, pp. 65-7) that such a task requires that full weight be accorded the values supported by those whose actions are the subject of inquiry. Indeed, the greater part of the *Moral Sentiments* was devoted to showing how a spectator can appreciate the character of those values (see Chap. II). Much of the analytic foundation of the

Wealth of Nations was derived from such an inquiry into "the rules which men naturally observe in exchanging..." (*WN*, p. 28). If it is useful to consider a contemporary parallel to Smith's theory of inquiry in natural philosophy, it would be advisable to compare his views with those of Thomas Kuhn (1962, pp. 91-109). Smith's essay on the history of astronomy was devoted to sketching and illustrating much the same thesis as Kuhn's on "the structure of scientific revolutions." A close contemporary parallel to Smith's theory of inquiry in moral philosophy may be found in the work of Peter Winch (1958a, pp. 86-91). Smith's "science of morals," to use Campbell's phrase, closely resembles Winch's "idea of a social science."

It is essential to recognize not only that Smith did insist upon formulating theories of human action consistently with the shared moral preferences of the community under investigation, but also why he did so. No theory which fails to take account of the life-situation and vital interests of men can hope to qualify as a theory of human action. At best such a theory treats human affairs as though they were merely a drama. In order to adequately understand human affairs an inquirer must, by a responsive exercise of imagination, take the moral preferences and the life situation of the relevant population into account. Nor is this necessary for theoretical reasons alone.

But if you have either no fellow-feeling for the misfortunes I have met with, or none that bears any proportion to the grief which distracts me; or if you have either no indignation at the injuries I have suffered, or none that bears any proportion to the resentment which transports me, we can no longer converse upon these subjects. We become intolerable to one another. I can neither support your company, nor you mine. You are confounded at my violence and passion, and I am enraged at your cold insensibility and want of feeling. (*MS*, 22)

"Adam Smith was not merely an economist, but a moralist and political theorist – a philosopher in the most comprehensive sense" (Gay 1966, p. 14). Until recently this type of remark usually conveyed a tolerant and sometimes apologetic connotation. A more sensitive generation of scholars is discovering that, contrary to the conventional wisdom, originality and humanitarian concern were the hallmarks of the Enlightenment (Cobban 1960; also see Morrow 1927). In the case of Adam Smith it may be that having been a philosopher has been the chief obstacle to understanding him. He seems to have been alive to this: "A philosopher is company only to a philosopher...." (*MS*, p. 43). Perhaps the capacity of our age to understand his work for what it was is a measure of our own philosophical acumen.

Adam Smith, the witless eclectic who by a clever application of the rationalism of his age managed a glimpse of those invisible forces which shape human conduct and unify the drama of society, is a myth which bears only a surface resemblance to that profoundly humane philosopher who gave initial impetus to what was soon to become, at the hands of less insightful men, the dismal science. Hopefully, we can yet restore the vision of his genius and, given time and similar motivation, put an end to that alienation which he aptly understood to be the necessary consequence of insensitive and mechanical methods of inquiry in the social sciences.

CHAPTER II

MORAL JUDGMENT

The philosophic foundations of Adam Smith's political economy are to be found in his *Theory of Moral Sentiments*. This thesis has seldom been seriously contested.[1] Unfortunately, very little progress has been made in explicating these foundations. This is due in large measure to the popular although mistaken belief that this work is, as Leslie Stephen proclaimed, sadly lacking in philosophic content.[2]

In the *Moral Sentiments* Smith addressed the subject of moral philosophy. Like the ancient Greeks, he believed that the task of the moral philosopher is to advise men how best to achieve happiness and perfection both as individuals and as members of various communities (*WN*, p. 726). According to Smith, to be happy is "... to be loved and to know that we deserve to be loved" (*MS*, p. 165). But since being loved is not within one's own power except to the extent that he can render himself deserving of it, each man is best advised to pursue that perfection of character which renders him worthy of the love of others, i.e., virtue. Thus, in Smith's estimate the motive of primary concern to the moral philosopher is the love of virtue and not the desire for happiness or the love of praise *(MS*, pp. 171, 193-4).

Adam Smith attempted to advise men how best to achieve virtue by delineating what had traditionally been called the rules of virtue. Eschewing the casuistic practice of prescribing recipes for righteous living, he recommended instead "describing, in a general manner, what is the sentiment upon which justice, modesty, and veracity, are founded, and what is the ordinary way of acting to which those virtues would commonly prompt us" (*MS*, p. 501; also pp. 391-2). He followed this

---

[1] "Smith's *philosophy* of riches and economic activity is there and not in the *Wealth of Nations*." (Schumpeter, 1954, p. 182)

[2] "But it is impossible to resist the impression, whilst we read his fluent rhetoric, and observe his easy acceptance of theological principles already exposed by his master Hume, that we are not listening to a thinker really grappling with a difficult problem, so much as to an ambitious professor who has found an excellent opportunity for displaying his command of language, and making brilliant lectures." (Stephen, 1876, Vol. II, p. 77)

approach throughout the *Moral Sentiments* reserving for another work the treatment of that one virtue the rules of which admit of more precise formulation, viz., justice. That more advanced division of moral philosophy was called "natural jurisprudence" one part of which is political economy (*MS*, pp. 501-3).

Smith's studies of earlier theorists convinced him that the moral philosopher must base his recommendations upon two general analyses – the one of virtue, the other of moral judgment (*MS*, pp. 391-2). He devoted the bulk of the *Moral Sentiments* to the latter largely because any description of the morally perfect character must ultimately rest upon an awareness of the factors which govern those judgments by which one mode of character and conduct is acclaimed as virtuous and others denounced as vicious.

The purpose of this chapter is to present a more accurate and philosophically adequate statement of Smith's analysis of moral judgments than is presently available. The doctrines of sympathy and the impartial spectator are of central importance in this regard. Accordingly, in the first two sections the current interpretations of these doctrines will be examined, deepened and revised. The third section provides an application of these revised views to the main types of moral judgments distinguished by Smith. This application provides indirect confirmation of the adequacy of these revised interpretations of sympathy and the impartial spectator as well as a brief exposition of the central content of the *Moral Sentiments*. The final section is devoted to a critique of several recent attempts at classifying Smith's analysis of moral judgments.

I

The doctrine of sympathy is typically thought to be simple and straightforward. The most popular interpretation is that sympathy is the same as empathy.[3] Smith introduced sympathy into his analysis of moral experi-

---

[3] O. H. Taylor's is the clearest statement of this view. "It [sympathy] is 'fellow-feeling' or an imaginative, vicarious sharing of another's feelings – or the feelings imputed to him – of *all* kinds, which occurs when and in so far as the subject, in observing the other person's conduct and inferring the feelings which that seems to express or manifest, imagines himself (the subject or observer) to be in that acting person's place or situation; and feels that in that situation he (the observer) would be impelled to feel and act just as the actual actor is acting and (apparently) feeling. In short, this sympathy is an acquisition into one's self – one's own feelings – of a kind of echo or reflection of the other, observed, active person's apparent feelings, which results from a successful, imaginative 'identification' of the self with that other person. I think it is that which a more modern

ence, according to this view, in order to explain the way one man comes to an appreciation of how another's man's circumstance actually affects him. Since no one is immediately aware of another man's sentiments, he must somehow simulate that knowledge. He does so by stimulating his own passions by an image of the other fellow's circumstance. Sympathy, considered as a device for circumventing this cognitive limitation, functions to provide one man with a reliable estimate of how others actually feel.

> By the imagination we place ourselves in his situation, we conceive ourselves enduring all the same torments, we enter, as it were, into his body and become in some measure the same person with him; and thence form some idea of his sensations, and even feel something which, though weaker in degree, is not altogether unlike them. (*MS*, p. 4)

This view, however, has lead interpreters to draw a number of conclusions all of which were rejected by Smith. First, were sympathy merely empathy it would be the same as approval. This view, first suggested by David Hume (letter to Smith, July 28, 1759), was rejected in a note added by Smith to the third edition of the *Moral Sentiments*.[4] Second, were sympathy the same as empathy it would be merely a psychological prerequisite of moral judgment. This contention is implicit in O. H. Taylor's account. Smith, however, consistently treated sympathy as an essential feature of moral judgments and not merely as a prerequisite. This is most evident in his discussion of moral judgments of one's own conduct, when one *is* possessed of an immediate awareness of the feelings of the agent.[5] Finally, were sympathy merely empathy morality would reduce to respectability, for the person acting from moral considerations would attempt to act in those ways with which his neighbors sympathize. This contention, explicitly sponsored by Glenn

psychological theory calls *empathy* ..." (Taylor, 1960, pp. 58-9; also see Morrow, 1923a, pp. 29-30 and 1923b)

[4] "It has been objected to me, that as I found the sentiment of approbation, which is always agreeable, upon sympathy, it is inconsistent with my system to admit any disagreeable sympathy. I answer, that in the sentiment of approbation there are two things to be taken notice of; first, the sympathetic passions of the spectator, and secondly, the emotion which arises from his observing the perfect coincidence between this sympathetic passion in himself, and the original passion in the person principally concerned. This last emotion, in which the sentiment of approbation properly consists, is always agreeable and delightful. The other may either be agreeable or disagreeable, according to the nature of the original passion, whose features it must always, in some measure retain." (*MS*, p. 63n)

[5] ... [W]e either approve or disapprove of our own conduct according as we feel that, when we place ourselves in the station of another man and view it, as it were, with his eyes and from his station, we either can or cannot entirely enter into and sympathize with the sentiments and motives which influenced it. (*MS*, p.161)

Morrow (1923 b, p. 69), however, neglects Smith's distinction between the love of praise and the love of praiseworthiness.[6] "To desire or even to accept of praise, where no praise is due, can be the effect only of the most contemptible vanity" (*MS*, p. 171).

The inadequacy of the empathy view, however interpreted, derives principally from the practice of generalizing from Smith's introductory description of sympathy, especially those given in the first three chapters of the book. More thorough attention needs to be given to the way in which he used the notion of sympathy in his analysis of moral judgment.

In the fourth chapter of the opening section of the *Moral Sentiments* Smith indicated that men have occasion to judge the actions of one another in two different ways. In the one case the object (by which Smith meant the entire situation in which the agent finds himself) which excites the sentiment and action of the agent is regarded as a matter of relative indifference by agent and spectator alike. Such objects include "all the general subjects of science and taste." Where the object is of this sort the spectator can assess the judgment or conduct of others by placing himself at the station of the agent by an act of sympathy,[7] noting how he is affected by the object confronted from that point of view, and then considering whether the agent's judgment or conduct is congenial with his own sympathetic sentiment. If it is, he is approved as a man of taste and judgment, if not, the reverse (*MS*, pp. 19-21).

This analysis would seem to lend support to the "empathy" interpretation of sympathy. That it does not is clearly indicated in a passage which has generally been overlooked.

We both look at them from the same point of view, and *we have no occasion for sympathy* or for that imaginary change of situations from which it arises, in order to produce, with regard to these, the most perfect harmony of sentiments and affections. (*MS*, p. 19) (Emphasis added).

Consideration of the second way in which men judge one another's conduct reveals the import of this denial. In that case the object which excites the sentiment and action of the agent is relevant to his well-being but not to that of the spectator. I will call these *objects of practical consequence* in contradistinction to those of science and taste. Where conduct is considered in relation to an object of practical consequence the inter-

---

[6] "Praise and blame express what actually are; praiseworthiness and blameworthiness what naturally ought to be the sentiments of other people with regard to our character and conduct. The love of praise is the desire of obtaining the favourable sentiments of our brethren. The love of praiseworthiness is the desire of rendering ourselves the proper objects of those sentiments." (*MS*, p. 183)

[7] Sympathy is an element of judgment not only in drama and the fine arts ("Imit. Arts," pp. 161-70), but also in the natural sciences ("Astron.," p. 61-2).

ests of agent and spectator in the object are not, as was true in the former case, originally the same. For the spectator the object is a matter of indifference, of no more consequence than the subjects of science and the arts. For the agent, however, it is a matter of vital concern. Upon such occasions the spectator may not presume to judge the conduct of the agent merely by comparing it to the sentiment which he excites in himself by the image of the agent's circumstance.

My companion does not naturally look upon the misfortune that has befallen me, from the same point of view in which I consider them. They affect me much more nearly. We do not view them from the same station, as we do a picture or a poem, or a system of philosophy; and are therefore apt to be very differently affected by them. (*MS*, p. 21)

Smith's description of judgments of the second type is quite similar to his account of those of the first type. The spectator places himself at a station different from his own by an act of sympathy, notes how he is affected by the object when confronted from that point of view, and then considers whether the agent's judgment or conduct is congenial with his sympathetic sentiment. The role of sympathy in judging both types of objects is to bridge the gap existing between the "points of view" or "stations" of agent and spectator thereby qualifying the latter to judge the conduct of the former.

The contrast which Smith drew between these two ways of judging conduct, however, makes clear that the terms "points of view" and "stations" were used in distinct although analogous senses. In the case of objects of science and taste they refer to the cognitive status of agent and spectator, i.e., to the kind of object which confronts the one but not the other. In that of objects of practical consequence they refer to the appetitive status of agent and spectator, i.e., to the interest taken in the object by the one but not by the other.

This observation leads to the further conclusion that in this discussion Smith also used the term "sympathy" in two distinct although analogous senses. In both cases "sympathy" refers to a mode of identification achieved between men by an exercise of imagination. The difference between the two senses derives from the difference in the modes of identifying. In the first sense, which I will call *aesthetic sympathy* and which is the same as empathy, it refers to an exercise of imagination whereby one man identifies with the cognitive status of another. In the second sense, which I will call *moral sympathy* and which is of paramount importance in the *Moral Sentiments*, it refers to an exercise of imagination whereby two or more men identify with a common appetitive status.

The observant reader will have noticed further and important differences between the two senses of sympathy. By aesthetic sympathy one man – the spectator – identifies with the concrete situation of another – the agent. By moral sympathy, on the other hand, both identify with a third disposition which is not (or at least is not necessarily) the disposition of any concrete individual. Furthermore, whereas aesthetic sympathy is performed by the spectator alone, moral sympathy is the joint responsibility of spectator and agent. The reconciliation of disparate interests can be achieved neither by the agent nor by the spectator alone. The unaffected spectator cannot possibly – no matter how sensitive he is – identify with the concrete, vitally interested agent. Neither can the agent possibly identify with the concrete, indifferent spectator. This diversity of interests can be reconciled only by mutual exercise of moral sympathy terminating in the joint adoption of that level of interest which both can support (*MS*, pp. 22-3).

Although agent and spectator do not share an immediate and vital interest in the agent's objective circumstance, they do share an interest in sustaining the bond of community between themselves. "Nature, when she formed man for society, endowed him with the original desire to please, and an original aversion to offend his brethren" (*MS*, p. 170). Both parties come to recognize that unless they can identify with a common level of interest in objects of practical consequence they can expect only one another's contempt. The passion of the agent's conduct will deeply offend the spectator's sensibilities, while the spectator's indifference will appear to the agent as cold insensitivity (*MS*, p. 22). The overriding interest to maintain society with one another moves each to cooperate with the other in defining and adopting that degree of interest in such an object which is mutually acceptable.

According to this interpretation the function of moral as opposed to aesthetic sympathy is to reconcile the disparity of interests which would otherwise persist among men in a practical situation. To the extent that men can adopt roughly the same interest in one another's practical circumstance, they are enabled to morally judge each other's conduct. Unless that identification is achieved neither moral judgment nor society is possible between them (*MS*, pp. 21-22). Having clarified the nature and function of moral sympathy [8] we turn to the even more puzzling doctrine of the impartial spectator.

---

[8] In section three of this chapter the various modes of moral sympathy – direct, indirect and reflexive – will be shown to be consistent with this account.

II

The figure of the impartial spectator bears directly upon the criterion of moral judgments, the measure by which a man decides whether an act is or is not one of "the ordinary ways of acting to which virtue commonly prompts us" (*MS*, p. 501). Only a few of Smith's interpreters have recognized the importance of this doctrine to his moral theory. After careful analysis Morrow (1923a, p. 37), Bonar (1926, p. 342), Bittermann (1940, p. 715), Macfie (1967, pp. 92-6) and Campbell (1971, pp. 134-9) concluded that the impartial spectator is the personification of the customary norms of performance honored within a society.

Although this identification of the spectator with mores entails the reduction of morality to the pursuit of respectability, a contention previously shown to be unacceptable, it is nonetheless partially correct. "Virtue," Smith proclaimed, "is excellence, something uncommonly great and beautiful, which rises far above what is vulgar and ordinary" (*MS*, p. 28). In order to decide whether an act is virtuous it must be submitted to two standards, viz., the idea of complete propriety and perfection and the degree to which the actions of men commonly approximate that idea (*MS*, pp. 29-30 and 362-3). The criterion of moral judgments, then, is a complex of two standards – the ideal of performance and the norm of performance. The figure of the impartial spectator refers more particularly to the first of these standards. Morrow, Bonar, Bittermann, Macfie and Campbell confused the criterion of moral judgment, which they took to be the same as the impartial spectator, with the norm of performance largely because they mistakenly assumed that criterion to be incomplex. This clarification reopens the question of how the ideal of performance is determined.

Smith consistently maintained that the temper of the impartial spectator is determined by each man, but that he does so with such facility that reflective analysis is required to discover how that determination is accomplished. He began that analysis by exploring an analogous case.

As to the eye of the body, objects appear great or small, not so much according to their real dimensions as according to the nearness or distance of their situation; so do they likewise to what may be called the natural eye of the mind; and we remedy the defects of both these organs pretty much in the same manner. (*MS*, p. 191)

When attempting to gauge the relative size of visual objects our judgment is apt to be severely distorted if it is based solely upon the relative size of the corresponding visual images. In his essay "On the External

Senses" Smith entertained the hypothesis that we compensate for this distortion by interpreting visual images according to certain "rules of perspective." He was troubled there, however, by the question of the origin of these rules ("Ext. Senses," pp. 202-223). By the time he composed the *Moral Sentiments* he had hit upon a better explanation.

In my present situation, an immense landscape of lawns and woods, and distant mountains, seems to do no more than cover the little window which I write by, and to be out of all proportion less than the chamber in which I am sitting. I can form a just comparison between those great objects and the little object around me, in no other way than by transporting myself, at least in fancy, to a different station, from whence I can survey both at nearly equal distances, and thereby form some judgment of their real proportions. (*MS*, p. 191)

The relative magnitudes of visual images distort our estimates of the relative size of the corresponding tactile objects only when the latter are situated at different distances from the observer. Were the observer situated at equal distances from the objects he could form a reliable estimate of their relative size by consulting only the relative size of the corresponding images. A man compensates for this distortion by an act of aesthetic sympathy. He simply imagines how these objects would appear to him were he located at equal distances from them. He constructs these images in two steps. First he recalls how both objects appeared to him when he was actually situated at opposite extremes, i.e., in the study and on the mountain. He then constructs an image of each object the size of which falls half-way between that of the recalled images. These constructed images are then regarded as representing the apparent magnitudes of the mountain and the study window when contemplated from a place midway between their actual locations. The determination of the point of propriety is accomplished in a similar way.

In the same manner, to the selfish and original passions of human nature, the loss or gain of a very small interest of our own appears to be of vastly more importance, excites a much more passionate joy or sorrow, a much more ardent desire or aversion, than the greatest concern of another with whom we have no particular connection. His interests, as long as they are surveyed from his station, can never be put into the balance with our own, can never restrain us from doing whatever may tend to promote our own, how ruinous soever to him. Before we can make any proper comparison of those opposite interests, we must change our position. We must view them, neither from our own place nor yet from his, neither with our own eyes nor yet with his, but from the place and with the eyes of a third person, who has no particular connection with either, and who judges with impartiality between us. (*MS*, p. 192)

The judgments of men as to the importance of an object of practical consequence are apt to be distorted only when their interests in the object differ. Were men to entertain the same degree of interest in the object each could form a reliable estimate of its importance by merely consulting the interest which he actually takes in it. Men compensate for this distortion by an act of moral sympathy. They imagine what interest they would take in the object were its relevance to the well-being of all the same. They construct this image in two steps. First, they recall the interest they took in the object when actually situated at opposite extremes, i.e., as agent and as spectator. They then construct an image of an interest in the object, the degree of which falls mid-way between that of the recalled images. This constructed image is then regarded as representing the interest which each would take in the object were it similarly relevant to the well-being of all.

Smith's parallel analyses of visual and moral judgments further clarify the contrast between the two types of sympathy. Both involve a "transport of imagination" to a "station" mid-way between the objects being compared, that station providing a stand-point from which that comparison can be reliably made. The methods of correcting visual and moral distortion differ, however, in one important respect. In the former case the observer neutralizes the factor of distance by constructing an image the size of which falls half-way between that of the recalled images. In that case it is appropriate to assume that the mean is the numerical average. In the latter case this assumption is not appropriate. The factor of "relevance to well-being" cannot be neutralized by merely striking an average. In matters of morality "equal" may or may not be the equivalent of "equitable." The equitable degree of interest in an object of practical consequence is not an average of the levels of interest which are or can be entertained in it.[9] The factor relevant to the determination of the moral mean is, as was stated earlier, the maintenance of community among men. The equitable degree of interest in such objects is the one which is expected to provide and sustain the basis of a concord of sentiment among men. This level of interest defines the image of the ideal disposition, i.e., the impartial spectator. It is, according to Smith, the maximum interest which the person making the

[9] The point here is not that a mean level of interest in an object of practical consequence cannot be determined statistically. Nor is it that the images of an equitable disposition adopted by a population cannot be described statistically. Rather, the claim here is that such a mean, often referred to as an emotional equilibrium (Taylor, 1960, p. 61; West, 1969a, p. 85), is not decisive in determining the equitable or proper level of interest in such objects. Confusion on this point has led many historians to believe that Smith provided only psychological foundations for his political economy in the *Moral Sentiments* (Taylor, 1960, p. 57; Grampp, 1965, Vol. II, pp. 3-23).

construction expects that a spectator can entertain in an object of practical consequence only to another (MS, pp. 161-2 and 386).

As already indicated a spectator can not be expected to entertain the same degree of interest in any object of practical consequence as does the agent or the patient. Smith identified two further limitations to which all spectators in all circumstances are subject. These too restrict the degree of sensitivity which even an ideally disposed and situated spectator can manage. First, any spectator's ability to morally sympathize with the plight of another is restricted by the extent to which his passions can be excited by mere images of their proper objects. Smith believed that the different passions are responsive in varying degrees to this type of stimulation. The passions which take their origin in the body cannot be excited by imagination at all, e.g., hunger and the sexual passion! (MS, pp. 33-8) Others are more or less susceptible to such excitation – the social passions more, the unsocial passions less, the selfish passions somewhere between these (MS, pp. 44-59). Second, any spectator's ability to approximate the degree of interest taken in an object by an agent is contingent upon his appreciation of the character of the interest the object holds for the agent. Spectators cannot be expected to appreciate the interest which an agent entertains in an object where that interest is rooted in a habit or circumstance of which the spectator is unaware. It was in this connection that Smith noted: "A philosopher is company to a philosopher only; the member of a club to his own little knot of companions" (MS, pp. 39-43).

In his treatment of the subject matter of moral philosophy Smith was intent upon showing the ordinary ways of acting to which virtue commonly prompts men. His analysis of moral judgment was designed to indicate the procedure for deciding whether a particular act is or is not consistent with those promptings. A man follows this procedure by adopting the temper of the impartial spectator, considering how such a spectator would respond in the situation of the agent and comparing the action at issue with that response (MS, p. 63n). Smith believed that this procedure was observed for the most part by men when issuing moral judgments. He admitted, however, that their performance was frequently marred by two irregularities. First, the distribution of well-being which prevails among men in a community affects the extent to which the average spectator can sympathize with particular types of interests. "The natural and ordinary state of mankind," is, Smith asserted, similar to that of "the man who is in health, who is out of debt, and has a clear conscience." Accordingly, the average spectator will find it more difficult to appreciate the sorrows of the miserable and much easier to appreciate the joys of the most fortunate than the ideally situated spectator (*MS*, pp. 60-9). Second, the original passions distort not only the judgment of the agent but also that of the concrete spectator, although to a lesser extent. This is especially clear in the case of acts which have a dramatic effect upon another (a patient). In such cases men are frequently so absorbed by the spectacle of the pleasant or painful consequences of the act that they neglect to give adequate attention to considering the propriety of the act (*MS*, pp. 136-51).

When morally judging an action each man formulates for himself that ideal of performance relevant to the situation of the agent and compares the act to that criterion. That ideal, however, is not a heavenly prototype which can never be achieved by merely human effort. The temper of the impartial spectator is an ideal which is attainable in principle by real people within the constraints of their natural circumstances. Still, although not unattainable this ideal disposition is seldom if ever fully achieved, especially by men in their capacities as agents. But one need not, in Smith's view, act in strict accordance with the sentiments of the impartial spectator in order to be the proper object of moral praise, not to mention mere approval. Those whose actions conform to that ideal to an extent which surpasses the degree normally attained by men qualify as virtuous. The impartial spectator, then, is the ideal of performance and as such is one of the two standards which compose the criterion of moral judgments, the other being the norm of performance.

III

Smith analyzed the phenomenon of moral judgment into two distinct actions. The first is moral sympathy. By this act a man qualifies himself to pass moral as opposed to merely aesthetic judgments by entertaining what he takes to be the maximum degree of interest which a concrete spectator can reasonably be expected to take in an object of practical consequence only to another. The second is comparison. By this act he decides whether and to what extent an actual or proposed response to a particular object is commensurate with the impartial level of interest in it (*MS*, p. 63n). The ability to perform these two acts constitutes a man's moral faculties.

It belongs to our moral faculties ... to determine ... when and how far every other principle of our nature ought either to be indulged or restrained. What is agreeable to our moral faculties, is fit, and right, and proper to be done; the contrary, wrong, unfit, and improper. (*MS*, p. 234)

Moral judgments are made in a variety of ways depending upon three factors: first, whether the act under consideration is one's own or that of another; second, whether the act is considered in relation to the one who performed it (agent) or in relation to those affected by it (patient); third, whether the act is being considered before or after it is performed. Variation among these factors requires that adjustments be made in the first component of moral judgment – moral sympathy – but not in the second – comparison. Thus, there are several modes of moral sympathy, viz., direct, indirect and reflexive. Smith's main concern, however, was not to explore and describe these modes of sympathy. His discussion of them was subsidiary to the objective of elucidating the three main capacities by virtue of which men are enabled to form moral judgments. These he divided according to the three principal moral sentiments, viz., the sense of propriety, the sense of merit and the sense of duty.[10]

Judgments of human conduct may be governed by three general considerations, viz., the observable movements of the body ("behavior" in the usage of contemporary psychology), the consequences which in fact result from these movements ("utility" in the usage of Bentham and the Mills) and the sentiment which occasioned these movements. Moral qualities are ascribed to an action, according to Smith, solely in terms of the sentiment from which it proceeds (MS, pp. 133-4). That sentiment may be considered in either of two relations, viz., to the cause or object which excited it or to the effect or end which the agent intended to promote by his action. Conduct found morally satisfactory in the former relation (the relation which is of immediate concern to the agent) is possessed of the quality of propriety. The capacity to judge conduct in this relation is the sense of propriety. Conduct found morally satisfactory in the latter relation (which is of immediate concern to the patient) is possessed of the quality of merit. The capacity to judge conduct in this relation is the sense of merit (MS, pp. 17 and 93). Smith treated these types of moral judgment first in relation to the past conduct of others.

Since judgments of the propriety of the past conduct of others have been the basis of our analyses of the doctrines of moral sympathy and the impartial spectator, they require little further comment. In order to perform this type of moral judgment a man considers whether the action in question is consistent with the impartial level of interest in the object which actually occasioned it. An appreciation of the impartial level of interest in the object is achieved by an act of "direct" moral sympathy (MS, p. 105). Where the act and the impartial level of interest are found

[10] The sense of justice and the sense of remorse are aspects of the sense of merit.

to be consistent the act is judged proper, where inconsistent, it is judged improper (*MS*, pp. 14-15).

In Smith's vocabulary merit and demerit were synonymous with "deserving of reward and deserving of punishment" (*MS*, p. 93). The sentiments from which reward and punishment proceed are gratitude and resentment. Within this context, then, judgments of merit bear upon the propriety of the resentment or gratitude which the patient is thought to feel. According to Smith, it is ordinarily proper to act on these sentiments if and only if two conditions are satisfied. These conditions define the impartial level of gratitude and resentment.

Actions of a beneficient tendency, which proceed from proper motives, seem alone to require a reward; because such alone are the approved objects of gratitude, or excite the sympathetic gratitude of the spectator. Actions of a hurtful tendency, which proceed from improper motives, seem alone to deserve punishment; because such alone are the approved objects of resentment, or excite the sympathetic resentment of the spectator. (*MS*, p. 112)

By specifying that only conduct which actually benefits another and also proceeds from proper motives is meritorious Smith insisted that neither ineffectual well-wishing nor unintentionally benefiting others is ordinarily deserving of reward. Likewise, in stating that only conduct which actually harms another and which also proceeds from improper motives is demeritorious Smith emphasized that neither ineffectual ill-will nor unintentionally harming others is ordinarily deserving of punishment. Although a patient may feel well-disposed toward the agent as a result of his wishing him well or having benefited from his actions or ill-disposed as a result of the contrary, neither sentiment is a proper basis for rewarding him on the one hand or punishing him on the other.

A man decides whether the agent's conduct is deserving of reward on the one hand or punishment on the other by considering whether the agent acted with propriety and whether the patient actually sustained benefit or harm as a result of the act. This compound act Smith termed "indirect" moral sympathy. If he decides in favor of the former alternative in both cases, the act is judged meritorious, if for the latter in both cases it is pronounced demeritorious (*MS*, pp. 105-8).

The principles by which a man judges his own past conduct are the same as those by which he judges that of others, viz., the senses of propriety and of merit (*MS*, pp. 161-2). The only difference between them is the way in which an agent comes to an appreciation of the impartial degree of interest in an object which was of practical concern to him. I will call this the *reflexive* mode of moral sympathy.

When I endeavor to examine my own conduct, when I endeavor to pass sentence upon it, and either to approve or condemn it, it is evident that, in all such cases, I divide myself, as it were, into two persons; and that I, the examiner and judge, represent a different character from that other I, the person whose conduct is examined into and judged of. The first is the spectator, whose sentiments with regard to my own conduct I endeavor to enter into, by placing myself in his situation, and by considering how it would appear to me, when seen from that particular point of view. The second is the agent, the person whom I properly call myself, and whose conduct, under the character of a spectator, I was endeavoring to form some opinion. The first is the judge; the second is the person judged of. (*MS*, pp. 164-5)

Smith was quite insistent that the distinction between judgments of past and of future conduct is of fundamental importance for morality – both in theory and in practice. Whereas distortion is always a major problem when moral judgments are attempted, it is much more of an obstacle when a person is in the throes of deciding how he will act. "The fury of our own passions constantly calls us back to our own place, where every thing appears magnified and misrepresented by self love" (*MS*, p. 221). In moments of decision one's immediate and vital interests are so much in the forefront of deliberation that they materially distort unaided imagination. It is for this reason that agents tend to confuse what is proposed by immediate sentiment with the appropriate course of action. "This self-deceit, this fatal weakness of mankind, is the source of half the disorders of human life" (*MS*, p. 223).

Unless a man can adequately compensate for this distortion of imagination he will not be able to attain a reliable estimate of the impartial degree of interest in the object of immediate and practical consequence to him and so will tend to act in ways which will be found profoundly offensive both by others and by himself when he later considers his conduct. This distortion is remedied by the implementation of certain general rules derived by induction from past moral judgments (*MS*, pp. 223-4 and 469-70).

The precise function of these rules is somewhat involved. They play an essential role in formulating a reliable estimate of the impartial degree of interest in the object which confronts the agent and a contingent role in maintaining civil behavior. The distorting effect of passion inclines every agent to expect a greater degree of interest on the part of the spectator in his situation than is reasonable. In order to avoid overreacting the agent must render his judgment more soberly. He enables himself to do this by reminding himself of how he and other concrete spectators have typically responded to acts similar to the one which he contemplates.

Those general rules of conduct, when they have been fixed in our minds by habitual reflection, are of great use in correcting the misrepresentations of self-love concerning what is fit and proper to be done in our particular situation. (*MS*, p. 226. Also see pp. 227 and 470)

The essential function of the general rules of morality then is to enable the agent to form a less fanciful image of the extent to which concrete spectators can take an interest in his situation. It is an essential function because no agent can rely completely upon his own image of the ideal of performance while he is in the throes of deliberation. If he is to be able to conform his conduct in any degree to that ideal, he must ordinarily settle for regulating his actions by these rules, even though they embody only the prevailing norms of performance and so fall short of that ideal. These rules, however, play a contingent role with respect to conduct quite apart from this consideration.

To the extent that men are either uncertain as to what is ideally required in their concrete circumstance or are insufficiently disciplined to act on their moral resolves, they are, according to Smith, best advised to avoid directing their conduct according to their own idea of what is praiseworthy and settle instead to defer to the general rules of morality (*MS*, pp. 178-83). Furthermore, since these conditions obtain for all men for the most part, acting out of reverence for the customary norms of approval and disapproval is the counsel of prudence.

The regard to those general rules of conduct is what is properly called a sense of duty, a principle of the greatest consequence in human life and the only principle by which the bulk of mankind are capable of directing their actions. (*MS*, p. 229)

Acting out of deference to the established rules of morality, however, qualifies as moral only in the minimal sense that the agent has acted out of a regard for one of the two standards which compose the criterion of moral judgment. The person who acts from a sense of duty avoids insinuating his own moral convictions into the determination of his conduct. Hence, while such acts may well be proper, they are never virtuous. This is the case not because such actions will fail to surpass the norm of performance, although that is certainly true, but because in determining them the agent takes no account of his ideal of performance. "No action can properly be called virtuous which is not accompanied with the sentiment of self-approbation" (*MS*, p. 254).

IV

Stephen's claim that Smith's *Moral Sentiments* was lacking in philosophic content, together with similar suspicions on the part of later readers, appears to derive from any or all of three sources. Such a belief may announce disappointment at not being able to confirm the hypothesis that in this work Smith propounded what is fundamentally a form of stoic moral theory. Attempting to interpret the *Moral Sentiments* by accommodating its various doctrines to those of the ancient Stoics has been a popular enterprise for some time (Hasbach 1891, pp. 129-47; Viner 1927, pp. 202-6; Gray 1931, p. 125; Grampp 1965, vol. II., pp. 5-38). The discovery that Smith's moral philosophy makes minimal sense when paraphrased in a Stoic idiom may well be the reason Stephen's claim is widely accepted.[11]

A second source of dissatisfaction in Smith's performance in the *Moral Sentiments* undoubtedly arises from the fact that he rejected outright one of the cornerstones of utilitarianism. Unlike utilitarians of the nineteenth and twentieth century, Smith rejected the claim that the relation between an action and its consequences is the fundamental consideration in moral discourse. For him an act's utility is posterior to the question of its propriety, whether utility be conceived as the aesthetic proportion between means and ends as Smith thought Hume had, or as productive efficiency as would later utilitarians and economists (*MS*, pp. 133-4, 269-72). The fact that Smith rejected at least one of the fundamental premises of that style of moral philosophy which has been fashionable in English speaking countries for the past century and a half has no doubt reinforced the inclination of many in their belief that there is nothing here of interest to so advanced a school of moral philosophy as ours.

A final source of skepticism about the profundity of Smith's analysis of moral judgments derives from the fact that it has been very difficult for us to conceptualize this particular aspect of his work within our own frame of reference. A few words of clarification with regard to three attempts in that direction, each of which proposed two claims one of which was true and the other false, may on this account be helpful.

Roderick Firth, in proposing what he called "the ideal observer" analysis of ethical statements, claimed that Smith as well as Hume accepted "an absolutist dispositional analysis of 'right' " (1952, p. 318n). Quite clearly Smith did support what Firth called a dispositional analysis of ethical statements. Throughout the *Moral Sentiments* Smith consistently proposed that the sentiments, disposition, or temper of the impartial spectator is the criterion in terms of which moral decisions are

---

[11] Should it seem desirable to search out ancient parallels for Smith's position, the Sophists, and Protagoras in particular, seem more likely to be useful than do the Stoics (see Plato's *Protagoras* and *Theaetetus*; Guthrie 1969, Part I).

taken. Equally clear, however, as Campbell observed (1971, pp. 128-39), is the fact that Smith supported a relativist analysis of ethical statements. For Smith the disposition of the impartial spectator was not that of a bloodless ideal observer, but the tone of temper which all parties to moral judgments would and to some degree do support. In claiming that moral statements include a reference to that disposition Smith very definitely did include what Firth called an "egocentric reference" and so must on Firth's grounds be identified with the position championed by Edward Westermarck, i.e., a relativist dispositional analysis, more popularly known as ethical, moral or cultural relativism.

Westermarck (1932, pp. 69-71; 81-3, 131-3, 168, 175) as well as Alexander (1933, pp. 248-51, 266-7) acknowledged a deep indebtedness to Smith's analysis of moral judgments. Westermarck was especially impressed by the profundity of that analysis. "For my part I maintain that Adam Smith's *Theory of Moral Sentiments* is the most important contribution to moral psychology made by any British thinker . . ." (1932, p. 71). His enthusiasm was due to his discovery that Smith had shown not only that but also how properly moral judgments are based on ordinary emotions considered, by a sympathetic transport of imagination, from an impartial point of view. In this Westermarck was correct. Westermarck, however, also believed that like himself Smith too was convinced that this analysis implied that moral judgments lack objectivity, that there is no basis upon which men might assess the correctness of normative claims.

Campbell correctly observed that Smith did not share this latter conviction. Smith did insist that the criterion of moral judgments is essentially different from that of judgments of truth and falsity (*MS*, pp. 467-71). He nevertheless claimed that the shared attitudes of men toward different modes of behavior in a variety of circumstances would and did provide a basis for agreement among men on questions relating to the moral status of those acts. Such agreement is possible insofar as those attitudes approximated the ideal temper personified in the figure of the supposed spectator (Campbell 1971, pp. 161-5). Campbell, however, regarded Smith's impartial spectator as the personification of the norms of performance customarily supported by men in a society (1971, pp. 134-39). Noting that Smith admitted that the different circumstances of societies result in the adoption of different mores, Campbell concluded that Smith had advocated "moral relativity" (1971, pp. 139-45). On the basis of this belief Campbell reasoned that Smith could not consistently disapprove as morally wrong any practice which is consistent with the mores of the society in which it occurs and certainly not the mores themselves. Observing that Smith did precisely that in opposing the liberal ethic of the rich and powerful and supporting the strict ethic of the lesser ranks (*WN*, p. 746; *MS*, p. 84), Campbell charged that Smith had "gone beyond the bounds of his own moral theory..." (1971, pp. 174, 176, 221).

In what follows I shall attempt to show that this criticism is not well taken because although he did support a relativist dispositional analysis of moral judgments he did not subscribe to moral relativity, at least not in Campbell's sense. Such a proposal may appear questionable on the face of it. Until recently it was popularly assumed that cultural relativity precluded the possibility of any uniformity of values among different societies, especially moral values. Kroeber and Kluckhohn (1952, pp. 174-9) and Wellman (1963) have shown, however, that this inference is invalid, unnecessary and incompatible with cultural anthropology as currently practiced. It is similarly invalid to argue that because Smith admitted that mores differ with circumstance, he must have rejected the conviction that all men share the same moral aspirations and achieve them to a degree within the varying constraints of their respective situations.

Campbell mistook Smith's admission that the moral quality of an act may vary considerably if the circumstances in which it is performed are radically different for an admission that the moral values of differently circumstanced societies are necessarily different. A closer reading of Smith's discussion of the extent to which custom, which is determined in large measure by circumstance, can distort a man's sense of propriety reveals several interesting points. Smith's conclusion was that on the whole custom has a very inconsiderable effect upon the moral sentiments of men. Even where it does occasion a divergence, that relates only to isolated practices and for a relatively short time (*MS*, pp. 290-306). For example, in ancient Greece the practice of abandoning infants continued to be permitted long after the insecurity of an earlier era had ceased to render the practice excusable. (*MS*, pp. 304-6). Smith's objection was not that such a practice is never excusable, nor that it was not consistent with the customary norms of performance, but that there is frequently a time lag between the cessation of circumstances which excuse a practice and the recognition of that fact by the public. On no reading does this discussion support any claim to the relativity of morals except in the ordinary sense that the moral value of an act must be decided in the context of the circumstances of the agent.

Although Smith was prepared to allow that limitation of circumstance and of awareness typically do limit the extent to which men in different situations manage to approximate that mode of conduct which is fully consistent with the ideal tone of temper personified by the impartial spectator, he was nevertheless convinced that every man, whatever his situation, in fact aspires to conform his conduct to the same ideal tone of temper and for that reason supports some set values which approximate that ideal to the full extent possible within the constraints of his concrete situation. Smith was convinced, on the other hand, that the specific content of the moral values which men in different circumstances can be reasonably expected to support admit of only slight uniformity. Although he rejected the tradition of moral casuistry for precisely this reason, Smith observed that while the rules of prudence and benevolence supported by men in different situations bear only a family resemblance to one another, those of justice are relatively "precise and accurate" (*MS*, p. 482). In particular he believed every society prohibits, in some form and to some extent, such deeds as murder, theft and lying (*MS*, p. 121). Even in these cases he admitted that there are situations in which exceptions are allowable. In time of war, for example, killing – even the killing of innocents – is excusable (*LJ*, p. 268).

Smith's belief that all men aspire to conforming their character to the same ideal disposition was rooted in his deep and abiding conviction that men are by nature social beings (*MS*, p. 170), that they recognize this in the ordinary course of their development (*MS*, p. 165) and that relating to one another through sympathetic identification with as intimate and as shared a temperament as circumstance permits and wit suggests, is the very essence of social life. Men who achieve such a relationship in any degree will, to that degree, find their life fulfilling and their conduct proper. Those among them who excel in their sociability are accorded praise and said to be virtuous. Those who act inconsistently with these formal conditions of social life are disapproved. Finally, any ethic which perverts the awakening of social consciousness by causing men to act inconsistently with the ongoing project of community, is the proper subject of moral critique.

Smith's analysis of moral judgments cannot be easily fitted into the foregoing categories of contemporary moral theory without distorting some essential aspect of his position. This has seemed to some to be sufficient warrant for acquiescing in Stephen's judgment that his analysis was, after all, quite superficial. A more plausible hypothesis is that this is so because Smith's analysis is possessed of a greater breadth of vision and depth of insight than these categories can easily accommodate.

CHAPTER III

PSYCHOLOGY

One of the few points upon which Smith's interpreters are in complete accord is in proposing that the psychological theories presupposed by the *Moral Sentiments* are the crucial link between that work and the *Wealth of Nations*. Morrow, who espoused the most enduring form of this view, claimed that the linkage turns in particular on "the place of self-interest in human excellence" (1923a, p. 7).

Notwithstanding the acknowledged centrality of Smith's psychological theories very little attention has been devoted to this aspect of his work. This is due to two circumstances. First, they seem to be so apparent as to require no great effort to comprehend them. His vocabulary appears to commit him to basically the same static and individualistic view of human nature proposed by Hume in his *Treatise* (Bonar 1926, p. 335).[1] Second, an accurate and reliable treatment of Smith's psychological theories is difficult to achieve. He referred to them only indirectly, always in the context of some other subject matter.

A few interpreters have suggested that the typically static reading of Smith's psychological theories is basically shallow. Morrow spoke of "a description of the several stages by which the social consciousness develops..." (1923a, p. 55). Grampp hinted that "economic man passed through three life-stages..." (1948, p. 317);[2] Taylor mentioned "his theory of a social-psychological process operating to produce convergence of the feelings of men in society..." (1960, p. 61). Campbell declared that Smith proposed "the outline of a developmental hypothesis of a type which is familiar in present-day social psychology" (1971, p. 148).

There appears to be good reason to suspect that these glimpses of a dynamic quality in Smith's psychological theories are trustworthy. In

---

[1] Cropsey (1957) went even further. He attempted, without notable success, to force Smith's psychological beliefs into a Hobbesian mechanistic model.

[2] Grampp later clarified this remark indicating that the development he intended was in Smith's thinking about man's psychological make-up (1965, vol. II, pp. 7, 10, 23).

his evaluation of previous accounts of moral judgment Smith rejected every attempt to explain them in terms of powers or faculties. The passions, reason and finally Hutcheson's moral sense were rejected (*MS*, pp. 463-81). Although Smith did refer to the capacity to pass moral judgments as our "moral faculties," the slightest appreciation of the role of sympathy in man's moral life must convince even the most cautious reader that this is an acquired capacity.

It is quite likely, therefore, that Smith's views on psychology did depart sharply from the older static doctrine of human nature and that this departure was in the direction of a developmental theory basically similar in its general outlines to that of Gordon Allport.[3] It is furthermore quite likely that formal acknowledgement of these aspects of his work will be of considerable assistance in specifying the relationship between the doctrinal content of the *Moral Sentiments* and the *Wealth of Nations*.

The purpose of this chapter is to present an orderly account of these developmental aspects of Smith's psychological theories. This account will be divided into what I take to be the three main phases of that developmental process. These will be referred to as the life of pleasure, the life of emulation and the life of virtue. The final section will be devoted to exploring the implication of these theories relative to the dispute over whether Smith did or did not subscribe to the method of individualism.

I

The behavior of the very young child results from the excitation of the passions either by internal stimuli, as in the case of hunger and thirst

---

[3] "The primary problem in the psychology of becoming is to account for the transformation by which the unsocial infant becomes an adult with structured loves, hates, loyalties, and interests, capable of taking his place in a complex ordered society" (Allport 1955, p. 29). Campbell correctly noted that the infant undergoes this transformation, according to Smith, by attempting to gain first the approval of others who care for it and later to maintain its own self-esteem. He went on however to incorrectly identify this view with that of Freud (1971, pp. 149-53). Like Allport (1937) Smith abandoned the conviction that adult motives are reducible to a set of original drives or instincts shared by all men. Both regarded adult motivation to be functionally autonomous of earlier drives or sets of drives. In the course of human maturation both believed that "activities and objects that earlier in the game were *means* to an end, now become *ends* in themselves" (Allport 1937, p. 144; also see Seward 1963). In the course of this chapter I will attempt to show that this assertion relative to Smith's psychological theories is basically sound. In Chapter IV I shall show that Smith believed that not only motives but also institutions can and do become functionally autonomous of their origins.

("Ext. Senses," pp. 219-20), or bij external stimuli. These stimuli activate or trigger the passions by stimulating pleasant or painful sensations (*MS.*, pp. 136-7). Accordingly, the very young child exercises no control over its actions. Its behavior is entirely reflex in nature. Furthermore, those acts which result in cementing pleasant or in dissolving painful relationships are totally spontaneous. There is no possibility that such consequences bespeak purposive actions on the child's part. The very young child, as will be shown shortly, is not even conscious of itself as an agent.

The experience of recurrent painful sensations in similar circumstances, especially where they are inflicted by parents, quickly alter this initial condition (*LJ*, p. 74). Smith was convinced that pain is the only effective instrument of moral education for the very young. "Hardships, danger, injuries, misfortunes, are the only masters under whom we can learn the exercise of this virtue [viz., self-command]" (*MS*, p. 215). The first lesson in the "great school of self-command" is reverence for others.

It is even of considerable importance that the evil which is done without design should be regarded as a misfortune to the doer as well as to the sufferer. Man is thereby taught to reverence the happiness of his brethren, to tremble lest he should, even unknowingly, do any thing that can hurt them, and to dread that animal resentment which he feels, is ready to burst out against him, if he should, without design, be the unhappy instrument of their calamity. (*MS*, p. 155)

Although an advocate of strict discipline, Smith did not regard discipline as coercion. A child who has learned to revere his father has not merely taken it upon himself to coerce his own actions as his father has. Much more is involved in moral education, as Smith understood it, than conditioning certain reflexes. Specifically, three changes occur in the very young child as it is effectively disciplined.

First, the child under the discipline of others, becomes conscious of itself as an agent. This occurs when the child associates its present painful sensation with its own previous action through the mediation of another person. It is only through this linkage of sensations that the child can become conscious of itself as an agent (*MS*, pp. 136-8). Although Smith was prepared to allow that a person might be able to manage some feeble awareness of the relative efficiency of one mode of conduct as opposed to another apart from any contact with other persons (*MS*, pp. 276-7), he everywhere insisted that the mediation of another person is a necessary condition of consciousness of self as agent. This is apparent not only in his repeated usage of the figure of the mirror in discussions of reflection and consciousness, but also in his complete rejection of the

"Robinson Crusoe" analogy which soon became popular among utilitarians and economists.

> Were it possible that a human creature could grow up to manhood in some solitary place without any communication with his own species, he could no more think of his own character, of the propriety or demerit of his sentiments and conduct, of the beauty or deformity of his own mind, than of the beauty or deformity of his own face. ... To a man who from birth was a stranger to society, the objects of his passions, the external objects which either pleased or hurt him, would occupy his whole attention. (*MS*, p. 162; also see p. 261).

The child becomes conscious of itself as an agent through discipline suffered at the hands of others in three distinct steps. He first recognizes that the other person responds differently to different stimuli. In particular, he strikes out to dissolve his relationship with painful stimuli. The sharp discomfort of the child causes it to acknowledge that it too responds differently to different stimuli. Next, the child notices that its own behavior has served as a stimulus for the other fellow. Again his present pain causes the child to acknowledge that the other fellow's behavior has stimulated its own painful sensation. Finally, connecting these observations, the child becomes conscious that it has been the indirect cause of its own present sensations (*MS*, pp. 136-8; 163-4).

The second change which occurs within the child as a result of discipline bears upon the criterion by which its conduct is determined. To the extent that the child is conscious that it has met with its present painful sensation because it has caused another person to suffer pain, the child will begin to take what it imagines to be the other fellow's sentiments into account when determining his future actions. This "regard to the sentiments of the real or supposed spectator of our action" introduces a "sort of impartiality between ourselves and others" into the process whereby the child as agent responds to various stimuli (*MS*, pp. 203, 196).

This regard for the sentiments of others provides the basis for the third change within the child to result from effective discipline, viz., a degree of self-determination. By introducing that consideration into the process of determining the response to a stimulus the child is enabled to exercise a degree of control over its conduct. By giving more and more weight to its concern for the sentiments of others, the child begins to govern its own passions. It begins to decide "where and how far every other principle of our nature ought either to be indulged or restrained" (*MS*, p. 234).

Complete self-control is not achieved until the child has completely subordinated its impulses to its concern for the sentiments of others.

There are many half-way houses between the initial condition of completely reflexive behavior and the final completely socialized condition. It is not unusual, for example to find that an older child or a young man pretends to be possessed of the qualities, talents and virtues known to exact the praise of others when he knows very well that he does not possess them. Such a person Smith termed vain. "He is guilty of vanity who desires praise for what, indeed, very well deserves it, but what he perfectly knows does not belong to him" (*MS*, p. 453; also see pp. 171, 374-5). Although vanity in grown men is among the most detestable of vices, in the maturing child is a sign of progress. The child would not even pretend to possess such qualities unless he earnestly desired to possess them. "Vanity is frequently no more than an attempt prematurely to usurp that glory before it is due" (*MS*, p. 379).

The vain young man's moral education is not yet complete. To complete it, however, discipline must be carefully administered. The youth needs to be encouraged to pursue the object of his desire – praiseworthy qualities – but more diligently. This is indeed a very delicate assignment, but an all-important one. "The great secret of education is to direct vanity to proper objects" (*MS*, p. 379).

In his discussion of Mandeville's *Fable of the Bees*, in which apparently public-spirited conduct is reduced to mere pandering in the service of self-gratification, Smith touched upon that feature of the vain young man which is most in need of attention. Although the vain man does take the sentiments of others into account, he views them only as a means to increasing his own pleasure and decreasing his own pain (*MS*, pp. 452-6). What the vain youth has yet to learn is to subordinate considerations of his own pleasure and pain to his desire to attain to those qualities which in fact exact the approval of others. The mentor of the vain youth is assisted in helping him to learn this lesson. The youth not only desires to attain those qualities to which he now only pretends, but deeply dreads being discovered for the fraud that he is (*MS*, pp. 171-2). Presumably, the mentor guides vanity to proper objects by carefully indicating to the youth that he recognizes the sham and by encouraging him to be more diligent in attaining to the qualities to which he now merely pretends.

II

The overall objective of moral education is to enable a person to govern his behavior by subordinating the spontaneous impulses of passion to considerations of what are or should be the sentiments of others.[4] This

---

[4] Accordingly, it is inconsistent with Smith's views to claim that "goal dis-

objective is achievable only over a long period of time. Years of experience are required first to enable the child to subdue its passions, This capability is acquired through the administration of punishment by others. Once a person has succeeded in regularly subordinating the impulses of his passions to his estimate of what is praiseworthy or blameworthy in the eyes of others, discipline administered by others has exhausted its usefulness as an instrument of moral education (*WN*, pp. 720-1). Moral education, however, is far from complete when a person is able to discipline his own passions. In fact, it has only begun. Such a person has next to formulate a more or less accurate estimate of which modes of conduct are praiseworthy and which blameworthy. He learns the standards of appropriate behavior through instruction, although not that typified by abstruse syllogism (*MS*, pp. 196, 203). Here again, as in the case of the discipline of the passions, he is first instructed by others and only later by himself (Campbell 1971, pp. 151-7).

Punishment effectively administered by others causes us "to examine our own passions and conduct, and consider how these must appear to them, by considering how they would appear to us if in their situation" (*MS*, p. 164). Once the passions are subordinated to sympathetic identification with others, the dominant motive of a man's behavior is the love of praise and the dread of blame. This motive must not be confused with vanity, since the latter motive grants only an instrumental value to consideration for the sentiments of others (*MS*, pp. 171, 183-4, 371-84, 451-6).

Every man, even the very young child, desires the approval of his fellows and dreads their disapproval for its own sake. The love of praise and dread of blame, although it burns very low initially and continues at a low level for some throughout their lives, is never fully absent. "The greatest ruffian, the most hardened violator of the laws of society, is not altogether without it" (*MS*, p. 3). Indeed it was this desire which enabled the child, responding to the discipline of others, to subdue his passions.

Nature, when she formed man for society, endowed him with an original desire to please, and an original aversion to offend his brethren. She taught him to feel pleasure in their favourable, and pain in their unfavourable regard. She rendered their approbation most flattering and most agreeable to him for its own sake, and their disapprobation most mortifying and most offensive. (*MS*, p. 170).

The young person who has effectively resolved to govern his conduct according to the sentiments of others can estimate what others regard as

placement," a necessary condition of social behavior, is essentially subversive of the values of the members of a society. (Becker, 1969, p. 71).

praiseworthy and blameworthy only by attending to what they actually praise and blame. First attempts to appraise and direct conduct by sympathetic as opposed to original sentiments must, therefore, regard public opinion as the standard of appropriate behavior. The young man who is motivated by the love of praise and adopts public opinion as his standard of action will judge the qualities which enjoy the acclaim of his fellows to be the ones which are most praiseworthy and will accordingly make every effort to attain and to act as befits a person possessed of those excellences of character. This is the life of emulation.

> The love and admiration which we naturally conceive for those whose character and conduct we approve of, necessarily dispose us to desire to become ourselves the object of the like agreeable sentiments, and to be as amiable and as admirable as those whom we love and admire the most. Emulation, the anxious desire that we ourselves should excell, is originally founded upon our admiration of the excellence of others. (*MS*, p. 166)

The conscientious youth who surveys public affairs quickly discovers that what qualifies men most often for acclaim is the possession of riches. He finds men stratified into two main groups or ranks depending upon whether they are possessed of wealth or not. Both the few who are rich and the many who are not appear to regard the possession of wealth as the appropriate warrant for praise and therefore as the proper object of emulation (*MS*, pp. 84-5). Men of all ranks are motivated by what Smith called the desire of bettering our condition, not because they believe that wealth will enhance their ease or pleasure, but because they observe that reputation is based upon its possession. "To be observed, to be attended to, to be taken notice of with sympathy, complacency, and approbation, are all the advantages which we can propose to derive from it" (*MS*, p. 71).

Although both those who are rich and those who are not view the possessions of wealth as the mark of excellence, as the measure of status or place in the community (*MS*, pp. 80-1), the ethic of the one differs markedly from that of those of others. In fact, Smith distinguished four such ethics, viz., that of the rich, that of the middle rank, that of the ambitious and that of the very poor.[5]

Those who, by virtue of their wealth, enjoy the sympathy and admi-

---

[5] Although he distinguished between the values of the middle rank and those of the ambitious on the one hand and those of the destitute on the other, Smith recognized that only two of the four ethics cited were articulated in developed moral systems, viz., the liberal system of the rich and powerful and the strict system of the common people (*WN*, pp. 746-8, 757). This does not indicate, however, as Campbell appears to have surmised, that Smith recognized only two classes, ranks or stations in society (1971, pp. 174-8).

ration of their fellows glory in their riches. These men cultivate the performance of small duties with a high degree of propriety. Their chief concern is to maintain an elegant and graceful air, manner and deportment. Above all, they avoid engaging in controversy or contest for they can never gain but only lose stature through them (*MS*, pp. 75-6).

Men of the middle ranks cannot hope to distinguish themselves in the same way. They can share in the attention and praise enjoyed by the rich only by imitating them. But in order to command fealty they must purchase it by their labor, both of mind and body. For this reason they cultivate superior knowledge, industry, patience, a competitive spirit and a keen sensitivity for the law and for the sentiments of others (*MS*, pp. 76-80). Most men of the middle ranks of society do not intend to improve their condition so much that they achieve a place among the rich. After a little experience most men easily recognize that little of value is to be gained by such exertions (*MS*, p. 70). For this reason their admiration of the rich is "disinterested." They defer to and serve the rich because the rich are believed to deserve it (*MS*, pp. 70-4, 84-5 and 258).[6]

Some men do not show such good sense. These are ambitious men who desire to change their rank (*MS*, p. 247). There are always a few young men who, as they contemplate the splendid palaces of princes, imagine that their accommodations are much superior to those of the common cottage. They are so charmed by this image of distant felicity that they commit their entire lives to the achievement of that much desired object (*MS*, pp. 259-63). Scratching and clawing their way toward that goal, they sacrifice health, friends and dignity. Such men realize their folly when at last they have attained the object of their ambition only to learn what others have known all along.

Power and riches appear then to be what they are – enormous and operose machines contrived to produce a few trifling conveniences to the body, consisting of springs the most nice and delicate, which must be kept in order with the most anxious attention, and which, in spite of all our care, are ready every moment to burst into pieces and to crush in their ruins their unfortunate possessor. (*MS*, p. 262).

So pervasive is the clamor for status that only a few escape it. The very poor, who are also anxious to enjoy the approval of their fellows, however, are ashamed of their poverty. The knowledge that they are either not noticed at all or are not accorded the compassion which is their due, mortifies them in their own eyes. Although in spirit and talent they are not significantly inferior to their neighbors, they often identify with the judgment of their fellows and sink into an overwhelming sense of their

---

[6] Deference to the wealthy will be discussed at length in Chapters IV and V.

own inferiority. This is the principal cause of "idiotism" (*MS*, pp. 381-2).

The conscientious young man who attempts to formulate a reliable estimate of which modes of conduct are praiseworthy and which blameworthy turns first to public opinion as his guide. Should he be so unfortunate as to adhere initially to the ethic of the rich, to that of the poor or to that of ambition, his moral education will quite likely be permanently subverted. If, on the other hand, he is born into the middle ranks of society and has the wit to discern the triviality of riches, he has a chance of maturing into a relatively wise and virtuous man. Fortunately most men adhere to the ethic of the middle rank (*MS*, p. 63).

The young man who adheres to the ethic of the middle rank exerts himself in an effort to approximate as best he can the lifestyle of the rich. He develops a degree of prudence as well as a strict sense of justice. Neither is he indifferent to his debts of gratitude. In his efforts to develop and to live consistently with these qualities, he always has an eye to their utility, but utility in quite a different sense than had been his concern earlier when he vainly attempted to usurp praise for qualities he did not possess. Instead of advantage his concern now is respectability. He prefers these qualities of character to others because, as Hume observed, they suggest to him the life-style of the rich, which they so delicately befit (*MS*, pp. 257-8; 269-71). He approves of his conduct and character because it is possessed of that species of beauty known as utility. His actions and personality befit his idea of excellence.[7]

Occasionally such people reject the life of emulation. Perhaps this is because they are ashamed of their complicity in the degradation of the poor, perhaps because they recognize that deference ought not be given to others merely because they possess a few trinkets and machines of pleasure, or perhaps it is because they yearn for more solid recognition than the cool esteem they have been able to manage in the shadow of an unreformed peerage. For whatever reason, such men on occasion begin to reflect and wonder. When they do they soon begin to resent being the subjects of praise for no better reason than utility. "It seems impossible . . . that we should have no better reason for praising a man than that for which we commend a chest of drawers." It is found upon investigation "that the usefulness of any disposition of mind is seldom the first ground of our approbation; and that the sentiment of approbation always involves in it a sense of propriety quite distinct from the perception of utility." All the qualities so intimately bound up with the ethic of the middle rank – superior reason, understanding and self-

---

[7] Smith's usage of the term "utility" will be discussed in Chapter IV.

command – "are originally approved as just and right and accurate, and not merely as useful or advantageous" (*MS*, p. 271).

The young man who asserts that the qualities recommended by the ethic of the middle ranks are praiseworthy, not because they fit into a scheme of things presided over by the rich, but because they are right, echoes the judgment of moralists of all ages.

This disposition to admire, and almost to worship, the rich and the powerful, and to despise or, at least, to neglect persons of poor and mean condition, though necessary both to establish and to maintain the distinction of ranks and the order of society, is, at the same time, the great and most universal cause of the corruption of our moral sentiments. That wealth and greatness are often regarded with the respect and admiration which are due only to wisdom and virtue, and that the contempt, of which vice and folly are the only proper objects, is often most unjustly bestowed upon poverty and weakness, has been the complaint of moralists in all ages. (*MS*, p. 84).

III

The final phase of development begins the moment a man breaks with the life of emulation. To the extent that he asserts that the habits promoted by the ethic of the middle ranks are approved not because they put one in mind of the way of life of the rich, but because they are right and just, to that extent he has also asserted the primacy of conscience over public opinion (*MS*, pp. 185-7) and rededicated himself to acting from a love of praiseworthiness and dread of blameworthiness (*MS*, p. 166). Such a man has thereupon embarked upon a life of virtue.

To the extent that a man fully enters upon this course he governs his conduct according to his own idea of propriety rather than merely by the norms of performance which prevail in his society. He subordinates the impulses of his passions to a sympathetic identification with the temper of the impartial rather than the actual spectator. He judges actions praiseworthy to the extent that they accord more nearly with that temper than is commonly attained (see Chapter II).

Before turning to a more concrete discussion of the life of virtue two of its distinguishing features deserve mention. First, it is with this phase of development that the individual fully attains to what Smith called his "moral faculties" i.e., the ability of self-determination (*MS*, p. 234). Now he not only subdues his passion, but does so in accordance with his own idea of propriety. Second, the mature individual strives to become virtuous not as a means to self-gratification, nor to merit the approval of others, but for its own sake. He strives to become virtuous because being virtuous and only that is praiseworthy. In this last phase of de-

velopment he at last recognizes that the prime motive of human life is
the love of virtue (*MS*, pp. 171, 194).

Smith nowhere provided a formal definition of virtue. Two of his
general remarks, however, supply an ample basis for constructing such
a definition. When stating the first of the two main questions of interest
to the moral philosopher Smith gave a paraphrase of such a definition.
"First, wherein does virtue consist, or what is the tone of temper and
tenor of conduct which constitutes the excellent and praiseworthy character, the character which is the natural object of esteem, honour, and
approbation?" (*MS*, p. 391).

Two points are included in this remark, one of which has been clear
all along. First, virtue is the proper object of praise. Second, virtue is
primarily a quality of the person, a "tone of temper," and only second-
arily a quality of his actions, a "tenor of conduct." [8] Smith agreed with
Aristotle in regarding virtue as the habit of moderating action according
to an impartial standard (*MS*, pp. 399-402). For Smith, of course, that
standard is the sentiment of the impartial spectator.

"Virtue is excellence, something uncommonly great and beautiful,
which rises far above what is vulgar and common" (*MS*, p. 28). The
point of this second remark is that virtue is a relative excellence or
superiority. Neither the degree of moderation typically attained by men
nor the supreme perfection personified by the impartial spectator alone
defines the level of accomplishment which determines the virtuous character. The criterion of moral judgment is a complex of both the ideal and
the norm of performance. Virtue approaches the ideal more closely than
is ordinarily attained by men (*MS*, pp. 28-30; 362-3; Campbell 1971, pp.
166-71).

A relatively complete definition of virtue may now be stated. Virtue
is the extraordinarily effective ability to regularly moderate one's actions
in accordance with the sentiments of the impartial spectator.

This ability is composed of two principal elements, the one cognitive
the other appetitive. To be possessed of virtue a man must have an
extraordinarily acute knowledge of what is ideally required of him in
his concrete circumstance. Still, as Aristotle saw, superior knowledge
alone does not make a man virtuous. To be virtuous such a man must
also be possessed of an extraordinary capability of acting in accordance

---

[8] It follows from these two points that the proper object of moral praise is the
habit of moderating one's actions in accordance with the sentiments of the impartial spectator. An action is an object of praise only in a secondary sense. A
generous act is praised only to the extent that it is regarded as befitting the agent's
habit of benevolence. It is in this sense that the beauty of utility constitutes an
essential, although subordinate, aspect of Smith's moral theory (*MS*, p. 480).

with that knowledge. "The most perfect knowledge, if it is not supported by the most perfect self-command, will not always enable him to do his duty" (*MS*, p. 349).

Smith distinguished four cardinal moral virtues, viz., prudence, justice, benevolence and self-command. Since, however, self-command is a necessary element of every virtue, we must conclude that there are but three distinguishable modes of character which may be termed virtuous.[9] These may be referred to under the titles of the other three cardinal virtues. Self-command is an element of each of these. "Self-command is not only itself a great virtue, but from it all the other virtues seem to derive their principal lustre" (*MS*, p. 354).

Prudence, justice and benevolence, considered as modes of character, are distinguished in point of what is ideally required of a man in his concrete circumstance. In general this amounts to promoting well-being through action. Prudence is the habit of promoting one's own well-being. Justice and benevolence are habits of promoting the well-being of others. Justice disposes a man to do so by restraining him from doing harm to others, benevolence does so by disposing him to contribute to their benefit (*MS*, pp. 310, 319-20).

The care of health, of the fortune, of the rank and reputation of the individual, the objects upon which his comfort and happiness in this life are supposed principally to depend, is considered as the proper business of that virtue which is commonly called prudence. (*MS*, p. 311)

Every man is inclined by his selfish passions to act in the service of his own present well-being (*MS*, pp. 55-59). The character of the prudent man is distinguished by the disposition to moderate these passions in accordance with the temper of the impartial spectator. The prudent man promotes his own well-being by taking approximately equal interest in both the short and the long term benefit of any action (*MS*, p. 314). His character is marked by two distinctive traits, viz., frugality and industry. Of these the former is controlling. Most men enjoy relative prosperity and therefore are more susceptible to loss than to gain (*MS*, pp. 60-9). "Security, therefore, is the first and principal object of prudence" (*MS*, p. 311). Still, security of one's own well-being depends primarily upon maintaining a reputation for reasonableness in the eyes of others. That in turn is best maintained by striving to improve one's "place" in society. For that reason industry is also an essential feature of prudence (*MS*, pp. 70-83, 311-12).

[9] Campbell argued that self-command is not a virtue because men can exercise it in pursuit of evil ends (1971, pp. 168-9).

A sacred and religious regard not to hurt or disturb in any respect the happiness of our neighbour, even in those cases where no law can protect him, constitutes the character of the perfectly innocent and just man ... (*MS*, p. 319-20)

Every man is inclined by his "unsocial passions" to harm anyone who threatens his own well-being (*MS*, pp. 44-51). The character of the just man is distinguished by the disposition to effectively restrain these passions in accordance with the temper of the impartial spectator. The just man permits himself to give vent to his resentment only when another fellow wrongly and effectively inflicts harm upon some other person (*MS*, pp. 93-108). Furthermore, he carefully measures his response according to the gravity of the injury actually suffered (*MS*, p. 121). By permitting himself to exercise resentment within these limits the just man effectively forces others to respect the well-being of their neighbors. It is on this account that justice, unlike benevolence, may be "extorted by force" (*MS*, p. 112).

Every man is inclined by his social passions to bestow benefits upon others (*MS*, pp. 52-4). The character of the benevolent man is distinguished by the disposition to moderate these passions in accordance with the temper of the impartial spectator. The benevolent man bestows benefits according to impartial priorities, i.e., an order according to which the good offices of the benevolent man are ordinarily due others. The order which Smith recommended was based upon the relative importance of the different services of the benevolent man to the various recipients (*MS*, p. 320). This importance ordinarily depends upon two principles, viz., the extent of one's knowledge of the situation of others and the extent of one's ability to effect that situation.

That wisdom which contrived the system of human affections, as well as that of every other part of nature, seems to have judged that the interests of the great society of mankind would be best promoted by directing the principal attention of each individual to that particular portion of it which was most within the sphere both of his abilities and of his understanding. (*MS*, p. 337)

The good offices of the benevolent man are due both to individuals and to societies. The order in which they are due individuals is as follows: self, family, friends, those of superior rank and those of inferior rank. In each case the higher priority of benevolence is ordinarily granted those individuals whose situation admits more of adequate understanding and of benefit by the actions of the benevolent individual. This is quite apparent as regards oneself as opposed to that of other members of one's family. It is equally the case in regard to the situations of those of superior as opposed to those of inferior rank. The best way to improve the condition of the miserable is ordinarily to work through the channels provided by the existing social constitution (*MS*, pp. 321-33).

The order in which the good offices of the benevolent man are due societies is based upon the same principle. They are due first to the nation in which he was born and educated and which provides him continued protection from both foreign and domestic threats. Although he may sympathize with the situation of citizens of other nations, he must resign their plight to others (*MS*, pp. 345-8). His efforts can seldom affect the situation of anyone beyond the sphere of his own nation. Furthermore, the well-being of groups within one's own nation depend upon the maintenance of the established constitution of the larger society. Accordingly, the benevolent man is ordinarily disposed to act in behalf of his nation and only then in support of one of its component groups (*MS*, pp. 334-44). Finally, Smith stated that the benevolent man ordinarily subordinates his obligations to individuals to his obligations to societies.[10]

The wise and virtuous man is at all times willing that his own private interest should be sacrificed to the public interest of his own particular order or society. He is at all times willing, too, that the interest of this order or society should be sacrificed to the greater interest of the state or sovereignty of which it is only a subordinate part . . . (*MS*, p. 346)

The completely virtuous man combines in his character all of these virtues in their perfection. Perfect attainment of any one of these in concert with even a slight degree of the others is seldom achieved by anyone. To be worthy of praise, however, one needs only attain to the character of the completely virtuous man more nearly than is commonly achieved. Besides distinguishing the ideal of performance with regard to the cardinal virtues, Smith mentioned what he took to be the degree to which these perfections are typically attained. Men are commonly able to maintain self-command in familiar and felicitous circumstances but fail to do so "under the heaviest and most unexpected misfortunes . . ." (*MS*, p. 220). Inferior prudence is the common care of one's own well-being exercised without concern for social justice and relief of the misery of one's fellow man (*MS*, pp. 315-16). Mere justice or lawfulness is the regard for only the legal rights of others (*MS*, pp. 319-20). Vulgar bene-

---

[10] Smith did not regard "the love of country" to be the same as nationalism or "the mean principle of national prejudice" (*MS*, p. 336). For him patriotism was composed of two sentiments which are not infrequently inconsistent with one another, viz., respect for the established constitution and concern for the welfare of one's fellow citizens (*MS*, p. 339). When these are in conflict the wise determination of the priorities of benevolence requires "the highest effort of political wisdom" and is left to individual conscience (*MS*, pp. 339-40).

volence limits one's allegiance to his nation to obeying civil authorities
(*MS*, p. 339).

To the extent that a man is disposed to act in ways which surpass
these norms, he is entitled not merely to our approval but to our praise.
Hence, although men enter upon the life of virtue by affirming the
independent rightness of those habits which are promoted by the ethic
of the middle ranks, they strive continually to attain to degrees of worth
well beyond what is common and vulgar.

IV

An unspoken assumption among most of Smith's interpreters has been
that he subscribed to what is known today as methodological individualism. Although seldom explicitly stated, Smith is commonly assumed to
have held, as had Hobbes, Locke, Mill and later micro-economists, that
the rules which govern the behavior of men in society are reducible to
(i.e., deducible from) the rules which govern individual behavior or to
what J. S. Mill called "The laws of the nature of individual men"
(*Science of Logic,* VI, 1, 1). One of the principal benefits of an explicit
study of the developmental aspects of Smith's psychological theories is
that it enables us to see that this assumption is untenable.

One of the most controversial of Morrow's conclusions was that Smith
abandoned the method of individualism in ethics and thereby committed
himself to an organic concept of society (1923a, pp. 12-38). Upon close
scrutiny it appears that Morrow at once overstated and understated his
case. He overstated his findings, as did Selby-Bigge before him (1897,
p. lx) and Bryson after him (1945, p. 160), by supposing that a denial
of methodological individualism is equivalent to affirming what is today
known as metaphysical holism, i.e., the belief that a social system is an
organic whole, the component parts of which are individual human
beings whose behavior is determined by the functional laws of the whole.
By employing an holistic vocabulary in describing Smith's view of the
relation of men in society Morrow provoked a negative response. Davenport declared talk about the organic unity of society or a group mind
to be meaningless (1925, pp. 608-9). Responding to similar claims in
other contexts, many denounced them as sinister overtures which portend
denial of individual autonomy and covertly support totalitarian politics
(Hayek 1944, 1948, 1952; Popper 1945, 1957; Watkins 1957). Such
disputes were unfortunate for two reasons. First, they were based upon
the acceptance of a logical fallacy. The denial of methodological individualism, as has since been shown repeatedly, does not entail meta-

physical holism (Gellner 1956; Mandelbaum 1957; Goldstein 1958; Brodbeck 1958). Second, in the course of this dispute one important issue has been neglected, viz., whether Smith did in fact abandon the method of individualism.

Morrow also understated his case by restricting his contention that Smith abandoned the method of individualism to the sphere of ethics. He correctly observed (1923a, pp. 29-33) that ethical conduct occurs, in Smith's judgment, only where and to the extent that men subordinate, as best they can, the impulse of their passions in accordance with the sentiments of the impartial spectator. To be sure it is the desire for praiseworthiness on the part of the individual which interests him in conforming his conduct and character to the temper of the impartial spectator. The point is, however, that he does not come to regard the sentiments of the impartial spectator as being of overriding importance because they conform to the impulse of his passions, but often in spite of the fact that they do not. It was for this reason that Smith insisted that self-command is an essential feature of all moral virtues.

> To act according to the dictates of prudence, of justice, and proper benevolence, seems to have no great merit where there is no temptation to do otherwise. But to act with cool determination in the midst of the greatest dangers and difficulties ... is the character of the most exalted wisdom and virtue. Self-command is not only itself a great virtue, but from it all the other virtues seem to derive their principal lustre. (*MS*, p. 354)

What Morrow failed to observe was that this same point applies to the action of individuals involved in the life of emulation. Smith devoted an entire chapter of the *Moral Sentiments* to opposing all attempts at "deducing" the satisfaction a person experiences when others sympathize with him "from certain refinements of self-love" (*MS*, pp. 10-13). Men involved in the life of emulation also subordinate, as best they can, the impulse of their passions in accordance with the sentiments of spectators, but here it is to those of real spectators – to public opinion. Here also men are interested in conforming their conduct and character to the temper of others, this time by the desire for praise. But again they do not accept the sentiments of others as being of overriding importance because they conform to the impulse of their own passions, but very often in spite of the fact that they do not.

Certainly the most interesting case of emulative behavior mentioned by Smith was the pursuit of wealth.[11] As indicated above, Smith ob-

---

[11] This observation contradicts the prevailing opinion that for Smith "the desire of bettering our condition," which is the motivational basis of commercial society (*WN*, pp. 81, 324-5, 326, 329, 379, 508, 638), is synonymous with self-love. Morrow, whose argument in favor of this view is representative, based this con-

served that the effort of men to better their condition by accumulating wealth is at root an attempt to obtain the acceptance and praise of their fellows and not, at least for the great bulk of men, an effort to satisfy their own passions (*MS*, pp. 70-83). The confirmation of this observation came to Smith when he discovered that the pursuit of wealth is, for those caught up in this way of life, usually disinterested. They regard the pursuit of riches not as the most efficient way to maximize their own satisfactions, but simply as the right way to behave (*MS*, pp. 84-90; 258). When carried to an extreme the pursuit of wealth becomes absurd by any reasonable standards (*MS*, pp. 259-63). Still, even when accompanied by good sense it is "vulgar" and "obvious" (*WN*, p. 325). Smith's fundamental objection to this plutocratic ethic was not that it failed to satisfy the primary needs of men. This appears to have been of relatively minor importance to Smith since, in his view, the necessities of life could be afforded by the wages of the meanest laborer (*MS*, p. 70; *LJ*, p. 158; *WN*, pp. 67-8, 74). His main objection was that under this ethic praise and blame were awarded on the basis of wealth and poverty instead of on the basis of virtue and vice (*MS*, pp. 84-5).

On the basis of these observations and the above analysis of Smith's psychological theories it appears certain that Smith did abandon the method of individualism both in ethics and in political economy. Stated negatively this means that Smith denied that the ethical and commercial rules according to which men govern their actions in society are explicable in terms of, reducible to or deducible from "the laws of the nature of individual man." In positive form it means that Smith regarded canons of ethical and commercial behavior to be *sui generis*. This seems to be what Selby-Bigge, Morrow and Bryson had in mind when they spoke of the relationship of men in society as being organic. In order to capture Smith's meaning here it is necessary to keep three points firmly in mind.

---

clusion upon a forced reading of a single sentence in the *Wealth of Nations*: "It is not from the benevolence of the butcher, the brewer, or the baker, that we expect our dinner, but from their regard to their own interest" (*WN*, p. 14). When studied in context it becomes apparent that the point Smith was trying to make here was that men who incline to amass their fortunes by enlisting the efforts of others in their behalf would be foolish if they tried to do so in any other way than on a *quid pro quo* basis. It was on the basis of this mistaken identification of commercial motivation with self-interest that the proposed compatibility between Smith's political economy and Mandeville's "ethics" has been erected (Morrow 1923a, pp. 7-8, 47, 65, 82: also see Cannan in *WN*, p. li). This wholly indefensible thesis has become so widely shared among historians of economic theory, with the notable exception of Gray (1948, p. 11), that W. F. Campbell could proclaim, without feeling the need to attempt textual justification, that "Adam Smith in many ways is Mandeville without paradox" (1967, p. 571).

First, all actions which occur in society are performed by individual human beings. Smith nowhere spoke of group entities in a literal sense. Certainly the impartial spectator and the invisible hand are not such entities. In supporting the view that canons of ethical and commercial behavior are *sui generis* he did not commit himself to what Brodbeck called "descriptive emergence," i.e., the view that there are attributes of group behavior which are not definable in terms of the individuals who compose the group (1958, p. 2). The "group mind" alluded to by Morrow (1923a, p. 57) would certainly have been as meaningless to Smith as it was to Davenport (1925, p. 609).

Second, except in the case of coercion, all actions of men in society are determined by criteria which they regard as their own. A man may regard such criteria as his own either because they are his own by nature, i.e., his original passions, or because they are the norms of conduct which obtain within a group or society with which he identifies. Thus, the voluntary conformity of a man's behavior to social rules, norms or canons may be explained in either of two ways. First, he may act consistently with group norms because he wishes to satisfy his passions and judges that that objective can best be achieved by submitting to those norms. In the case of groups in which norms of behavior are supported for this reason, those norms can, at least in principle, be explained in terms of "the laws of the nature of individual man." Second, he may act consistently with group norms because he accepts those norms as defining the right way to behave independently of whether they provide for the satisfaction of his passions. In the case of societies in which norms of behavior are supported for this reason, those norms have the status of the prevailing conventions of correct behavior. They simply are the rules which men in that society accept as defining the right way to act and they are accepted as such because men identify with the group or society constituted by them. The point ordinarily missed by those who doctrinairely advocate individualism – whether political, sociological or methodological (Schumpeter, 1954, pp. 888-9) – is that an act is no less a man's own, i.e., it is not coerced, merely because his decision to perform it is determined by received criteria even though those criteria have little or nothing to do with the satisfaction of his original passions, provided only that they are the rules which define the right way to behave for a group or society with which he genuinely identifies. The idea of a society in which social choices are ruled by conventions is not, as Arrow (1963, pp. 28-9; also 1967, pp. 221-23) and others who shared his liberal persuasion fear, incompatible with citizen sovereignty.

As stated above, there are two ways in which the voluntary conformity of individual behavior to group norms can be explained. As Brodbeck correctly observed, the question of which type of explanation is appropriate is a question of fact (1958, p. 20). It seems apparent in the light of what has gone before that Smith's experience led him to the judgment that, as a matter of fact, men typically govern their conduct according to the ethical and commercial norms which prevail within their society because they accept those norms as defining the right way to behave. In supporting this factual judgment Smith espoused the view that not only are the scientific and aesthetic norms which prevail within any society ultimately a matter of convention (Chap. I), but so also are its ethical, commercial and, as will be shown in the next chapter, political norms. Each of these norms is a set of rules in terms of which particular practices are justified. The norms themselves are in need of no further warrant beyond being accepted by individual members. In this way all such norms are "institutional rules" (Searle, 1964) and are perceived as "societal facts" (Mandelbaum, 1955).[12] It has been the burden of this entire chapter to show how, in Smith's view, men are brought to accept such norms as their own and to govern their conduct according to them.

Third, when and to the extent that individuals govern their conduct according to criteria which they accept because they are the prevailing conventions of a society with which they genuinely identify they surrender neither their identity nor their autonomy. In fact the opposite is the case. As was shown above, the capacity to govern one's own conduct is acquired only when and to the extent that the individuals consciously subordinate the impulses of their passions to their estimates of what the sentiments of others either are or should be. Furthermore, it is only in this way that they can ever become the proper object of respect and praise in the eyes of others, but most especially in their own eyes.

Respect for what are, or for what ought to be, or for what, upon a certain condition, would be, the sentiments of other people is the sole principle which, upon most occasions, overawes all those mutinous and turbulent passions into that tone and temper which the impartial spectator can enter into and sympathize with (*MS*, p. 386).

[12] The basic affinity between much of the work of Smith and that of modern sociology has not gone altogether unnoticed (Small, 1907; Salomon, 1945). Heimann credited Smith with fathering not only modern economics, but also modern sociology (1945, p. 245). More recently Samuels has explored what he termed "nonlegal forces of social control" in the writings of Smith and others (1966, ch. 2). Unfortunately Samuels persists in regarding such "forces" as frameworks which constrain choice rather than rules which enable and even constitute choice (p. 67).

When and to the extent that an individual governs his conduct by the norms of his society he becomes and becomes conscious of himself as a member of that society. By subordinating his private well-being to what is required by these norms he consciously elevates the well-being of the community as a whole to a position of overriding importance (*MS*, p. 346). This is what I take Morrow to have meant when he said:

Sympathy leads the individual to identify himself with the welfare of others, and eventually to appreciate his own existence as part of a larger whole whose welfare is of supreme importance; and it is his organic relation to this larger whole which accounts for the compelling character of the good. (1925, p. 611).

When Morrow, Selby-Bigge and Bryson spoke of the relationship in which individuals hold themselves in society as being "organic" and indeed of society itself as an "organic" whole, they did not mean to suggest that Smith thought of society as an animal the parts of which are individual men. Rather, they intended to allude to the fact, as Smith saw it, that insofar as individual men act socially they act from a consciousness of themselves as members of a community. What they meant was that this relation of membership is, in their estimate, more adequately comprehended by means of the biological model than by that of static mechanics or for that matter fluid dynamics or cybernetics. The regularized and preserved relationships which men support in communities bear a greater similarity to the vital interdependencies which exist among the organs of an animal than they do to the frameworks which constrict movement in any of the other models listed above.

Adam Smith clearly felt at home in his society and believed the great bulk of his fellows did as well. He regarded the conventions of that society as vehicles by which each and every man could lead a basically satisfactory existence.[13] This is not to suggest that he had no serious grievances with the received conventions. Clearly he did and they were more far-reaching than is generally acknowledged. But he was also convinced that fundamental improvement of those conventions was possible not because the powerful are wise, but because the men of the middle ranks of society are good. He did not tremble lest their quest for recognition should chip away at the lingering vestiges of aristocratic privilege and eventuate in what De Tocqueville and Mill feared most – a tyranny of the majority. It was perhaps his quiet confidence in the basic righteousness of the middle ranks of society more than his avoid-

---

[13] "There is no protest in Smith, as there is in Marx, that work is 'forced labour'. The offer of the best value of one's work in exchange for another's services via the market was made willingly in an atmosphere of self-respect and prudent exchange" (West, 1969b, p. 104; also see 1969a, ch. 8).

ance of rationalism as Morrow suggested (1923a, 88-90) which marked the most profound difference between Smith's perception of the relation of men in society and that of that long line of doctrinaire advocates of individualism from Hobbes through Locke and Mill to Hayek and beyond.

Important though it may be to stress that Smith would probably have preferred the biological model to all others for representing social phenomena, it is still more important to recognize his deep and abiding conviction that although all social values are conventional, men are by nature social beings and this in two senses. First, men cannot attain happiness and perfection except in community (*WN*, p. 726). "What so great happiness as to be beloved, and know that we deserve to be loved?" (*MS*, p. 165) "It would be difficult," wrote Macfie, "to represent human desires as seeking a form of satisfaction more social" (1967, p. 56). Second, not only are all men able to benefit by joining in community with their fellows, but all are genuinely anxious to do so.[14]

How selfish soever man may be supposed, there are evidently some principles in his nature, which interest him in the fortune of others, though he derives nothing from it, except the pleasure of seeing it. . . . That we often derive sorrow from the sorrow of others is a matter of fact too obvious to require any instances to prove it; for this sentiment . . . is by no means confined to the virtuous and humane . . . The greatest ruffian, the most hardened violator of the laws of society, is not altogether without it. (*MS*, p. 3)

[14] Smith criticized Mandeville and Rousseau on the one hand for failing to acknowledge that man is possessed of a "powerful instinct which necessarily determines him to seek society for its own sake . . ." ("Letter," p. 24). and Hobbes and Pufendorf on the other for neglecting the "natural love which he bears to his own kind" (*MS*, p. 463).

CHAPTER IV

GOVERNMENT

Interest in Smith's political thought stems from the realization that his advocacy of a roughly laissez faire policy is not fully intelligible in terms of the arguments adduced in the *Wealth of Nations*. That policy position was advocated there on the basis of his opposition to certain types of government activity. That argument, however, presupposes an overall orientation toward government. After having indicated this, Viner forwarded a rough description of that orientation and suggested that it can be understood only by an investigation of Smith's political thought.

There is no possible room for doubt, however, that Smith in general believed that there was, to say the least, a strong presumption against government activity beyond its fundamental duties of protection against foreign foes and maintenance of justice. (1927, p. 219)

The purpose of this chapter is to develop a reliable statement of the political theories, beliefs and convictions which brought Smith to this orientation. In order to accomplish this objective consideration will be devoted to his views on political obligation, the nature and function of government and the justification of governmental authority. In the course of these considerations fresh light will be shed on such issues as the sociological basis of politics, the enforcement of morals and the rise of government through a division of labor.

In order to develop a reliable statement of Smith's political theories, beliefs and convictions, it is necessary to draw upon fragments, i.e. statements which occur either in ethical and economic contexts or in a set of early lectures which Smith judged unworthy of publication. Clearly any account of this nature amounts to a reconstruction, the truth of which is at best probable. This caution need not deter the historian. It does, however, draw attention to one point of major importance. In reconstructing what may reasonably be regarded as Smith's political thought, the investigator must weigh, assess and interpret fragmentary statements. He must decide which of these statements is of greater and which is of less overall importance. He must also identify the nature of the logical relations which bind these statements into a coherent whole. In order to make these decisions and identifications the investigator must organize these fragmentary statements within some frame of reference. The selection of such a frame of reference, therefore, is an important juncture in developing a reliable account of Smith's political thought.

Previous Smithian interpreters have selected one of three frames of reference each of which seems plausible. The earliest and still most popular strategy is to locate Smith in the natural law tradition.[1] The plausibility of this view derives from Smith's references to Grotius and Pufendorf as well as to the natural order, natural price and the system of natural liberty. Viner (1927) and Bittermann (1940), however, have already shown that belief in natural law played no significant role in either the *Wealth of Nations* or the *Moral Sentiments* (also see Chap. I and VII). Should any doubts about the accuracy of these critiques remain, the reader is referred to Smith's sharp criticism of Stoic moral theory (*MS*, pp. 402-28).

A more recent strategy locates Smith in the social contract tradition which emphasizes natural rights (Cropsey 1957, 1963; Grampp 1965; vol. II, pp. 43-50). The plausibility of this view derives from the similarity, noted by Cannan (*WN*, p. 674n; *LJ*, p. 15n) and Viner (1927, p. 219), between Smith's assertions that the end of government is the protection of property and statements by John Locke to the same effect. The adoption of this frame of reference is based upon three premises each of which is false. First, it is claimed that Smith subscribed to the same psychological views as had the earlier contract theorists, i.e., that men are fundamentally avaricious, mean and belligerent, but clever in serving their own interests. That Smith subscribed to nothing of the sort was shown in Chapters II and III above. Second, it is claimed that Smith too believed that men are possessed of certain natural rights and that it is the function of government to secure these. It is quite accurate to suggest that Smith regarded the function of government to be the restraining of acts regarded as the proper object of public resentment (*MS*, p. 319). But it is not the case that Smith regarded resentment, however compellingly felt by an individual, to be the sufficient condition for regarding the object which occasioned that sentiment as the proper object of public resentment. According to Smith the question of whether a man's claim ought to be defended by government turns on whether his fellows

---

[1] Leslie 1888, pp. 21-40; Zeyss 1889, pp. 107-9; Hasbach 1891, pp. 6-7; Bonar 1893, pp. 172-77; Ingram 1908, p. 89; Morrow 1923a, pp. 52-3; 1927, pp. 333-35; Myrdal 1954, pp. 43-5; Gray 1931, p. 125; Strong 1932, pp. 63-8; Gide and Rist n, d., p. 89; Barnes and Becker 1952, vol. I, pp. 523-4; Schumpeter 1954, p. 182; Hutchison 1964, pp. 24-5, 130-32.

approve his resentment as proper.[2] Third, it is claimed that Smith believed that political obligation derives from an implicitly contractual arrangement. Twice in the course of his lectures Smith attacked this theory charging that it was both insufficiently comprehensive and incoherent (*LJ*, pp. 11-13, 69-70).

Grampp found it convenient, as have others, to treat the political theories of Smith and David Hume together as though they reflected basically the same orientation. This practice presupposes the belief that Smith subscribed to Hume's views on the nature of political obligation, viz., that it is rooted in the perception of its social utility. Of all the strategies mentioned so far this appears to be the most promising. The main thrust of Smith's argument in the *Wealth of Nations* is that his policy recommendations ought to be adopted by governments because they promise greater efficiency in augmenting national wealth. Hume's very warm reception of the book certainly indicates that he liked it. Even this interpretive scheme, however, is inappropriate (Campbell 1971, pp. 199-200). Smith agreed with Hume that governments are socially useful, often indispensable. He even agreed that consideration of its utility often confirms and reinforces our willingness to obey our sovereign. But he denied that men obey their sovereign originally or principally because they are convinced of its social utility. Hume's analysis was, in Smith's judgment, rooted in an illicit interference and resulted from considering human actions from an abstract point of view (*MS*, pp. 124-30). In political as well as ethical affairs, utility is subordinate to propriety (*MS*, p. 271). Men support the punishment of criminals, for example, not be-

---

[2] This is especially clear in Smith's discussion of one of the earliest forms of property right. "Occupation seems well founded when the spectator can go along with my possession of the object and approve me when I defend my possession by force" (*LJ*, p. 108). It may be argued that many of Smith's objections to the existing commercial system appear to commit him to at least the more modest natural rights position of H. L. A. Hart (*WN*, pp. 121-2, 141, 497, 549; see Hollander 1971, pp. 282-3). His allusions to the "sacred right of property" and "natural liberty and justice" seem at first reading to presuppose "the equal right of all men to be free" (Hart 1955, p. 175). A more careful reading reveals, however, that Smith did not use the concept of "a right" in the same way as does Hart, viz., "to determine when a person's freedom may be limited by another and so to determine what actions may appropriately be made the subject of coercive legal rules" (Hart 1955, p. 177). What Smith pressed in those criticisms was only that there can be no moral justification for hindering men – whether individually or collectively – from acting on their own moral sentiments. Hart allows that it is not necessary that a moral code employ the concept of a right and so it is not necessary that a moral code recognize the equal right of all men to be free, but asserts that such a code (and presumably a moral theory rooted in such a code) must appear "imperfect" to men whose perspective has been formed in the liberal tradition (Hart 1955, pp. 176-177).

cause it is expected to deter crime (although it probably will), but because crime is universally regarded as hateful (*MS*, pp. 108-10).

A comprehensive study of Smith's writings not only disqualifies these frameworks for interpreting his political fragments, but suggests one which is more reliable viz., his own ethical theory. According to him political economy is a branch of natural jurisprudence which is in turn a branch of ethics (*MS*, pp. 501-3; *LJ*, pp. 1-3; *WN*, p. 397). One further point needs to be borne in mind especially by those whose perspective on political theory is geared to post-revolutionary political arrangements. Smith's analysis bore upon a political situation which was dominated by monarchies (*LJ*, pp. 55-6, 274). When he thought and spoke of governments his paradigm was monarchy. This is not to suggest that his political views are no longer relevant or even less so than they once were, but only that to understand him correctly this paradigm and not one of constitutional democracy must be kept in mind.

I

When Smith inquired into what he called the foundations or original principles of government he was concerned to answer what is perhaps the most fundamental question of political theory, viz., why should anyone obey anyone else? Although Smith failed to reach a complete and satisfactory answer to this question – few have – he did achieve a degree of clarity on several aspects of the problem. He recognized that political obligation is a special case of moral obligation, that civil government is a special way of organizing the political authority of the community and that both moral obligation and political authority vary according to the mode of social stratification which prevails within a community. Smith's analysis of political authority was based upon what today is called sociological analysis (Cropsey 1957, pp. 57-64; Wolin 1960, pp. 286-94).

Moral obligation derives, according to Smith from "respect for what are, or for what should be, or for what, upon a certain condition, would be, the sentiments of other people . . ." (*MS*, p. 386). Mutual respect for shared preferences and aversions is the basis of moral obligation because that respect is the very bond of community and the maintenance and enhancement of community with one's fellows is the very essence of morality (see Chap. II). Many different preferences and aversions or sentiments are shared by members of a community but not all are held to be equally binding. Although every community will tolerate violation of certain preferences and aversions, there are always some which are held to be so essential to the social bond that any violation of them is the proper object of resentment and punishment. Every member of a community is expected to carefully avoid actions which are inconsistent with those preferences and aversions which are held to be inviolable. Respect for those sentiments constitutes each man's political obligation or duty in justice (*MS*, pp. 112-14).

The designation of the precise sentiments which qualify as inviolable within any community depends mainly upon what I shall call the *deference structure* which happens to prevail in that society. By deference structure I mean the rule according to which the several strata, classes or "ranks" of society are distinguished and the duties of members of each class is specified. This rule is discovered by induction from the sentiments actually expressed by the different members of society with respect to one another's actions. I prefer "deference structure" to Smith's term – order of subordination – because it is less likely to be confused with the distribution of men in a stratified community which results from the application of the rule. The most convenient way to show how Smith understood the entire deference phenomenon is to begin with what he termed "the principle of authority," for obedience to civil authority derives largely from this source (*LJ*, pp. 9-13).

The concrete situations of the various members of any society are not identical. They range over a spectrum from most miserable to most fortunate. Neither is the distribution of the members on that spectrum equitable or what the statisticians call a standard distribution. Rather, it is markedly skewed toward the less fortunate end of the spectrum such that "the state of the greater part of men" is that of the man who "is in health, who is out of debt, and has a clear conscience" (*MS*, pp. 62-3). When this circumstance is combined with the fact that sympathizing with joy is more agreeable than sympathizing with sorrow (*MS*, pp. 63-9) we can understand why it is that the actual situation of those who enjoy the most fortunate situation is more apt to be fully appreciated by members of a community than is that of anyone else. Furthermore, since the condition of the most fortunate "rises above what is common" it is the object of admiration (*MS*, p. 28; "Astron.," p. 30). Admiration of their condition in turn excites emulation. "Emulation, the anxious desire that we ourselves should excell, is ordinarily founded in our admiration of the excellence of others" (*MS*, p. 106). In this way the most fortunate of men come to be regarded as superiors and their preferences and aversions are thereby endowed with a social significance which is out of all proportion to their number. This is especially the case when the most fortunate boast that their good fortune accrues to them because of their peculiar habits and dispositions (*MS*, pp. 366-7). Their way of life becomes the model for all to emulate. They are regarded as proper objects of disinterested deference and reverence – even worship and adoration (*MS*, p. 74, 367).[3] "We are eager to assist them in completing a system of happiness that approaches so near to perfection; and we desire to serve them for their own sake, without any other recompense but vanity or the honor of obliging them" (*MS*, pp. 73-4; also pp. 85, 258).

It is in this way that a deference structure arises within a community and certain preferences and aversions come to be designated as most important, viz., those of the most fortunate.[4] The immediate consequence of this designation is the definition of the duties in justice of the various members of the community in terms of the strata, class or rank in which they are placed because of their concrete situation.

The moral basis of political obligation and political authority follows from the foregoing analysis. The social bond of every community depends upon the maintenance of respect for those preferences and aversions specified by the prevailing deference structure. Any violation of these sentiments will amount to an injustice for it will eventuate in giving someone less than is his due. Such acts are regarded as attacks upon the very existence of the community and on that account are judged to be the proper object of resentment, public outrage and punishment. The use of force and coercion is morally justified in the case of all acts which are inconsistent with the duties which are directly entailed by the prevailing deference structure because the maintenance of that structure and those duties which follow from it is the *conditio sine qua non* upon which the very existence of the community depends (*MS*, p. 125).

Each community can and does more or less effectively secure those elements of the social bond which are held to be inviolable or sacred. It does so through its collective judgment and the use of its collective

[3] In Chapter VII it will be shown that Smith regarded the principle of authority as a basically religious habit. This accounts for the continued influence of religion in political as well as moral affairs (*MS*, pp. 232-42, 367-9; *WN*, pp. 747-66).

[4] Cropsey asserted that equality was one of Smith's "watchwords" (1957, p. 64). Although it is difficult to specify the precise sense in which Cropsey used such terms as "equality" and "democracy," it seems reasonably clear that he associated both very closely with the egalitarian conviction that unequal treatment of members of a society is at the very least avoidable. If this is a fair reading, Cropsey was clearly mistaken. Like Dahrendorf (1962, pp. 100-09), Smith was convinced that social stratification is a necessary feature of every society. Unlike Dahrendorf Smith reached that conclusion from an analysis of the role of leadership rather than that of coercive power. In Smith's view communities can reach accord on which sentiments are essential to the social bond and so define duties in justice only by granting greater weight to the preferences and aversions of some members and less to those of others. Unless some "regular order of subordination" exists within a community that accord will be wanting and "confusion and misrule" will result. ("Astron.," p. 51; also see *WN*, p. 670 and Campbell 1971, pp. 172-3).

power, i.e., by the exercise of the community's political authority. The fundamental mission of political authority is, according to Smith, as Lord Devlin more recently put it – the enforcement of morals.[5]

> Proper resentment for injustice attempted, or actually committed, is the only motive which, in the eyes of the impartial spectator, can justify our hurting or disturbing in any respect the happiness of our neighbour. To do so from any other motive is itself a violation of the laws of justice, which force ought to be employed either to restrain or punish. The wisdom of every state or commonwealth endeavours, as well as it can, to employ the force of society to restrain those who are subject to its authority from hurting or disturbing the happiness of one another. The rules which it establishes for this purpose constitute the civil and criminal law of each particular state or country. (MS, p. 319; also see pp. 501-2)

A member of any community is morally obliged to obey the directives of governmental officials and the community is morally justified in coercing that obedience if and to the extent that such directives accurately articulate those duties which are entailed by the prevailing deference structure of the community. Should anyone or any group attempt to force compliance with directives which are inconsistent with that deference structure, men may find it convenient to observe them from considerations of utility or expediency, but they are not morally obliged to obey them. Smith acknowledged that men often obey laws and support governmental policies and practices from the latter types of considerations (LJ, pp. 9-10; MS, pp. 263-8). The Scots prior to union with England, for example, tolerated the oppressive rule of an aristocracy based on "religious and political prejudices" (WN, p. 897). Such accommodation to the coercive power of the state is not in itself sufficient to justify the exercise of such power by the state or to confirm the state's claim to political authority.[6] The exercise of power by the state is

---

[5] On the issue of punishment one point requires emphasis. Smith rejected as atypical the popular justification of punishment, viz., that it is a distasteful task undertaken solely for the sake of deterring infractions of duties in justice. Although he acknowledged that punishment does have that effect, he denied that it is with a view to that end that criminals are punished. Instead he argued that punishment is an expression of resentment. "To punish ... is to recompense, to remunerate ... to return evil for evil that has been done" (MS, p. 94). When a community punishes a criminal it does so out of sympathetic resentment, out of public outrage (MS, pp. 105-11). Smith's opposition to the deterrence theory of punishment was rooted in the same conviction as was Lord Devlin's opposition to H. L. A. Hart's utilitarian position (Hart 1963; Devlin 1965).

[6] Smith's concept of political authority closely corresponds to that of Peter Winch (1958b). Both regarded the internal relation of moral ideas, upon which legitimacy depends, as the primary attribute of authority and the power to exact performance as a secondary and perhaps unnecessary attribute. Failure to recognize the fact that Smith regarded legitimacy rather than power as the essential characteristic of the political has permitted many to mistakenly propose that in political theory Smith supported a form of utilitarian analysis (Campbell 1971, pp. 205-10).

authorized only to the extent that it is used to enforce the moral preference and aversions of the community. Communities attempt to assure
the conformity of state power with moral values by prescribing procedural rules which are to be observed by the officers of the state.

To prevent the confusion which would attend upon every man's doing justice to
himself, the magistrate, in all governments that have acquired any considerable
authority, undertakes to do justice to all, and promises to hear and to redress
every complaint of injury. In all well-governed states, too, not only judges are
appointed for determining the controversies of individuals, but rules are prescribed
for regulating the decisions of those judges; and these rules are in general intended to coincide with those of natural justice. (*MS*, pp. 501-2)

II

Smith was thoroughly convinced that the manner in which communities
exercise political power depends upon the prevailing mode of social
stratification. The deference structure specifies not only what that power
will be used to secure, but also how it will be deployed and by whom.
He stated this explicitly in the *Moral Sentiments* [7] and illustrated how
the exercise of political authority has changed with changes in deference structures in the course of the development of European nations
both in his "Lecture on Justice" (pp. 14-55) and in the *Wealth of Nations*
(pp. 373-96).

The key variable in terms of which deference structures are distinguished is that difference among members of the community which is
regarded as the distinguishing mark of superiority. According as one
or another of these is designated, political authority will be differently
constituted. Smith claimed that only two of the differences which exist
among men have been regularly and successfully employed to constitute
genuinely political authority, viz., age and fortune (*LJ*, p. 10; *WN*, pp.
670-74).[8] Accordingly, he recognized only two politically significant
modes of social stratification – gerontocracy and plutocracy.

[7] "Upon the manner in which any state is divided into the different orders and
societies which compose it, and upon the particular distribution which has been
made of their respective powers, privileges, and immunities, depends what is called
the constitution of that particular state" (*MS*, p. 338).

[8] He mentioned three other differences which might but in fact have not served
this purpose. Birth has long served to differentiate among men, but always as a
subsidiary mark of distinction (*WN*, p. 673). Smith generally dismissed physical
force as uninspiring apart from mental qualifications (*WN*, p. 671). Nevertheless,
he admitted that military might has not seldom excited the admiration and deference of men (*WN*, p. 667; *MS*, p. 371; *LJ*, pp. 30-32). Wisdom and virtue have,
in point of fact, never been considered marks of superiority in any society (*WN*,
p. 671). Smith appears to have been torn on this point. He allowed that this is

In the course of history the deference structure of Western communities changed. Primitive societies of hunters, both in ancient times and among modern North American Indians, (*WN*, p. 653) were stratified according to a gerontocratic deference structure, whereas more civilized communities have become more and more plutocratic (*LJ*, pp. 14-15; *WN*, pp. 373-96). A full account of Smith's philosophy of history would be interesting and perhaps rewarding (cfr. Forbes, 1954; Meek, 1967; 1971). In the interests of brevity it shall be neglected except to observe that this change in the basic pattern of social stratification resulted in the rise of civil governments. "Civil governments supposed a certain subordination" (*WN*, p. 670). They exist only in plutocratic societies.

Civil government is but one of the ways in which communities have exercised political power. Smith's theory of the nature and purpose of civil government can best be understood by showing why the change from gerontocratic to plutocratic stratification made it necessary for communities to exercise their political power in the form of civil governments. In order to expedite that consideration two distinctions must be noted. First, Smith distinguished three "powers of government." Since, however, these are exercised even where political authority did not take the form of civil government, they should be regarded as the three functions of political authority.

The powers of government are three, to wit, the legislative, which makes laws for the public good; the judicial, or that which obliges private persons to obey these laws, and punishes those who disobey; the executive, or as some call it, the federative power, to which belongs the making of war and peace. (*LJ*, p. 17)

Second, the way in which political authority is exercised in a community is called its constitution. While Smith allowed that a variety of mixed constitutions can be distinguished, he recognized only three main types. Although his classification is far from satisfactory, it is useful for present purposes.

Monarchial government is where the supreme power and authority is vested in one who can do what he pleases, make peace and war, impose taxes, and the like. Aristocratical government is where a certain order of people in the state, either of the richest or of certain families, have it in their power to choose magistrates who are to have the management of the state. Democratical government is where the management of affairs belongs to the whole of the people together. These two last forms may be called republican, and then the division of government is into monarchical and republican. (*LJ*, p. 14).

probably a good thing since these qualities are ever so difficult for even trained minds to recognize (*MS*, p. 232). Still, he was convinced that social stratification on any other basis is an abomination (*MS*, pp. 84-6).

The rise of civil governments can best be understood by applying these distinctions to the analysis of political authority in the two main types of societies, i.e. to gerontocracies and plutocracies. Smith believed, for reasons he did not disclose, that gerontocracies were possesed of democratic constitutions. Such peoples were awed and impressed most profoundly by the mere presence of village elders. In such communities decisions on public affairs were made at public meetings. "The whole society interests itself in any offense; if possible they make it up between the parties, if not they banish from their society, kill or deliver up to the resentment of the injured, him who has committed the crime" (*LJ*, p. 15). In such societies all functions of political authority were jointly exercised directly by the people as a whole.

The political status of the village elders was significant, but fell far short of that of later sovereigns. At public meetings the opinions and dispositions of the elders carried greater weight than did those of their juniors. Still, the elders could never "do anything without the consent of the whole" (*LJ*, p. 15). They could tip the balance of controversy sufficiently to allow the population to reach accord, but could not make determinations on public affairs on their own.

Smith believed that plutocracies are possessed of either monarchical or aristocratic, but never democratic constitutions. He based this belief on his reading of history. In every civilized society he found the same patterns of deference. Whenever a man managed to amass a considerable store of life's necessities and had no alternative use of what he could not himself consume, he always used that excess to maintain his neighbors – not out of benevolence, but in order to enhance his own social status by increasing their dependence upon him. As they accepted his excess they came to depend upon his favor for their ease and survival. His great power and providence over their lives excited their overriding admiration and deference (*LJ*, pp. 16, 21, 24, 35, 36-40, 42-3, 253-5; *MS*, pp. 73-4, 84-5, 331-2; *WN*, pp. 356-96, 652-66).

In such communities decisions on public affairs were made quite differently than in gerontocracies. In plutocracies the exercise of the three functions of political authority came to be more and more the exclusive prerogative of superiors, i.e., the rich or those designated by the rich. Even in earliest times the political status of Titan chieftains was far greater than that of village elders. "At their public meetings there will always be one of superior influence to the rest, who will in a great measure direct and govern their resolutions . . ." (*LJ*, p. 16). The political influence of the rich in a plutocratic society differed from that of the elders in a gerontocratic society in one important respect, viz., they could make and enforce determinations on public affairs without "the consent of the whole." The political status of superiors in plutocratic societies, therefore, is that of a sovereign (*LJ*, pp. 16-21, 34-5).

The importance of this comparison comes to light when we recall that Smith said that there were no civil governments in the nations of hunters, but that there always are in more civilized societies.

Thus among hunters there is no regular government ... The appropriation of herds and flocks which introduced an inequality of fortune, was that which first gave rise to regular government. Till there be property there can be no government, the very end of which is to secure wealth, and to defend the rich from the poor. (*LJ*, p. 15; also see *WN*, pp. 670-74)

Since political authority was exercised both in gerontocracies (nations of hunters) and plutocracies (civilized societies), but only the latter were possessed of governments, it must be that the essential difference between the constitutions of the two is the distinctive mark of that mode of exercising political authority which Smith referred to as civil government. That difference is the one in terms of which democratic constitutions (of gerontocracies) are distinguished from aristocratic and monarchical constitutions (of plutocracies). In the former all functions of political authority are exercised directly by all members of the community, in the latter they are the proper functions of only a few. Civil government obtains, therefore, only where the political authority of a community becomes the special function of some but not all members. Accordingly, by civil government Smith meant an institution, the function of which is the exercise of the political authority of the community.

This definition is considerably enriched by considering the purpose which brought men to support the institutionalization of political authority. According to Smith two factors combined to necessitate it, both of which obtain only in plutocratic societies, viz., diversificaton of productive roles and an increase in the volume of public affairs. In gerontocracies all members performed the same functions – all hunted, all went to war, all participated in the disposition of public affairs (*WN*, pp. 653-5). In such societies, furthermore, the volume of public business was slight. Since title to social status was rooted in age, it was inalienable. For that reason crimes were few.

Men who have no property can injure one another only in their persons or reputations. But when one man kills, wounds, beats, or defames another, though he to whom the injury is done suffers, he who does it receives no benefit ... Men live together in society with some tolerable degree of security, though there is no civil magistrate to protect them from the injustice of those passions [i.e., envy, malice and resentment]. (*WN*, pp. 669-70)

In plutocracies, on the other hand, neither of these circumstances obtain. The diversification of productive roles is of the essence of this mode of stratification, i.e., the rich maintain the poor out of their excess, while the poor perform the labor and provide the service required of them by the rich. Furthermore, in plutocracies the volume of public affairs increases significantly. Title to deference in plutocracies is alienable and that circumstance encourages forcible usurption of social status. "The affluence of the rich excites the indignation of the poor, who are often driven by want, and prompted by envy, to invade his possessions" (*WN*, p. 670). This same circumstance also prompts invasion by other nations (*WN*, p. 659; *LJ*, p. 23). These two factors combined to necessitate the institutionalization of political authority.

... [B]ut as men were generally employed in some branch of trade or another, without great detriment to themselves they could not spare time to wait upon them. All causes must be left undecided, which would be productive of inconvenience, or they must fall upon some other method more suitable to the several members of society. The natural means they would fall upon would be to choose some of their number to whom all causes should be referred. The chieftain ... would naturally be one of those who were chosen for this purpose. (*LJ*, p. 19)

The institutionalization of political authority resulted in a more efficient strategy for dealing with the increased volume of public affairs in plutocracies. Notwithstanding, men did not support this change in their political constitution because they foresaw that it was necessary to dispatch the general business of society. "The consideration of that necessity comes no doubt afterwards to contribute very much to maintain and secure that authority and subordination" (*WN*, p. 674). The purpose which the founders of civil governments had in mind was quite different and, once more, provided moral justification for the exercise of political power by the state. They were concerned to assure that the deference structure of their plutocratic society, together with all the duties entailed by it, would be effectively secured against violation. Any attempt to infringe upon the status of the rich, to alienate from them their title to deference, to violate "the sacred right of private property," was regarded as the proper object of public outrage which must be punished through the exercise of the community's political authority. As they could see no way of guarding against acts contrary to their plutocratic deference structure other than by institutionalizing that authority they did so and expected their public officials to deploy the political power of their community to that end. "Civil government ... is in reality instituted for the defense of the rich against the poor ..." (*WN*, p. 674; also see *LJ*, p. 15). Again "law and government, too, seem to propose no other object but this; they secure the individual who has enlarged his property, that he may peaceably enjoy the fruits of it" (*LJ*, p. 160).

III

The exercise of political power is morally justified, according to Smith, if and to the extent that it is consistent with the deference structure which prevails within the community. Political authority was originally institutionalized, in his estimate, for the purpose of assuring the maintenance of the deference structure according to which the moral sentiments of a basically plutocratic society were ordered. Thereafter some members of society were charged to exercise the power of the community in support of those preferences and aversions which were generally regarded as inviolable. Hence, Smith reasoned, so long and insofar as governments deploy the political power of the community to enforce its morals, governments are morally justified in directing even coercing the conduct of citizens and citizens are morally obliged to obey and otherwise support their government. In Smith's judgment, however, governments have often, and increasingly so as they become more complex, violated those very sentiments which they were established to secure.

The violence and injustice of the rulers of mankind is an ancient evil, for which, I am afraid, the nature of human affairs can scarce admit of a remedy (*WN*, p. 460)

Smith's disenchantment with big government and other complex institutions as well should not be dismissed as mere nostalgia for the simpler life. Although he did prefer that life his discontent with modern governments was based upon his considered rejection of their claims to moral justification. If I understand Smith correctly it was his belief that as political authority becomes increasingly institutionalized it becomes less responsive to the moral sentiments of the community subject to it and thereby increasingly undermines its own legitimacy. In order to establish the credibility of this interpretation two points need to be clarified. First, as political authority is increasingly institutionalized the disposition of public affairs ceases to be determined by consideration of propriety and comes to be determined instead by considerations of utility. Second, insofar as governmental affairs are conducted from considerations of utility the function of government ceases to be the enforcement of the public morality and becomes instead the maintenance of its own power.

In the preceding section civil government was shown to result, in Smith's view, from the assignment of a set of functions which had previously been exercised by everyone to only a few who thereupon exercised them as their exclusive responsibility. This change has all the ear-marks of a division of labor.[9,10] The rise of government was there shown to be attended by the main advantage of a division of labor, viz., increased efficiency. It was, however, also attended by its disadvantages, one of which is particularly worthy of notice here. The scope of activities a man is able to understand is commensurate with the variety of functions

---

[9] Smith's concept of the division of labor has ordinarily been too narrowly construed. The discussion of the division of labor in the pin-factory was clearly intended as an illustration of the patterns of development discernible "in the general business of society" (WN, pp. 3-4). The broader significance of the division of labor has not gone altogether unnoticed. "The greatest work dealing with social problems, that Great Britain produced in the Eighteenth century, was Adam Smith's *Wealth of Nations*, and his luminous expositions of the effects of the division of labour was the most considerable contribution made by British thinkers of the age to the study of human development." (Bury 1932, p. 220; also see Cannan 1903, p. 44; West 1964; Rosenberg 1965; Hamowy 1968). What Bury and the others failed to acknowledge was that the pattern of development which is called the division of labor is discernible in every product of human effort whether a social institution, a system of philosophy, a machine or a language ("Astron.," pp. 66-7; "Lang.," p. 246). Had he noticed that even broader applicability he might have appreciated that the disadvantages which accrue to the division of labor in social functions (WN, 734-5) are the same as those which result from its application to language ("Lang.," p. 251) and that accordingly a division of labor in both of these cases brings about a less rather than a more perfect result ("Lang.," p. 249).

[10] By division of labor Smith meant a particular kind of change in the internal organization of group behavior. A division of labor occurs whenever a group function which had been performed by each member of the group comes to be divided into distinct although related operations and these are distributed among the members of the group who thereupon become specialist (WN, pp. 4-5). Such changes are typically the cumulative result of actions taken by individuals who intend to enhance their status in the group by excelling in the performance of only a few tasks (WN, pp. 13-16; MS, pp. 70-2). This type of change at once promotes productive efficiency and social fragmentation (WN, pp. 7-10, 743-40). This description, however, fails to capture the intricacies and preconditions of such changes. Both the group and the group function are divided into a complex of related members and sub-functions. These in turn are combined into sets of members and of sub-functions each of which contain at least one but less than all of the members and sub-functions. Each set of members thereupon undertakes to perform one and only one set of sub-functions. The change will not be complete, however, unless two further conditions are satisfied. viz., all sub-functions must be performed by some set of members and the sub-functions must be ordered properly with respect to one another. These conditions can be satisfied in the absence of control by centralized authority if and only if the rule which constituted the original group function continues to govern the actions of individuals throughout the phases of role differentiation and integration. A division of labor as Smith conceived it is possible, therefore, only in a community, only where each agent observes and continues to observe the canons implicit in the prevailing order of subordination. "It seems clear (though Adam Smith barely touches the point) that division of labour assumes a society or at least a common understanding ready formed, and does not itself create such" (Bonar 1893, p. 155).

which he himself performs. As the latter is reduced, so also is the former. Furthermore, as different men come to perform exclusive functions, each will become less able to understand why others act as they do. As a consequence of this each will become incapable "of forming any just judgment concerning many even of the ordinary duties of private life. Of the great and extensive interests of his country he is altogether incapable of judging . . ." (*WN*, pp. 734-5).

As political authority becomes institutionalized the activities and responsibilities of sovereign and subject become increasingly diverse. The immediate consequence of this separation of functions is that each begins to cultivate those habits and perspectives which are peculiarly suited to their separate functions. But to the extent that the habits and perspectives of sovereign and subject diverge it is impossible for either to appreciate the interest which the other takes in an object of practical consequence. Each acts from "a particular turn or habit" and that forecloses the very possibility of either being able to morally sympathize with the concrete practical situation of the other. (*MS*, 39; also see Chapter II). As a result neither those who administer the affairs of government nor those whom they purportedly serve can formulate a reliable and impartial estimate of what the other can support. But if the sovereign cannot morally sympathize with the concrete situation of his subjects, he cannot appreciate which of their preferences and aversions are generally held to be inviolable and so cannot assure that the political power of the community is deployed in accordance with the prevailing deference structure. Isolation from the moral sentiments of the community, however, does not release a public official from the responsibility of administering the operations of government. If he cannot know the moral sentiments of the community he must direct those operations according to criteria which are at his disposal. These are the same ones as are employed in the natural sciences and the arts, viz., comprehensiveness, coherence, familiarity and beauty (*MS*, pp. 19-21; also see Chapter I). When affairs of state come to be directed according to these standards alone, utility has replaced propriety as the overriding concern of government.

The same principle, the same love of system, the same regard to the beauty or order, of art and contrivance, frequently serves to recommend those institutions which tend to promote the public welfare. . . . The perfection of police, the extension of trade and manufacturers, are noble and magnificent objects. The contemplation of them pleases us, and we are interested in whatever can tend to advance them. They make part of the great system of government, and the wheels of the political machine seem to move with more harmony and ease by means of them. We take pleasure in beholding the perfection of so beautiful and grand a system, and we are uneasy till we remove any obstruction that can in the least disturb or encumber the regularity of its motions (*MS*, pp. 265-6).

Smith's contention that commercial institutions tend to become autonomous loci of power, the function of which increasingly becomes inconsistent with the purposes of their founders, often of those who manage them and certainly of those they purportedly serve, is common knowledge (*WN*, pp. 595, 692, 712). Becker correctly noted that this tendency, which he called "goal displacement" following contemporary sociological usage, is not peculiar to commercial institutions (1969, pp. 70-4). The function of institutions of all types – governmental, military, commercial, educational and religious – tends to become the maintenance and enhancement of their own power (*MS*, p. 266; *WN*, pp. 667-8, 691-2, 718, 744-5). Becker incorrectly maintained, however, that Smith felt the cause of "the corporation spirit" to be the "dissociative force of self-interested motives – the propensity to invade . . ." (1969, p. 76). A more accurate understanding of the consequences entailed in conducting the operations of institutions, and those of government in particular, according to considerations of utility leads to quite a different analysis of the causes of the corporation spirit and the tendency of institutions to become "functionally autonomous" of the purposes which men have in mind for them.

Particularly close attention must be devoted to discerning what Smith meant by the term "utility" for he used it quite differently than did Bentham, Ricardo, J. S. Mill and later utilitarians and economists. Having rejected Hume's claim that moral judgments are founded upon a perception of utility (*MS*, pp. 270-1), Smith located utility in the vocabulary of aesthetics. "[U]tility is one of the principal sources of beauty. . . ." (*MS*, p. 257). Some attention to Smith's aesthetic theories is therefore necessary in order to achieve a clear understanding of the precise way in which he used the term "utility." Since those theories were discussed in some detail in Chapter I a brief summary of the relevant points will suffice.

Objects are said to be associated with one another if the perception of the one excites the image of the other. If this condition is satisfied the former is said to resemble the latter. The observation of a resemblance between objects is a source of satisfaction to men because they are concerned that their experience be orderly or systematic. Men associate objects and events either by inquiry or art. In both cases objects of one kind are made to excite images of objects of quite a different sort. The observation of that kind of resemblance arouses a special kind of pleasure, satisfaction or sentiment, viz., admiration. The resemblances produced by the artist are called imitations and differ from those which result from inquiry in only one respect. In the case of art the imitating object openly displays the manner in which it excites the image of the imitated objects. Objects of this kind are said to be possessed of the quality of beauty because they excite the pleasure, feeling or sentiment of admiration.

That pleasure is founded altogether upon our wonder at seeing an object of one kind represent so well an object of a very different kind, and upon our admiration of the art which surmounts so happily that disparity which nature had established between them. The noble works of statuary and painting appear to us a sort of wonderful phaenomena, differing in this respect from the wonderful phaenomena of nature, that they carry, as it were, their own explication along with them, and demonstrate, even to the eye the way and manner in which they are produced. The eye, even of an unskillful spectator, immediately discerns, in some measure, how it is that a certain modification of figure in statuary, and of brighter and darker colours in painting, can represent, with so much truth and vivacity, the actions, passions, and behaviour of men, as well as a great variety of other objects. ("Imit. Arts", p. 146)

Products of the applied arts excite the same pleasure as do those of the fine arts and for the same reason. Any system which is skillfully designed to promote a state of affairs which is quite different from itself is possessed of that same quality of beauty. The perception of the former (the means) excites the image of the latter (the end) and openly displays the manner in which that image is excited. "That the fitness of any system or machine to produce the end for which it was intended bestows a certain propriety and beauty upon the whole, and renders the very thought and contemplation of it agreeable, is so obvious that nobody has overlooked it" (MS, p. 257).

Any productive system may be appraised in either of two ways. On the one hand it may be judged as a productive system in terms of the efficiency with which it actually produces the end for which it was designed. On the other hand, it may be judged as a symbol of that end in terms of its capacity to excite the image of that end in the mind of the beholder. Following the usage attributed to Hume, Smith employed the term "utility" to denote the symbolic capacity of a productive system.

The utility of any object, according to him, pleases the master by perpetually suggesting to him the pleasure or convenience which it is fitted to promote. Every time he looks at it, he is put in mind of this pleasure; and the object in this manner becomes a source of perpetual satisfaction and enjoyment. The spectator enters by [aesthetic] sympathy into the sentiments of the master, and necessarily views the object under the same agreeable aspect. (MS, pp. 257-8).

Once the precise meaning which Smith assigned to the term "utility" is grasped the cause of the "goal displacement" phenomenon becomes apparent. A productive system comes to be possessed of an autonomous value to the extent that it is appraised solely in terms of its utility. Smith was somewhat puzzled that what was to him so obvious had not been noticed before.

But that this fitness, this happy contrivance of any production of art, should often be more valued than the very end for which it was intended . . . has not, so far as I know, been yet taken notice of by anybody. That this, however, is very frequently the case may be observed in a thousand instances, both in the most frivolous and in the most important concerns of human life. *(MS, p. 258)*

Two instances of this phenomenon, which might with greater accuracy be termed *value displacement,* which concern the more important aspects of human life are worthy of mention. In the pursuit of wealth commercially ambitious men desire to acquire commodities possessed of exchange value not because their possession is expected to improve the quality of their private lives, but as symbols which excite in them the image of public respect. The desire for bettering one's own condition which is the great force that turns the wheels of commerce is not rooted in rational self-interest, but in this phenomenon of value displacement *(MS, pp. 259-65, 70-3; also see Chapters III and V).*

Another instance of value displacement occurs in the case of governments. Subjects do not ordinarily obey the directives of their sovereign because, after careful deliberation, they conclude that the behavior commanded is indeed in keeping with the sentiments of the impartial spectator. They obey him because his condition is the object not of moral approval but of admiration. His way of life is the symbol of all that is fine and good. It is for that reason that he is emulated and obeyed. Smith termed this basis of obedience "the principle of authority" in his lectures, distinguishing it there from "the principle of utility" *(LJ, pp. 9-11).* It is now clear that these two principles are not altogether unrelated. Although emulation of, deference to or obedience toward the sovereign, who is regarded as the paradigm of the good life, is most often a spontaneous act, it can and does result from the deliberate employment of the principle of utility when considering whether or not the sovereign should be obeyed. When considered in terms of utility, the proposition – "the sovereign ought to be obeyed" – reduces to a tautology.

Value displacement as regards government does not affect only subjects. As was mentioned above, those who administer the affairs of government are also isolated from those whose preferences and aversions are supposed to measure the deployment of the power under their control. Being isolated from their subjects such administrators have no option except to direct the operations of government according to considerations of utility. Those who administer governments, indeed any institution, must of necessity undergo value displacement the moment they accept institutional responsibilities. As those responsibilities are accepted governing comes to be perceived as either a machine to be tended or a game to be played. In either case their habits and perceptions come increasingly to be dominated by a "love of system" (MS, pp. 265-6, 342-3). It is because of this isolation that "man is generally considered by statesmen and projectors as the materials of a sort of political mechanics" (from the manuscript of a lecture given by Smith in 1755 as recorded by Stewart 1858, p. 68).

IV

It would be indeed difficult to read very widely in Smith's works and fail to become aware of his general disenchantment with governments. Viner and others interpreted this "strong presumption against government" as having resulted from the extension of governmental power into areas of community affairs in which Smith believed political authority had no legitimate concern. This interpretation appears to rest upon the mistaken assumption that Smith subscribed to the belief, shared by many political theorists, that the limits of the legitimate exercise of political authority can be established in principle. To the contrary, Smith allowed that political authority can be legitimately exercised in whatever ways are necessary to secure the deference structure of the community. That position allowed Smith to acknowledge that political authority may be legitimately employed not only to secure national defense and to provide effective administration of justice, but also to promote trade and commerce, public health, public education and even to administer a state religion (WN, pp. 651, 653, 669, 691, 734-40, 746-50, 759). Indeed in his lectures Smith flatly denied that the limits of the legitimate exercise of political authority can be established in principle.[11]

[11] Neither was Smith's disenchantment with governments or other types of institutions rooted, as is popularly believed, primarily in the fact that they are often administered by witless, self-seeking men, although he was keenly aware that they were. Becker's contention that goal displacement is caused by the "dissociative forces of self-interested motives" puts the cart before the horse (1969, p. 76). According to Smith administrators, whether of governmental, military, commercial, educational or religious institutions, act to preserve and enhance the autonomy of their institutions because they cannot meet their responsibilities in any other way given the fact that their situation effectively denies to them any reliable access to moral sentiments of the community. Thus after criticizing the rule of the East

In England it can be exactly ascertained when the king encroaches on the privileges of the people, or they on that of the king, but none can say how far the supreme power of king and parliament may go. In like manner, where the absolute power of sovereignty is lodged in a single person, none can tell what he may not do, with accuracy. (*LJ*, pp. 66-7).

Smith's disenchantment with governments did not derive from their function – the exercise of the political authority of the community – but from the fact that they were institutions. Whenever an essentially moral function of a community undergoes a division of labor, is sub-divided and distributed among separate individuals, it becomes impossible for anyone to judge whether the entire function is being exercised in accordance with that complex of moral sentiments which is the very bond of the community. Because of that circumstance those charged with the responsibility of administering the affairs of the institution must rely upon considerations of utility rather than propriety. The institutional function thereby becomes autonomous and replaces rather than maintains the deference structure of the community.

The rise of "civilized" society has brought about a value displacement. Considerations of efficiency, proficiency and beauty have replaced considerations of propriety, merit and virtue. This is evident not only among men of affairs but also among moral philosophers. Although most evident in the moral theories of the ancient Stoics, Hobbes, Mandeville and Hume, the love of system also played a significant although a more subtle role in the theories of the Epicureans, Cudworth and Hutcheson (*MS*, pp. 406-10, 464, 184, 270-1, 438, 468-9, 445). Social theorists, especially reform-minded theorists, are especially prone to this value displacement. Not infrequently they perceive social institutions in the same way as does every man of system, i.e., in abstraction from their moral foundations (Wolin 1960, pp. 298-9).

The man of system ... is apt to be very wise in his own conceit, and is often so enamoured with the supposed beauty of his own ideal plan of government that he cannot suffer the smallest deviation from any part of it. He goes on to establish it completely and in all its parts, without any regard either to the great interests or to the strong prejudices which may oppose it; he seems to imagine that he can arrange the different members of a great society with as much ease as the hand arranges the different pieces upon a chess board; he does not consider that the pieces upon the chess board have no other principle of motion besides that which the hand impresses upon them; but that, in the great chess board of human society, every single piece has a principle of motion of its own

India Company, Smith remarked: "It is the system of government, the situation in which they are placed, that I mean to censure; not the character of those who have acted in it" (*WN*, pp. 605-6). For recent discussions along these same lines see Blau (1956, pp. 85-96; 1963, pp. 231-49) and Merton (1968, pp. 251-4).

altogether different from that which the legislature might choose to impress upon it. If those two principles coincide and act in the same direction, the game of human society will go on easily and harmoniously, and is very likely to be happy and successful. If they are opposite or different, the small will go on miserably and the society must be at all times in the highest degree of disorder (*MS*, pp. 342-3)

In his *Wealth of Nations* Smith advocated significant reforms in the commercial policies of governments. That he should have devoted such a massive study to further *that* objective may appear puzzling in view of his disenchantment with governments, his disgust for ideologues and his conviction that legislators are typically incapable of even recognizing a morally normative statement. Certainly untold numbers of lesser men who supported similar attitudes have thought such efforts futile and promptly abandoned them. That Smith did not reveals a great deal about the manner of man he was, about his fundamental temperament and about the strategy he so effectively employed in the *Wealth of Nations*.

Smith observed that, although not necessary in every type of society, governments are necessary in "civilized" societies for the reason that these are structured plutocratically. He further observed that as the political authority of a society becomes the special function of only a few members it necessarily becomes an instrument of oppression. These observations must have been a source of continuing torment to Smith. He acknowledged that the love of country is one's first duty in benevolence (Chapter III). But for him the love of country involves two commitments; "first, a certain respect and reverence for that constitution or form of government which is actually established; and, secondly, an earnest desire to render the condition of our fellow-citizens as safe, respectable, and happy as we can" (*MS*, p. 339). His observations must have shown him that in "civilized" societies these commitments are in conflict which in turn could not but have occasioned within him something akin to that profound distress which is visited upon every sensitive man during times of public discontent, faction and turmoil. Whether experienced in one's own soul or in the streets the resolution of this form of turmoil "requires perhaps the highest effort of political wisdom to determine when a real patriot ought to support and endeavour to re-establish the authority of the old system, and when he ought to give way to the more daring but often dangerous spirit of innovation" (*MS*, p. 340).

Smith's deliberations led him to favor, for reasons which will be discussed in succeeding chapters, the latter course, one which entailed recommending changes in the established practices of governments which in turn would alter the respective "powers, privileges and immunities" of the different ranks of society, i.e., the constitution of the state (*MS*, p. 338). Such a decision could not have come easily to a man who was convinced that "the peace and order of society is of more importance than even the relief of the miserable" (*MS*, p. 331). Nor could it have been taken with the intention of making society conform to some ideal model he fancied would relieve all social ills or at least finally initiate those patterns of institutional practice which would eventuate in the ultimate achievement of some social condition he fancied to be ideal. To have done so would have ensnared him in those same delusions which prompt ideologues to become fanatics (*MS*, pp. 340-42).

In deciding to take action to alter the prevailing constitution Smith did not, either by intent or in actual practice, erect "his own judgment into the standard of right and wrong." (*MS*, p. 343). In this as in other cases one is permitted to regard his own preferences and aversions as morally relevant only if others will support them. For the same reason he resolved not to force endorsement of his plan, but, observing "the divine maxim of Plato, never to use violence to his country, no more than to his parents" (*MS*, p. 342), to attempt to persuade others of its advisability. In this way he would follow the proper course of action for any publicly spirited man.

> He will accommodate as well as he can his public arrangements to the confirmed habits and prejudicies of the people, and will remedy as well as he can the inconveniences which may flow from the want of those regulations which the people are averse to submit to. When he cannot establish the right, he will not disdain to ameliorate the wrong; but, like Solon, when he cannot establish the best system of laws, he will endeavour to establish the best that the people can bear. (*MS*, p. 342)

Having come this far Smith confronted still another dilemma. The only way the changes he supported could be effected was by legislators and they, as he already knew, could not be persuaded of the advisability of any policy change on the basis of appeals to moral considerations. Legislators in particular and administrators of institutions generally decide on matters of institutional practice solely on the basis of considerations of utility, typically in the aesthetic sense which Smith attributed to Hume. Recognizing these constraints, Smith hit upon a strategy whereby he could enlist the support even of men who regard those subject to governmental power as the parts of a great machine or as pieces in a grand game of chess.

You will be more likely to persuade, if you describe the great system of public police which procures these advantages, if you explain the connections and dependencies of its several parts, their mutual subordination to one another, and their general subservience to the happiness of the society; if you show how this system might be introduced into his own country, what it is that hinders it from taking place there at present, how those obstructions might be removed, and all the several wheels of the machine of government be made to move with more harmony and smoothness, without grating upon one another or mutually retarding one another's motion. (*MS*, p. 267)

In the *Wealth of Nations* Smith recommended that governments relinquish in large measure the prerogative of administering the commercial affairs of their respective peoples. He argued his case for this change mainly upon the grounds that the resulting arrangement would be at once more coherent and more conducive to the enrichment both of the sovereign and of the people (*WN*, pp. 397, 651). Clearly considerations of utility played a prominent role in the *Wealth of Nations*.[12] This prominence of considerations of utility in the *Wealth of Nations* as contrasted with Smith's sharp critique of utility in the *Moral Sentiments* has been a source of puzzlement from the day John Millar declared that Smith's political economy was based upon considerations of expediency and not justice (Stewart 1858, p. 12), through the long debates on "Das Adam Smith Problem," to our own day when now and again someone declares that Smith was a utilitarian after all (Campbell 1971, pp. 205-20). This puzzlement is relieved the moment we recognize three points. First, although Smith rejected the claim that utility and not propriety is the fundamental consideration in moral judgments, he nevertheless recognized that utility, where consistent with propriety, can be an important subsidiary consideration (*MS*, pp. 479-81). Second, the proposed policy changes were consistent, as will be shown in subsequent chapters, with the requirements both of propriety and of utility. Third, Smith argued for those changes on the basis of their utility not because he regarded utility as the sole criteria relevant to public policy decisions, but because he wished to persuade others who did support that belief of the advisability of those reforms – reforms he supported on the basis of considerations of propriety. In my judgment it is much more likely that the prominence accorded considerations of utility in the *Wealth of Nations* reflects a rhetorical [13] strategy on Smith's part and not a doctrinal change or inconsistency.

[12] Macfie's claim that utility is not the link between the *Moral Sentiments* and the *Wealth of Nations* (1967, p. 59) is, therefore, false. Macfie and others have neglected to analyze the precise sense in which Smith used the term "utility" and thereby missed the value displacement phenomenon.

[13] "Rhetorical" is here used in Smith's sense as discourse the primary purpose

If this be the case then the *Wealth of Nations* was conceived and executed not so much as a scientific treatise, although it was certainly that too, as a masterful piece of moral propaganda. Although this may appear to be a scandalous remark to the layman, many economists have come to recognize that this description applies to most major treatises in political economy. (Myrdal 1954; Robinson 1962; Hutchison 1964). Be that as it may, propagandizing even in a moral cause and even where consistent with a scrupulous sense of propriety is, like the spirit of innovation itself, a dangerous strategy. Even when it is effective in promoting reforms which are just and proper such an approach creates mis-impressions and is frequently counter-productive. In Smith's case it has permitted utilitarian ideologues as well as those who live by and/or administer capital to cite Smith as an early champion of their cause. "Now such was the tragedy of Adam Smith, who was praised by the descendents of his enemies, and scorned by the descendents of his friends" (Ginzberg 1934, p. 198). Having decided upon a rhetorical strategy of appealing to the a-moral mentality of men of system, Smith must share the responsibility for this "tragedy." Having recognized this we may now be able to discern who is on the side of the angels.

of which is persuasion (*LR*, p. 58). Both rhetorical and didactic discourse attempt to prove a proposition but do so differently. "Didactic discourse emerges from the attempt to prove a proposition when proof can be accomplished by putting both sides of a question before an audience, and by giving each side its true degree of influence. Rhetorical discourse emerges from the attempt to prove a proposition when proof can be accomplished only by magnifying one side and by diminishing or concealing the other. Didactic discourse seeks conviction, rhetorical discourse, persuasion." (Howell 1971, p. 554). Campbell, who adopted the popular view that Smith's primary purpose in the *Wealth of Nations* was to instruct, claimed that its style was didactic and in particular imitated that style which Smith attributed to Newton (Campbell 1971, pp. 29-32). In view of the argument adduced above and substantiated in the next two chapters it appears more likely that Smith's primary intention in that book was to persuade and that he adopted the rhetorical style attributed to Socrates. "In this method we keep as far from the main point to be proved as possible, bringing on the audience by slow and imperceptible degrees to the thing to be proved, and by gaining their consent to some things whose tendency they cannot discover, we force them at last either to deny what they had before agreed to, or to grant the reality of the conclusion" (*LR*, p. 140-1).

CHAPTER V

COMMERCE

The *Wealth of Nations* is the principal basis of Smith's reputation as a seminal social theorist. In it he addressed the general subject of political economy. This has seemed to most of his interpreters to suggest, indeed to demand, that the analyses and doctrines presented in that work be interpreted from the perspective of economic theory. On the basis of that assumption the *Wealth of Nations* has been represented in our century as one of the foundation stones of economic liberalism, free enterprise or competitive capitalism.

This reading has become increasingly difficult to sustain for three reasons. First, it fails to elucidate a number of Smith's more important doctrines. His labor theory of value is rejected as hopelessly confused (Schumpeter 1954, p. 188); his claim that value in exchange is independent of value in use is rejected as either meaningless (Stigler 1950, p. 308) or mistaken (Taylor 1960, p. 103); and his distinction between productive and unproductive labor is declared inconsistent with his own concept of wealth (Cannan 1903, pp. 18-31). Second, it fails to give full weight to the very grave reservations Smith had about the commercial life of his day which reservations were expressed in the *Wealth of Nations*. Ginzberg discovered that Smith disdained merchants and traders (1934, pp. 11-12); Gray found that Smith held the pursuit of wealth in contempt (1948, p. 16); and Grampp observed that Smith not only disliked the arrogance and ostentation of the rich but was also deeply disturbed by the intellectual and moral tone of commercial society (1965, vol. II, pp. 7, 32). Third, it ascribes ethical, psychological and methodological positions to Smith which are inconsistent with views he in fact espoused in his earlier writings. These views have been discussed in the foregoing chapters. Among the more important of these were Smith's rejection of stoic and utilitarian ethics (Chap. II, IV) his analysis of commercial motivation (Chap. III), his abandonment of the method of individualism (Chap. III) and his conventionalistic epistemological position (Chap. I).

Although the strategy of interpreting the *Wealth of Nations* by accommodating the views expressed in it to the methods, interests, cate-

gories and paradigms of subsequent economic theorists has by no means
been exhausted, it seems clear that the combined weight of these difficulties strongly suggests that this approach does not afford an altogether
reliable way of discovering the meaning Smith intended to convey in
that book. A more reliable technique for at once discovering how Smith
understood the *Wealth of Nations* and avoiding these and other difficulties is to approach that work from Smith's own perspective and to
treat it consistently with his own method.

Smith's perspective on political economy was quite different from
that which has prevailed since J. S. Mill. To Smith political economy
was a branch or application of ethics. In particular Smith understood
political economy as that area of moral philosophy which is concerned
with the articulation of the rules of justice as they relate to the practices
of government, specifically to those practices which concern the provision of a more plentiful supply of the material necessities and conveniences of life to the citizenry (*MS*, pp. 501-3; *LJ*, pp. 1-4, 153-6; *WN*,
pp. lvii-lix, 396). Smith's primary concern as a political economist was
not with the efficiency with which a given population might provide
itself with the necessities and conveniences of life by acting in accordance
with one set of social practices or another, but with the consistency of
those practices with the rules of justice supported by that population.
He regarded the question of the justice of commercial practices to be
more important than the question of their efficiency because he was
convinced that justice and not efficiency is the *sine qua non* of any
society whatsoever (*MS*, pp. 124-6). He devoted such enormous energy
to the project of political economy because he was also convinced, as
I will show in the course of this chapter, that the commercial practices
of his day were in flagrant violation of the established rules of justice
and so posed a serious threat to the survival of society itself.

When the *Wealth of Nations* is considered apart from the *Moral
Sentiments* this emphasis is not readily apparent. Indeed it appears that
Smith there argued for certain reforms in the commercial policies of
governments chiefly on the basis of increased efficiency. This appearance has reinforced the general practice of neglecting Smith's other
works when interpreting the *Wealth of Nations*. It explains in large part
the mistaken belief that that work is self-contained, thoroughly intelligible apart from his other writings. In the last section of chapter four
I argued that this reversal of emphasis resulted from a rhetorical strategy
on Smith's part and not a doctrinal change or inconsistency. Although
allowance must be made for this strategy when interpreting the *Wealth
of Nations*, it must no longer be allowed to obscure the fact that Smith's

primary concern in political economy was with matters of justice. Except
for rhetorical purposes, considerations of utility or efficiency were always of secondary importance to him.

The purpose of this and the next chapter is to present a brief but
accurate statement of the central features of Smith's political economy
considered as an application of his own moral philosophy. If allowance
is made for Smith's rhetorical strategy, this may reasonably be regarded
as the equivalent of an account of the central project of the *Wealth of
Nations*. Although these brief chapters do not pretend to elucidate all
or even most of the details of Smith's political economy, they do provide
an historically correct statement of the philosophical context in terms of
which those details can most profitably be pursued whether by philosopher, economist or sociologist.

Smith's understanding of political economy emerges only when his
own method of inquiry is employed in interpreting the *Wealth of Nations*.
Indeed, this technique is suggested in the full title of that work. Smith's
method of inquiry in moral philosophy was discussed in chapter one.
The structure of these chapters follows a four part outline suggested by
that discussion. First, Smith's critique of what he took to be the prevailing outlook on commerce and commercial policy will be recounted.
Second, I show how he developed a revised outlook on commerce, one
which he believed superior to the received view on all criteria relevant
to moral inquiry, viz., coherence, comprehensiveness, familiarity, beauty
and propriety. The third part treats Smith's proof that his outlook
provides a more powerful tool on the very grounds which the mercantilists claimed as the chief distinction of their own view, viz., for ex-
plaining the causes of the increase of the wealth of nations. Finally, I
will discuss the full range of revisions in public policy which Smith felt
were entailed by his own outlook on commerce.

The order in which Smith's doctrines are treated in these chapters
and the emphasis given to each is justifiable solely in view of their
purpose. These chapters are not structured to highlight original contributions to Smithian literature. On several occasions I attempt to advance
the discussion of disputed issues in footnotes and dwell at length on
matters in the text on which there is general agreement. Nor are they
designed to reveal the relevance of Smith's analyses for topics of contemporary interest. The separation of value theory from growth theory
is probably very awkward for any other purpose. Still, it is only by
treating these theories separately that we can achieve a firm grasp of how
Smith came to his views on political economy and so to an understanding of the central project of the *Wealth of Nations*. Although Smith

shows that the commercial policies which he proposed would, if implemented, promote conditions which allow maximum economic growth, he conceived and supported those policies primarily because those same conditions would assure the viability of a pricing procedure which satisfied the demands of justice.

I

In a commercial society each man typically satisfies his various wants "by exchanging that surplus part of the produce of his own labour, which is over and above his own consumption, for such parts of the produce of other men's labour as he has occasion for" (*WN*, p. 22). In such a relationship men "exchange good offices according to an agreed valuation" (*MS*, p. 124). The value of different objects in this type of arrangement is whatever men agree will exchange for them on an equitable basis. That judgment is reached, however, "not by any accurate measure, but by the higgling and bargaining of the market, according to that sort of rought equality which, though not exact, is sufficient for carrying on the business of common life" (*WN*, p. 31). As the volume and variety of goods and services offered in exchange for the surplus produce of others increases, the inconvenience of barter becomes more acute. Too often the goods which a man offers to barter do not interest the owners of the commodities which he desires. Smith believed that money was originally invented to ease this inconvenience. In order to expedite trade a universally desired commodity – which for convenience I will call silver – came to be used as an intermediary or medium through which all other commodities could be exchanged. In this way commodities desired by anyone could always be exchanged for silver because silver was desired by everyone (*WN*, pp. 22-3).

The essential function of money in a commercial society is as a medium of exchange or as Smith called it, an instrument of commerce. It frequently acquires an altogether different function, viz., as the measure of value. As the volume and frequency of exchange increases the most frequently exchanged commodity is silver. In this situation men most frequently assign value to commodities in relation to the quantity of silver men agree to exchange for them. "Hence it comes to pass, that the exchangeable value of every commodity is more frequently estimated by the quantity of money, than by the quantity either of labour or any other commodity which can be had in exchange for it" (*WN*, p. 32). This tendency to associate the instrument of commerce with the measure of value was particularly pronounced among those who were in the habit of keeping accounts in terms of silver (*WN*, pp. 40-1), i.e. those whose principal occupation was, by the division of labor, limited to exchanging commodities for silver and among those who attempted to compare the relative wealth of ancient nations (*WN*, pp. 406-7; 181-6). The result of this association was that men became habituated to the practice of assessing the value of their possessions and those of others in terms of the amount of silver for which they would exchange. This was in Smith's judgment the origin of the popular notion that wealth is the power to command money. "To grow rich is to get money; and wealth and money, in short, are, in common language, considered as in every respect synonymous" (*WN*, p. 398).

This popular conviction affected not only the outlook and actions of merchants and economic historians, but also the policies of governments. By the fifteenth and sixteenth centuries European governments had, in an attempt to enhance their wealth as a hedge against future military contingencies, adopted policies designed to increase their store of silver. To this end the export of silver was prohibited (*WN*, pp. 398-400) and colonies were established in the hope of exploiting more fertile mines (*WN*, pp. 523-31). The former, however, was a source of considerable frustration to merchants engaged in foreign trade because it placed them on a barter footing, thereby reducing the volume of that trade. By 1663 these merchants and their apologists had persuaded Parliament to abolish the prohibition upon the export of silver and to initiate in its stead two other policies designed to more efficiently increase the quantity of silver in the nation's possession by assuring what they called an "advantageous balance of trade" (*WN*, pp. 400-02, 607). The two strategies designed to achieve this objective were restraints upon importing and encouragement to exporting certain commodities. These were designed to generate a surplus of receipts from foreign trade over payments (*WN*, p. 418).

Smith examined both the arguments and the policy recommendations of the merchants as represented in the writings of certain of their apologists, eg., Mun and Locke (*WN*, pp. 399-400; *LJ*, pp. 195-8). He found their arguments favoring abolition of the prihibition of the export silver to be sound (*WN*, p. 402). He agreed, furthermore, that under certain circumstances limited restraints upon imports were justified, eg., to protect an industry essential to national security and "infant industries" (*WN*, pp. 429-37; 712). Beyond that he agreed that certain types of encouragements to exporting were reasonable, eg., drawbacks (*WN*, pp. 466-71). With these exceptions, however, he was convinced that the practices sponsored by the mercantile interests were enormously detrimental to the enrichment of the nation. Smith went to great length to establish this point (*WN*, pp. 420-626). Beyond that he charged that their contention that the nation would be enriched by fostering a favorable balance of trade was self-serving and patently "sophistical" (*WN*, pp. 402, 460-1, 481).

In arguing for the implementation of policies which were clearly designed to enhance their own profits, the merchants and their apologists represented them – no doubt in good faith (*WN*, p. 602) – as being in the best interests of the nation. Their arguments prevailed in Parliament for a variety of reasons. It resulted partly from the ignorance and gullibility of the nobility and gentry; partly from the quick-wit and articulate skill of the merchants; partly from the air of credibility projected by the exactitude of their calculations; and partly from the failure of anyone to consider in what manner foreign trade contributes to the enrichment of a nation (*WN*, pp. 402-3, 250, 473). The credulity of Parliament allowed the glib apologists of mercantile interests to win the day by playing upon the popular confusion of wealth and money (*WN*, pp. 398-400). As a result the merchants became a formidable lobby as well as the principal advisors to the government on commercial affairs (*WN*, pp. 438, 550). In that capacity they successfully erected the "sneaking" and "rapacious" arts of "underling tradesmen" in the place of political wisdom (*WN*, pp. 460-1) and persuaded the British government to enter upon a "project of empire" (*WN*, pp. 898-900) "for the sole purpose of raising up a nation of customers" (*WN*, p. 626) – a project so palpably abhorrent as to be unfit even for a nation of shopkeepers, "but extremely fit for a nation whose government is influenced by shopkeepers" (*WN*, p. 579).[1]

Smith leveled three types of charges against the prevailing commercial system of Great Britain. The first, mentioned above was that it was an inefficient method of augmenting national wealth, but only of enriching merchants. The second, which also occupied Smith's attention to quite

[1] Smith rejected the extreme views of both the physiocrats and the mercantilists as to the value of manufacturers, merchants and traders in commercial society. Against the former he insisted that these men do contribute significantly to the process of enriching a nation (*WN*, pp. 638-42). Against the latter he insisted that the interests of those who live by profits are almost always at odds with those policies which most effectively promote national wealth (*WN*, pp. 249-50). On balance the *Wealth of Nations* neither advocates nor denigrates the role of owners of capital. The bulk of Smith's criticism was directed against the then current commercial policies of Great Britain and indirectly against the practice of formulating public policy on the advice of men who live by profits. Smith himself described the *Wealth of Nations* as "the very violent attack I had made upon the entire commercial system of Great Britain" (Letter to A. Holt, October, 1780. Scott 1937, p. 283).

some length (*WN*, pp. 176-246), was that the outlook upon which those
policies were based was predicated upon a fallacious inference and was
therefore incoherent. The third and by far the most important to Smith
was that the practices which resulted from the application of mercantile
policies were unjust. This last charge was deemphasized in the *Wealth
of Nations* as a part of Smith's rhetorical strategy (see Chapter IV).

The ultimate objective of the commercial system advocated by the
mercantile interests was represented as being "to enrich the country by
an advantageous balance of trade" (*WN*, p. 607). The plausibility of
this strategy did not derive from the confusion of wealth and money in
popular language. That ambiguity is so obvious as to be apparent to all
who had command of the language (*WN*, pp. 398, 274, 406). The
plausibility of this strategy derived mainly from "the popular notion,
that as the quantity of silver naturally increases in every country with
the increase of wealth, so its value diminishes as its quantity increases"
(*WN*, pp. 181, 188, 237-8).

Unlike the belief that wealth consists in silver or money, this notion
is far from ridiculous. In any commercial society which employs money
as an instrument of commerce the value of any commodity is ordinarily
measured by the quantity of silver for which it will exchange. The practice of estimating the magnitude of a man's wealth in terms of the
quantity of silver he can purchase with it is valid and useful within
certain limits. "At the same time and place, therefore, money is the
exact measure of the real exchangeable value of all commodities. It is
so, however, at the same time and place only" (*WN*, p. 37). Within
these limits the quantity of silver in the market does necessarily vary
directly with the value of all commodities in that market, and it does
so because silver is the instrument of commerce. Thus, if and insofar as
the quantity of silver increases solely "in order to circulate a greater
quantity of commodities," it can be used as an index to fluctuations in
the magnitude of the wealth in the given market (*WN*, pp. 188, 328).
By contending that the value of all commodities in all markets of a
nation increases as the quantity of silver in those markets increases over
time, the mercantilists exceeded these limits, ignored the fact that the
quantity of silver frequently increases as a result of the discovery of
more productive mines, and thereby fell victim to what logicians today
term the fallacy of composition (*WN*, pp. 188-9, 236-7). The quantity of
silver in a nation's possession bears no necessary relation to the magnitude of its wealth. In no case is an increase in the quantity of silver the
cause of an increase of a nation's wealth and that in spite of the fact
that the two did occur simultaneously (*WN*, p. 238).

Smith also objected to the commercial system supported by mercantile policies on the ground that it violated what he took to be the rudiments of justice. His most strenuous objection, stated in a most subdued tone in the *Wealth of Nations*, was that that system violated equity by supporting a grossly unfair distribution of wealth among the different ranks of society.[2] "It is but equity, besides, that they who feed, cloath and lodge the whole body of the people, should have such a share of the produce of their own labour as to be themselves tolerably well fed, cloathed and lodged" (*WN*, p. 79; also see p. 49).

His second objection was that in its operation this system of commerce hindered the ability of men – both individually and collectively – to conduct their affairs consistently with their own moral sentiments. He pointed to three specific instances of such hinderances. The statutes of apprenticeship were, perhaps, the most obvious case.

The property which every man has in his own labour, as it is the original foundation of all other property, so it is the most sacred and inviolable. The patrimony of a poor man lies in the strength and dexterity of his hands; and to hinder him from employing this strength and dexterity in what manner he thinks proper without injury to his neighbour, is a plain violation of this most sacred property. (*WN*, pp. 121-2; also see p. 497).

The settlement provision of the poor laws, by encouraging relocation of the labor force, violated the right of every citizen to live in the community of his choice. "To remove a man who has committed no mis-

---

[2] This same judgment was expressed in earlier versions in much less guarded language. These statements show that Smith was not insensitive to questions of distributive justice.

"In a civilized society, though there is a division of labour, there is no equal division, for there are a good many who work none at all. The division of opulence is not according to work. The opulence of the merchant is greater than that of all his clerks, though he works less; and they again have six times more than an equal number of artisans, who are more employed. The artisan who works at his ease within doors has far more than the poor labourer who trudges up and down without intermission. Thus, he who as it were bears the burden of society, has the fewest advantages." (*LJ*, pp. 162-3)

"But with regard to the produce of the labour of a great Society there is never any such thing as a fair and equal division. In a Society of a hundred thousand families, there will perhaps be one hundred who don't labour at all, and who yet, either by violence, or by the more orderly oppression of law, employ a greater part of the labour of the society than any other ten thousand in it. The division of what remains too, after this enormous defalcation, is by no means made in proportion to the labour of each individual. On the contrary those who labour most get least. . . . [T]he poor labourer who has the soil and the seasons to struggle with, and who while he affords the materials for supplying the luxury of all the other members of the common wealth, and bears, as it were, upon his shoulders the whole fabric of human society, sees himself to be pressed down under the ground by the weight, and to be buried out of sight in the lowest foundations of the building." ("Draft of the Wealth of Nations," Scott 1937, pp. 327-8).

demeanor from the parish where he choses to reside, is an evident violation of natural liberty and justice" (*WN*, p. 141). Colonial practices
resulted in the depravation of entire communities of the ability to
administer their own affairs.

> To prohibit a great people, however, from making all that they can of every part
> of their own produce, or from employing their stock and industry in the way that
> they judge most advantageous to themselves, is a manifest violation of the most
> sacred rights of mankind. (*WN*, p. 549)

The third and perhaps the most insightful of Smith's objections to the
existing commercial system on the grounds of justice was that it habituated men – both individually and collectively – to employing the categories and the decision making procedure of the entrepreneur in all
spheres of human affairs. By promoting this habit this commercial
system prompted men to substitute the values of the entrepreneur in the
place of the moral sentiments of the larger community thereby seriously
corrupting the moral character of the very community it purports to
serve (*MS*, p. 84). In short, the existing commercial system, because it
received the unqualified endorsement and support of governments,
promoted value displacement (see Chap. IV) not only in the case of
ambitious individuals (*MS*, pp. 259-63), but also and more importantly
in the case of governments themselves.

> By such maxims as these, however, nations have been taught that their interest
> consisted in beggaring all their neighbours. Each nation has been made to look
> with an invidious eye upon the prosperity of all other nations with which it
> trades, and to consider their gain as its own loss. Commerce, which ought naturally
> to be, among nations, as among individuals, a bond of union and friendship, has
> become the most fertile source of discord and animosity. (*WN*, p. 460).

II

The heart of the outlook on commerce which Smith sponsored is set
down in what has come to be known as his theory of value. The key
doctrines of that theory emerge from his critique of the received outlook. Unlike the merchants and their apologists Smith did not regard
the money or nominal price of commodities as the appropriate measure
of their value – as their real prices. Still, he did believe that the money
prices of commodities in the same market and in the intermediate term
did approximate their real values or prices. Smith's differences with the
mercantilists were rooted in a disagreement over the nature of wealth,
over what price measures, and not, as is frequently urged, over which
commodity provides the most useful index to fluctuations in real wealth

(Stigler 1952, p. 205; Schumpeter 1954, p. 188; Robertson and Taylor 1957, pp. 194-5). Accordingly, the best access to Smith's theory of value is through a discussion of his definition of wealth, of his view on the nature and determinants of real price and of his account of how nominal price is made to approximate real price.

Smith conceived of wealth quite differently than either the mercantilists and physiocrats before him or the great majority of orthodox economists since.[3] For him wealth was a mode of power, i.e., the ability to direct the actions of others. Indeed, wealth had been the decisive mode of power in "civilized" societies ever since the rise of the "nations of shepherds" with the ancient Tartar, Arab and Hebrew tribes (*WN*, pp. 653-4; *LJ*, pp. 14-15). In every society which is based upon a plutocratic deference structure the custom is that the power to decisively influence mores, tastes and institutions and thereby to exercise control over the actions of other men in society is conferred on the condition that the recipient possesses a stock of such materials as are currently admired and sought after (see Chapter IV). Although the type of possessions which has been regarded as the warrant for the conveyance of this power had changed over the centuries, the type of power conveyed and the manner in which it was exercised has remained constant. Those possessed of greater fortunes enjoyed the benefit of the services of those of lesser affluence and in return distributed that portion of their revenue from which they could derive no use or amusement to those who labored in their behalf. In this way the rich become the benefactors of the poor and the poor their dependents. Although this pattern was more apparent in the less complex "nations of shepherds" (*WN*, p. 671), it is also discernable in modern commercial societies.

Those, therefore, who have the command of more food than they themselves can consume, are always willing to exchange the surplus, or, what is the same thing, the price of it, for gratifications of this other kind [conveniences and ornaments].

[3] Smith is generally held to have subscribed to a definition of wealth which is roughly equivalent to the more recent concept of national income. This belief originated, as far as I can tell, with Leser (1874, pp. 7-8) and was popularized by Cannan (1903, pp. 11-18). Once accepted this belief leads directly to the observation that this concept of wealth is inconsistent with several of Smith's other principal doctrines, viz., the labor theory of value, the distinction between productive and unproductive labor and the independence of value in exchange from value in use. Having arrived at this observation an interpreter may either reconsider the accuracy of the initial belief concerning Smith's concept of wealth or charge that Smith committed major blunders concerning these subsidiary doctrines. Smith's commentators have typically followed the latter course (see, for example, Taylor 1960, pp. 90-109). In this and the following chapter I shall show how more careful attention to Smith's definition of wealth reveals a somewhat different concept of its nature, one which is quite consistent with these subsidiary doctrines.

What is over and above satisfying the limited desire [of food], is given for the amusement of those desires which cannot be satisfied, but seem to be altogether endless. The poor, in order to obtain food, exert themselves to gratify those fancies of the rich, and to obtain it more certainly, they vie with one another in the cheapness and perfection of their work. (*WN*, p. 164).

Throughout the experience of "civilized" societies, then, the term wealth has been used to denote the power which propertied men enjoy over the activities of others. Men have not been called wealthy to the extent that their wants were satisfied, but to the extent that they could, by transferring some of their surplus, direct the energies of others. Accordingly, the word "wealth" denoted not the possessions which were the prior condition of the conveyance of this power, but the power conveyed upon the satisfaction of that prior condition and exercised by the transfer of those possessions. Smith's definitive statement of the essential nature of wealth relates to the way that power existed in the commercial society of his own day.

Wealth, as Mr. Hobbes says, is power. ... The power which that possession [of fortune] immediately and directly conveys to him, is the power of purchasing; a certain command over all the labour, or over all the produce of labour which is then in the market. His fortune is greater or less, precisely in proportion to the extent of this power; or to the quantity either of other men's labour, or, what is the same thing, of the produce of other men's labour, which it enables him to purchase or command. The exchangeable value of every thing must always be precisely equal to the extent of this power which it conveys to its owner. (*WN*, p. 31)

To be sure Smith used the labor theory of property to advantage in communicating this perception. That theory, however, was not the basis of his definition of wealth as Myrdal suggested (1954, p. 72). For one thing he recognized that the institution of property was not based upon that theory. Owners of land and of capital had a valid claim upon the produce which resulted from the use of their property even though they invested none of their own labor in its production (*WN*, p. 49). It is understandable and may perhaps be excusable that men who consider commerce as merely a machine for allocating resources should fail to fully appreciate what to the working poor is so obvious, viz., that market relations are as surely power relations as are those between sovereign and citizen or nation and nation. Smith adopted their point of view in approaching commercial affairs mainly because he was convinced that they were suffering profound injustices due to abuse of commercial power and was intent upon doing whatever he could to alleviate that situation.

Wealth, then, is at root the power to command labor. The extent of that power is, by definition, the extent to which others can be persuaded to toil in exchange for the commodity the possession of which conveys this power. Labor, therefore, is the appropriate measure of the value of any commodity – its real price. "The real price of every thing, what every thing really costs to the man who wants to acquire it, is the toil and trouble of acquiring it" (*WN*, p. 30).[4] Clearly Smith did not declare that labor is the real price of commodities because he felt that the price of labor is a more satisfactory index of economic growth than are those of silver or corn. Indeed, the money price of labor is a less reliable index of real growth than is that of corn. When he claimed that labor alone never varies in its own value he was speaking of its value "to the labourer" (*WN*, p. 33). Although Smith did offer some advice to economic historians on how to compare the money prices of a given market basket over time with a fair degree of accuracy (*WN*, pp. 33-7, 186-7), the specification of a set of rules whereby the observer of commercial affairs could render the spectacle most coherent and orderly was not, as is widely held, his principal concern (Stigler 1952, p. 205; Schumpeter 1954, p. 188; Robertson and Taylor 1957, p. 194). His main concern in the first book of the *Wealth of Nations* was to show how, in the same neighbourhood and in the intermediate term, the money or nominal prices of commodities approximate their real prices. In order to show how and why this happens – rather than merely to assume that it does – he had to inquire into the rules which market agents actually followed, into the rules which governed their behavior and not merely the rules which might generate an aesthetically sound theory of the "behavior" of prices.

What are the rules which men naturally observe in exchanging [goods] either for money or for one another, I shall now proceed to examine. These rules determine what may be called the relative or exchangeable value of goods. (*WN*, p. 28)

The exchange value of commodities in a commercial society is whatever men agree will exchange for them on an equitable basis. In a barter situation, i.e., where commodities are exchanged directly for one another without the intervention of money, the equality of the values of com-

---

[4] In 1817 David Ricardo, who failed to recognize that the "labor command theory" was a definition of wealth, claimed that Smith proposed two theories of value, the labor command and the labor cost theories, and furthermore that these were incompatible with one another (*Principles of Political Economy and Taxation*, Ch. 1). This view has been repeated ever since (Douglas 1927, pp. 63-9; Schumpeter 1954, p. 188; Myrdal 1954, p. 67; Taylor 1960, p. 105). On my reading "labor command" is a definition of wealth and "labor cost" is the specification of the appropriate measure of wealth, a specification which is not only compatible with but inferred from the definition of wealth. These are not two theories, but two aspects of the same theory.

modities exchanged is based upon a comparison of the labor which was
expended upon the production of each. On such a basis the exchange
ratio is inversely proportional to the ratio of the labor cost of producing
the commodities. "If among a nation of hunters, for example, it usually
costs twice the labor to kill a beaver which it does to kill a deer, one
beaver should naturally exchange for or be worth two deer" (WN, p. 47).
In that case the labor commanded by one beaver is equal to that commanded by two deer.

In such a situation the worth of the labor invested in the production
of a commodity is neither obvious nor the same for all men in all cultures.
Clearly the amount of time devoted is one of the relevant considerations,
but it is not the only one, for the same amount of time expended in one
way is worth more than it is when expended in other ways. Accordingly,
in order to provide a basis for agreement on the relative merits of two
commodities in a barter situation all parties must first agree on what
weight will be given to different kinds of labor. These agreements enable
barter to occur. They take the form of customs according to which such
considerations as the degree of exertion, ingenuity, cleanliness, skill, risk,
and responsibility involved in a given mode of laboring will qualify its
produce as worth more or less (WN, pp. 31, 47). Such customs were still
operative in the commercial society of Smith's own day (WN, pp. 100-07).

These customs constituted the rules by which men in a primitive barter
situation determined the exchange value of commodities. When men
exchanged commodities on a ratio of labor costs which costs were
determined according to these customs the exchanges were and were
known to be equitable according to mutually accepted standards. Commodities were then sold for what they were worth. This was the case in
spite of the very inelegant way their value was decided "It is adjusted,
however, not by any accurate measure, but by the higgling and bargaining
of the market, according to that sort of rough equality which, though
not exact, is sufficient for carrying on the business of common life"
(WN, p. 31).

With the division of labor in society the process of deciding the relative
worth of different commodities became severely complicated. As capital
was accumulated and land appropriated the commodities brought to
market came to be the product of the cooperation of laborers and
owners of capital and/or owners of lands. Supported by customs and
later by law the owners of capital were considered to have contributed
to the worth of the product by providing materials and advancing wages
to the laborers. Likewise owners of land were considered to have contributed to the worth of the product by allowing the laborers to use their

land while producing the commodity. In this way each came to be allowed a share of the return from the sale of a jointly produced commodity because like the laborers they too had contributed to its production (*WN*, pp. 47-54).

As the price for which a commodity exchanged became factored into two or three components the rules by which the worth of the commodity was determined became considerably more complex. The older customs by which the relative merits of different modes of laboring were weighted were no longer sufficient to decide the real worth of a product which resulted from the cooperation of laborers with owners of real property for their investment was not one of labor. Here again there is a need for a set of rules according to which men could agree on the relative merits of two commodities. Such a set of rules must weight the relative value of the contribution of each factor of production in terms of the labor it is worth (*WN*, p. 50). They must, furthermore, be agreed upon by all parties to any exchange. These qualities will assure that exchange ratios will be based upon the real value of each factor's contribution and that the exchange of commodities will be and will be known to be equitable.

The rules by which the real value of the contributions of land, labor and capital to the product of their joint venture was decided were of the same type as were those by which the worth of labor was decided in more primitive arrangements, viz., customs. These customs, some of which came to have the force of law, developed in each society and neighbourhood over the centuries in response to changing political constraints. During any era they determined what Smith called the natural rates of wages, profits and rents.

In Smith's day the natural rate of rent was the maximum the land owner could deduct from the gross sales of his tenants (*WN*, p. 144-5). This monopoly rate was rooted in property laws which dated from the fall of the Roman Empire (*WN*, pp. 361-72, 393-5). The exercise of this prerogative to exploit had by Smith's day been moderated by the prudence of land owners who, desiring to maximize their long term gains, allowed tenants to retain the expense of maintaining the productivity of the land (*WN*, pp. 270-1) and by the cunning of tenants who exaggerated the magnitude of that expense (*WN*, p. 144). The natural rate of profit in Smith's day was twice the rate of return on the principal which is necessary to cover occasional losses where that principal is lent at interest, i.e., double interest (*WN*, pp. 96-7). This rate too depended largely upon the legal and financial institutions which had developed in the towns as a secure outlet for the surplus revenue of land owners since the feudal era (*WN*, pp. 373-83). The natural rate of wages was determined by two sets of customs. On the one hand, there were the older rules which designated different modes of laboring as more or less worthy depending upon ease, cleanliness, etc. (*WN*, pp. 100-07). On the other hand, there were moral restraints upon the minimum wage which an employer could press upon those who entered a labor contract with him, viz., something more than the price of subsistence for the laborer. This is "the lowest which is consistent with common humanity" (*WN*, p. 67-8).

As indicated on a number of occasions already, Smith was not pleased that these were the prevailing customs of evaluating the worth of contributions to products of joint ventures. He was particularly unhappy with the prerogatives of land owners who "like all other men, love to reap where they never sowed, and demand a rent even for its natural produce" (*WN*, p. 49). Grampp found the attitude noteworthy for the times (1965, vol. II, p. 20). Notwithstanding, these were the prevailing conventions and hence the rules by which the real price of the contribution of the factors of production to the product of their joint venture were determined. The real or natural price, what that product is really worth, is the sum of the prices of these components at their natural rates.[5]

When the price of any commodity is neither more nor less than what is sufficient to pay the rent of the land, the wages of the labour, and the profits of the stock employed in raising, preparing, and bringing it to market, according to their natural rates, the commodity is then sold for what may be called its natural price. The commodity is then sold precisely for what it is worth . . . (*WN*, p. 55)

III

The exchange value of commodities in a commercial society is whatever men agree will exchange for them on an equitable basis. In a barter situation the equality of the values of commodities exchanged is based upon a comparison of the cost of producing them, which costs are measured in terms of the labor each type of cost is worth to others. In the primitive situation the worth of these costs was decided by a simple set of customary rules according to which different types of labor were

[5] Marshall claimed that Smith understood natural price as "the average which economic forces would bring about if the general conditions of life were stationary for a run of time long enough to enable them all to work out their full effect" (1920, p. 289). This reading clearly abstracts from the normative function evidently intended by Smith and furthermore ignores the fact that the market prices of some commodities are permanently in excess of their natural prices. Any commodity which requires exceptionally rare materials and/or productive circumstances falls into this category. Smith cited French wines as an example (*WN*, pp. 60-1).

assigned different degrees of worth. After the division of labor the relative worth of different types of costs were again decided by applying a set of customary rules. Although much more complex in the latter case, it was still custom which ultimately governed the determination of exchange value in both the simple and the complex cases of barter. In both cases the ratio at which commodities should exchange is inversely proportional to the ratio of production costs at customary rates. Although the introduction of the division of labor complicated the task of determining the real price of commodities, it did not disrupt it totally.

Another effect of the introduction of the division of labor, however, threatened the very foundations of commercial society, i.e., the advent of the use of money as the ordinary measure of value. As indicated above Smith believed that money was invented to overcome the inconveniences of barter. Its original function was as an instrument of commerce. But as money or silver became the most frequently exchanged commodity people fell into the habit of estimating the exchange value of commodities in terms of the silver it would purchase instead of the labor it would command (*WN*, pp. 31-3). This made it much more difficult for men to be assured that exchange transactions were equitable and that commodities sold for what they were worth. Unless men can assure that the silver, nominal or market prices of commodities are roughly equal to their real or natural prices they cannot be confident that the consideration given and received in such exchanges is just. But unless *that* is assured the very fabric of commercial society would "crumble into atoms" and each man would then enter the market place "as he enters a den of lions" (*MS*, pp. 124-6).

One of the most significant analytic advances of the *Wealth of Nations* occurs in Book I, Chapter 7. There Smith indicated the precise way in which men assured that rudimentary justice is maintained "by a mercenary exchange of good offices according to an agreed valuation" (*MS*, p. 124),[6] i.e., how the nominal or market prices of commodities are made to approximate their real or natural values in the intermediate term and to the extent that market procedures are not hampered by any of a variety of irregularities most of which result from the unfortunate commercial policies of governments.[7] The core of this analysis is set forth in three observations.

[6] The value of this analysis is widely acknowledged among economists, although frequently for quite different reasons. (See, for example, Hayek 1944, pp. 36, 49; Schumpeter 1954, p. 189; Taylor 1960, p. 110; Grampp 1965, vol. II, p. 32).

[7] Those policies which most immediately disrupted these procedures resulted in the restriction or the increase of the numbers of sellers, in the restriction of

The market price of every particular commodity is regulated by the proportion between the quantity which is actually brought to market, and the demand of those who are willing to pay the natural price of the commodity . . ." (*WN, p. 56*)

When the quantity brought to market is just sufficient to supply the effectual demand and no more, the market price naturally comes to be exactly, or as nearly as can be judged of, the same with the natural price. (*WN, p. 57*)

It is the interest of all those who employ their land, labour, or stock, in bringing any commodity to market, that the quantity never should exceed the effectual demand; and it is the interest of all other people that it never should fall short of that demand. (*WN, p. 57*)

In a market in which the exchange value of commodities is measured in terms of money and jointly decided among prospective buyers and sellers by a process of "higgling and bargaining," the market price of each commodity is the greatest quantity of money which sellers can interest buyers in exchanging for their wares. Now it so happened that the money price buyers were typically willing to pay for commodities varied inversely with the quantity of those commodities which were available. Thus, as a commodity became rarer buyers were willing to pay more money in exchange for it and as it became more common, less. Sellers, for their part, were interested in maximizing their own revenue but were willing to settle for a price which afforded them as little as what was by custom [8] their due, i.e., the natural price. Sellers pursued this interest by adjusting the quantity of each commodity which they produced and brought to market. Thus, if the market price received for a commodity was less than its natural price the seller decided to reduce the quantity produced during subsequent days or seasons in the hope of encouraging buyers to pay more and if it was higher than its natural price he decided to increase the quantity produced in order to increase his revenue. In time both strategies have the same result. The quantity supplied approximates that desired by effective demanders and the market price these buyers are willing to pay for commodities is approximately equal to their natural prices. (*WN, pp. 56-8*)

Grampp suggested that this account of the procedures by which market prices are decided is "almost identical with the conception of perfect competition in modern price theory" (1965, vol. II, p. 32). Insofar as this widely shared belief relates to the organizing effects of market procedures this view is clearly sound. But insofar as it is further

the flow of accurate market information and in restrictions on the ways men could employ their energies or property in markets (*WN, pp. 118-43*).

[8] Both Taylor (1960, pp. 78, 81) and Samuels (1966, Chapter II) observed that Smith believed market decisions to have been restrained by "moral" or "non-deliberative" forces. Neither noticed, however, that these restraints were operative as the rules which determined the natural rates of wages, profits and rents.

maintained that Smith subscribed to the same explanations as modern price theorists on why the consumer demand curve has a negative slope and why producers attempt to maximize their revenue whether on the average or at the margin, this view is demonstrably incorrect for two reasons. On the one hand, Smith did not postulate the rules which define rational market conduct as recent price theorists frequently do, but inquired into the rules which men in the market places of his society actually followed. On the other hand, the rules which he found men following in market places differ sharply from those which are typically postulated today.

Smith insisted that the above description relates the rules which men, in a particular sort of market situation, actually employed in deciding the exchange value of commodities. He also insisted that men in those situations had an interest in following these rules and procedures. The remainder of this section will be devoted to a discussion of what he understood that interest to have been, i.e., why men acting in the capacity of producers attempted to maximize their revenue beyond their natural rates and acting in the capacity of consumers were willing to pay more or less for commodities depending upon how scarce or plentiful they were.

Smith consistently denied that in either capacity men were principally intent upon supplying the very limited "necessities of nature" (*MS*, p. 70; *WN*, p. 164). Men attempted to maximize their revenue by servicing the desires of others because they wished to augment their own fortunes and because they recognized that servicing the desires of others was the most reliable way of doing so (*WN*, p. 14). Their wish to augment their own fortunes was rooted in the "desire to better our own condition" which most men believed could best be accomplished by an "augmentation of fortune (*WN*, pp. 324-5; also 81, 326, 329, 379, 508, 638). But this desire to better one's own condition by accumulation of fortune was not, as was shown in Chapter III, a sophisticated form of the love of pleasure, but a perverse form of the love of praise.

Smith was profoundly convinced that the overriding concern of human beings is to sympathize with the joys and sorrows of others and to enjoy being sympathized with by others (*MS*, p. 3). This concern could not, in Smith's view, be explained in terms of self-love (*MS*, pp. 10-13). As men mature they strive to fulfill this concern by becoming "both respectable and respected" (*MS*, p. 84). In doing so they govern their actions by what they imagine others will find respectable. But when observing the object of the respectful attention of their fellows they discover that, as a matter of cold and to moralists lamentable fact, it is the rich who enjoy the deference and admiration of the greater part of men (*MS*, pp. 84-5). "His actions are the objects of the public care. Scarce a word, scarce a gesture, can fall from him that is altogether neglected. In a great assembly he is the person upon whom all direct their eyes..." (*MS*, p. 72). Observing this most men formulate their rules of conduct or their image of correct behavior by associating the distinctive qualities exhibited with such noticeable effect by the rich with the idea of respectability (*MS*, pp. 84-6). By governing their conduct according to this image men emulate the rich and the rich are "enabled to set or lead what is called fashion" (*MS*, p. 87).

It was in Smith's judgment because of this, together with the fact of unequal distribution of fortune, that men inclined to "make parade of our riches and conceal our poverty" (*MS*, p. 70). It was also because of this that they typically pursued an augmentation of fortune well beyond supplying the necessities of nature – which the wages of the meanest laborer could in fact satisfy (*MS*, p. 70; *LJ*, p. 158; *WN*, pp. 67-8, 74). They were "disinterested admirers and worshippers, of wealth and greatness" (*MS*, p. 85). The anxious toil and bustle of the commercial society of Smith's day was plainly directed toward the acquisition of "equipage" and not the satisfaction of such modest needs. (*WN*, pp. 163-4, *LJ*, pp. 157-9). Such luxuries were desired, finally, not because they were thought to render the life of their possessor more pleasant – for if anything they rendered it more unpleasant (*MS*, pp. 259-63) – but because status or "place" was, as a matter of fact, accorded to people in that society on the condition that they were possessed of a greater or lesser supply of such objects (*MS*, pp. 80-1). Spengler (1959, p. 399n), Grampp (1965, vol. II, pp. 6, 19) Rosenberg (1968, pp. 364-7) and Campbell (1971, pp. 171-4) appear to have arrived at this same interpretation.

From whence, then, arises that emulation which runs through all the different ranks of men, and what are the advantages which we propose by that great purpose of human life which we call bettering our condition? To be observed, to be attended to, to be taken notice of with sympathy, complacency, and approbation, are all the advantages which we can propose to derive from it. (*MS*, pp. 70-1).

The overriding interest of those who produced and brought commodities to market in Smith's day was, in his judgment, to increase their stock of those symbols of status which, in a society whose values are determined by the rich, is a stock of equipage. They sought to increase their equipage because equipage commanded the attention and respect of their fellows and it was that attention and respect rather than any petty pleasure they might derive from such trinkets that most men desired above all else. What Smith identified as the primary motive for the pursuit of fortune in his day is quite similar to what Veblen described as the primary motive for that same pursuit over a century later, viz., "pecuniary emulation" (*The Theory of the Leisure Class,* Chapter II).

The profound influence of the rich was equally evident in the behavior of men in their capacities as consumers. Here too the relative usefulness of commodities in satisfying the very limited "necessities of nature" was not typically one of the considerations to which men gave significant weight when deciding upon their exchange values. Smith reported what others call the "paradox of value" i.e., that value in exchange was independent of value in use, as a description of how men in his day decided upon market prices (*WN*, p. 28). If anything was paradoxical there it was their behavior and not his description of it.[9]

Smith was convinced that men in his day were interested in acquiring commodities principally as symbols of status. Commodities were wanted mainly because and to the extent that their possession excited or commanded the attention, respect or esteem of others (Robertson and Taylor 1957, pp. 196-7). In deciding upon the relative value of com-

---

[9] During our century Smith has been roundly criticized for claiming that value in exchange was independent of value in use. The objections appear to derive from the fact that this claim directly contradicts the utilitarian postulate that all value derives from utility, which postulate has occupied an honored place in the theory of consumer demand since Jevons and Menger. At first Smith was patronized – the poor fellow had not considered utility at the margin and for that reason failed to resolve the paradox of value (Douglas 1927, p. 54; Gray 1931, pp. 128-9; Bladen 1938, p. 40; Kauder 1953, p. 650; Schumpeter 1954, pp. 307-8). Recently stronger objections have been raised. Stigler termed Smith's claim "meaningless" (1950, p. 308). This judgment appears to have been based upon a construction of "utility" which renders it synonymous with "desirable." On this construction Robertson and Taylor were of course right when they proclaimed that utility is essential "for any satisfactory treatment of value..." (1957, p. 186) and so also was Stigler. However acceptable among contemporary economists this construction may be, it is unacceptable in the context of moral philosophy (Rawls 1958, p. 186n) on at least two scores. First, it abstracts from the question of whether the desired and the good are the same (Morrow 1925, pp. 610-11). Second, the practice of lumping the objects of all wants together under the head of utility so as to identify what is wanted with what is useful results in an empirically vacuous tautology (Myrdal 1954, p. 16; Robinson 1962, p. 47). The only valid function of this utilitarian postulate so construed is that of a purely logical canon. Taylor, on the other hand, dismissed Smith's claim as a mistake (1960, p. 103). Presumably the basis of this allegation was its incompatibility with the utilitarian postulate of the currently orthodox theory of consumer demand. If so, this objection is clearly untenable. Smith claimed that, as a matter of fact, men in his day did not give any significant weight to considerations of usefulness when deciding the prices of commodities. As such his claim may have been either correct or incorrect. Its correctness, however, cannot be decided apriori. Nor for that matter can the correctness of recent empirical studies of consumer and managerial behavior (Barnard 1938; Simon 1947, Katona 1951; McClelland 1953) be dismissed merely because they are inconsistent with the orthodox definition of economic rationality (Tobin and Dolbear 1963).

modities each prospective buyer considered the extent to which they conformed more or less closely to his image of "a perfect and happy state" (MS, p. 72). In doing so, however, he did not consider the relative efficiency with which each commodity would actually produce that state, but only the extent to which it was fitting for a man who entertained such an image to possess such commodities. Smith considered this observation as an original discovery, viz., that in commercial as well as political affairs the value of means was in fact decided on the basis of how well they reminded men of their idea of the good life and not on the basis of how well they actually produced a condition which corresponds to that image (MS, pp. 258-68). Pricing decisions, then, were governed by considerations of "utility" in the peculiar sense of that term attributed to Hume (MS, pp. 257-8; also see Chapter IV). Commercial society, therefore, was maintained among men "from a sense of its utility" in this very special sense of the term (MS, p. 124).

The relative value of commodities was decided on the basis of the degree to which they conformed to the buyer's image of respectability. But since that image was typically modeled after the distinctive qualities of the rich their relative value in the judgment of all prospective buyers was the same as their relative value in the judgment of the rich, for the rich "set or lead what is called fashion" (MS, p. 87). It was for this reason that the price men were willing to pay for any commodity varied inversely with the quantity available. "Fashion is different from custom, or rather is a particular species of it. That is not fashion which every body wears, but which those wear who are of a high rank or character" (MS, p. 282).

By any measure the most significant discussion in the *Wealth of Nations* which illustrates this point is Smith's account of how the value of precious metals is set independently and antecedently to their use as money. Although the same points apply to the valuation of diamonds and any other commodity (WN, pp. 172-3; LJ, pp. 158-9), including "necessaries" (WN, p. 56), the discussion of the valuation of precious metals is most significant because they were actually employed as an instrument of commerce and one of the necessary conditions of that employment was that they were desired by all who entered into commercial transactions (WN, pp. 22-3).

The demand for those metals arises partly from their utility, and partly from their beauty. If you except iron, they are more useful than, perhaps, any other metal. As they are less liable to rust and impurity, they can more easily be kept clean; and the utensils either of the table or the kitchen are often upon that account more agreeable when made of them. A silver boiler is more cleanly than a lead, copper, or tin one; and the same quality would render a gold boiler still better than a silver one. The principal merit, however, arises from their beauty, which renders them peculiarly fit for ornaments of dress and furniture. No paint or dye can give so splendid a colour as gilting. The merit of their beauty is greatly enhanced by their scarcity. With the greater part of rich people, the chief enjoyment of riches consists in the parade of riches, which in their eye is never so complete as when they appear to possess those decisive marks of opulence which nobody can possess but themselves. In their eyes the merit of an object which is in any degree either useful or beautiful, is greatly enhanced by its scarcity, or by the great labour which it requires to collect any considerable quantity of it, a labour which nobody can afford to pay but themselves. Such objects they are willing to purchase at a higher price than things much more beautiful and useful, but more common. These qualities of utility, beauty, and scarcity, are the original foundation of the high price of those metals, or of the great quantity of other goods for which they can everywhere be exchanged. This value was antecedent to and independent of their being employed as coin, and was the quality which fitted them for that employment. (*WN*, p. 172; also see *LJ*, pp. 178-9)

In Smith's day men, acting in the capacity of consumers, considered relative scarcity to be the determining consideration when deciding the exchange ratios of commodities because they were interested in commodities largely as symbols of status, as the "decisive marks of opulence." As such the power to command the attention, respect and esteem of others in the concrete form of labor which their possession conveyed was greater or less in proportion to their rarity or commonness, i.e., depending upon how few or how many others could afford them. It was for this reason that men acted on the rules which Smith observed governed the market prices of commodities. This was Smith's explanation of why the consumer demand curve has a negative slope. "The idea of 'conspicuous consumption' was not new," observed Cole, "with Thorstein Veblen" (1958, p. 5; Veblen, *The Theory of the Leisure Class*, Chapter IV).

IV

The current commercial policies of the British government were based upon the counsel of the merchants and their apologists who promised "to enrich the country by an advantageous balance of trade" (*WN*, p. 607). The cogency of this strategy in the view of the nobles and gentry in Parliament derived from its conformity to the popular habit of considering the value of commodities in particular markets in terms of the quantity of silver they could command. They were easily lead to fallaciously infer that the wealth of the nation is great or small depending on the quantity of silver within its command and to conclude that any measure which would increase the nation's silver, e.g., an advantageous balance of trade, must increase its wealth.

After showing the incoherence of the outlook on commercial society which subtended the mercantilist policy recommendations Smith presented his own outlook based upon the view that wealth is indeed the power to command, but it is labor and not silver which is ultimately commanded. His outlook on commerce was represented as superior to that of the mercantilists on all five criteria appropriate to evaluating the relative preferability of moral perspectives (see Chapter I). It was more comprehensive because it embraced not only money but also barter economies. It was more coherent because it did not confuse the medium of exchange with the measure of value (the medium with the message as it were). It was more familiar because the command over one's own labor exercised by those possessed of high-status commodities is an experience no one in a plutocratic society can fail to fully appreciate. It was more beautiful because it showed how objects of one kind – silver – represent objects of a very different kind – labor. Finally, it conformed more closely to the rules of propriety, although by no means as closely as Smith would have preferred. It showed how wealth – the decisive power in "civilized" societies – was allocated consistently with the deference structure which prevailed within the community and was thereby rendered legitimate (see Chapter IV).

The above interpretation of Smith's account of the considerations which governed the commercial behavior of men in his day differs sharply from the popular image of Smith as an early champion of competitive capitalism. Several of these differences warrant explicit mention.

Adam Smith's laws of the market are basically simple. They tell us that the outcome of a certain kind of behavior in a certain social framework will bring about perfectly definite and foreseeable results. Specifically they show us how the drive of individual self-interest in an environment of similarly motivated individuals will result in competition; and they further demonstrate how competition will result in the provision of those goods that society wants, in the quantities that society desires, and at the prices society is prepared to pay. (Heilbroner 1953, p. 46).

This caricature is untenable as an historical judgment on three counts. First, according to Smith commercial behavior was motivated by the profound need for attention, respect and recognition. In Smith's day neither producer nor consumer behavior was motivated by a hedonistic pursuit of pleasures no matter how rare or exquisite. Second, the function of competition in Smith's view is not to specify the ratios at which commodities and factors of production exchange on an equitable basis, but to assure that the ratios at which they are exchanged approximates that at which they should exchange, the latter being specified by custom.

Both custom and competition are necessary to assure a viable market economy but they play different roles. That of competition is to enforce the precepts specified by custom. Smith's opposition to any diminution of the competition which is attendant to commercial affairs, whether by act of government, business or labor (*WN*, pp. 56-7; 60-2; 118-30), was not based on a Spencerian abdication of conscience to the winds of chance in the name of the principle of natural selection (Bonar 1893, p. 174; Marshall 1920, pp. 200-1) nor was it based on the view that competition is the only reasonable substitute for arbitrary authority (Hayek 1944, p. 36). He opposed any diminution of competition because he recognized it not as the regulator of the market mechanism but as an effective check against the advance of the "monopoly spirit," i.e., the delegation of the power of decision to institutions which cannot exercise that power justly because they inevitably fall victim to value displacement (*WN*, p. 147; also see Chapter IV). Third, according to Smith producers who respond to fluctuations in market prices above and below natural price levels, by altering the ways in which the labor and property at their disposal were allocated, did indeed provide the kind of commodities wanted and in the quantities desired but not by society. Consumer sovereignty did not extend to every member of society who might have wanted or even needed a commodity but only to those who could pay the piper, i.e., only to effective demanders (*WN*, p. 56). In commercial society the rich call the tune.

Smith was convinced that the commercial society of his day was in imminent danger of collapse as a society. In order that any society at all be maintained among men each must restrain his conduct and act only on those passions with which others can be reasonably expected to sympathize and, if not admire, at least tolerate (*MS*, pp. 124-26). One of the principal reasons Smith favored the expansion of commerce was that by exposing men to the constant scrutiny of his neighbours this habit of subordinating the impulse of passion to the sentiments of others would be enhanced (*MS*, pp. 86-7; *LJ*, pp. 155-6, 223, 253-4; *WN*, pp. 95; 96-7).[10] So long as men subscribe to the same customs and by an

---

[10] This discipline results for most men in the development of such morally praiseworthy habits as prudence, justice, temperance and fortitude. "In the middling and inferior stations of life, the road to virtue and that to fortune – to such fortune, at least, as men in such stations can reasonably expect to acquire – are, happily, in most cases very nearly the same" (*MS*, p. 86). Over the centuries, as Ginzberg observed (1934, p. 173), Smith's intention has been obscured. He did not intend to suggest that growth in national wealth was intrinsically good or to suggest, as Mandeville had, that private aggrandisement is in the end the same as virtue (Gray 1948, pp. 11, 16). He supported a market economy partly because

act of at least aesthetic sympathy take the situation of others into account when deciding upon their courses of action, they can live in a society with one another – albeit a minimally satisfactory society. But that act of sympathy is essential not only to moral judgments but also to judgments of taste (*MS*, pp. 19-20). Should even that become impossible, as it does when men insist upon acting on the impulse of those passions which cannot be appreciated by others – the passions which take their origin in a state of the body or idiosyncracy (*MS*, pp. 33-43) – then men would become intolerable to one another (*MS*, p. 22) society would become impossible to maintain and "a man would enter an assembly of men as he enters a den of lions" (*MS*, p. 126).

In Smith's judgment commercial society had not yet become a den of lions, although it was fast becoming one under a regime "influenced by shopkeepers" (*WN*, p. 579). More importantly, however, he did not regard the pricing procedures observed by men in his day as an "apparatus of registration which automatically records all the relevant effects of individual actions and whose indications are at the same time the result of and the guide for, all the individual decisions" (Hayek 1944, p. 49). Such caricatures of social relations can appeal only to "men of system." In our day this is but the old concept of society as a game of chess (*MS*, pp. 342-3) except that now the game is played by computers. Fortunately for all of us it has again become socially acceptable to challenge the legitimacy of the "indications" of these machines for making social choices – be they market or voting mechanisms (Arrow 1963, 1967; Wolin 1960; Wollheim 1962; Macpherson 1967). What has yet to be fully recognized by those who are painfully extricating themselves, and hopefully the rest of us as well, from the mad fantasy that society is but a complex machine and that men are but "the materials of a sort of political mechanics," [11] is that there is precedent for this line of thinking in the writings of Adam Smith. Contrary to popular belief, Smith supported what Arrow called the "conventionalist ideal of social

"on balance it promoted the good life – the life of learning, beauty, personal virtue, and good works" (Grampp 1965, vol. II, p. 7), but mainly because it would insure that merchants and traders observe the moral sentiments of the larger population. Since Smith economists have typically, in their pursuit of scientific respectability, lost sight of these humanistic foundations. Polanyi dated that shift in concern with the rise of Townsend's Robinson Crusoe analysis of man in 1780 (1957, p. 111-15). Macpherson traced the tendency to prefer the model of possessive individualism to Hobbes (1962). In all likelihood this tendency to abstract from moral considerations in the practice and theory of commerce is as ancient as the division of labor itself (see Chapter IV).

[11] Dugald Stewart recorded this remark from the manuscript – now lost – of a lecture which Smith delivered to the Glasgow Economic Society in 1755. (Stewart 1858, p. 68).

choice" and opposed, at least in its early form what would become after the French and industrial revolutions the ideal of "capitalist democracy" (Arrow 1963, pp. 1-2). Before the integrity of cultural bonds were wrenched by these twin upheavals society and community were still a reality and were eminently worth defending – at least in the view of Adam Smith. Once those customary bonds were severed it has proven very difficult indeed to maintain even the appearance of legitimacy.

CHAPTER VI

COMMERCIAL POLICY

Adam Smith considered the current commercial policies of Great Britain abhorrent largely because they promoted and sustained grave injustices. He considered his *Wealth of Nations* a very violent attack upon the entire system of commerce supported by those policies (Letter to A. Holt, October, 1790. Scott 1937, p. 283). His intent, however, was not merely to condemn. In the *Wealth of Nations* Smith set out to persuade Parliament to not only reject those policies but to adopt others in their stead, policies which would allow the legitimacy of commerce to be maintained directly by those whose sense of justice had not yet been subverted by institutional responsibilities – the middle ranks of men. In order to establish the preferability of his policy recommendations over those which had long been supported by the mercantile lobby he argued, as was shown in the preceding chapter, that the outlook upon which his recommendations were based was superior to theirs not only on aesthetic grounds but also on moral grounds. Throughout the *Wealth of Nations* he stressed the former attributes and de-emphasized the latter in order to strengthen the persuasive impact of his case upon the "men of system" in the Parliament. Notwithstanding this rhetorical strategy, however, it was the consideration of justice which he considered to be the most compelling recommendation for the outlook which he set forth. On the basis of that outlook on commercial affairs Smith proposed an alternative definition of the nature of national wealth, indicated the factors which had contributed to the augmentation of national wealth and deduced the public policy implications of his entire analysis. The purpose of this chapter is to explore these steps thus completing the account of the central project of the *Wealth of Nations* begun in the preceding chapter.

I

The opening paragraphs of Smith's "Introduction and Plan of the Work" are generally regarded as containing Smith's statement of the nature of the wealth of a nation. This is only partially correct but it is a convenient place to begin.

The annual labour of every nation is the fund which originally supplies it with all the necessaries and conveniencies of life which it annually consumes, and which consist always either in the immediate produce of that labour, or in what is purchased with that produce from other nations.

According therefore, as this produce, or what is purchased with it, bears a greater or smaller proportion to the number of those who are to consume it, the nation will be better or worse supplied with all the necessaries and conveniencies for which it has occasion. (*WN*, p. lvii)

As indicated in the preceding chapter, wealth consists not in the commodities in a person's possession but in the purchasing power enjoyed by that person by virtue of his possessions. The "fund" referred to above does not constitute the wealth of a nation but only the objects which confer wealth. The wealth of the nation is the purchasing power of that fund of commodities. In Book II Smith referred to that fund as "The stock which may be reserved for immediate consumption." That stock was distinguished from "capital stock" or that stock from which members of the nation expect to derive revenue.[1] Capital stock was subdivided into fixed and circulating capital depending upon how it was expected to generate a revenue, or what is the same thing, how it was expected to augment the volume of produce placed in the stock or fund which may be reserved for immediate consumption (*WN*, p. 262-7).

This relation of capital to the other fund was regarded as necessary and exhaustive. Augmentation of the latter stock was, in Smith's view, the sole function and entire justification for the existence of capital. "To maintain and augment the stock which may be reserved for immediate consumption, is the sole end and purpose both of fixed and circulating capitals" (*WN*, p. 267; also see p. 625). Smith's belief that the performance of this function by capital justified the claim of its owners to a revenue in the form of profits defined the main difference between Smith and the physiocrats (*WN*, pp. 638-40). This relation of capital to the "fund which originally supplies [every nation] with all the necessaries and conveniencies of life" is also an exhaustive account of its reasonable and justified uses. "A man would have to be perfectly crazy who, when there is tolerable security, does not employ all the stock which he commands, whether it be his own or borrowed of other people, in some one or other of these three ways" (*WN*, p. 268).

The wealth of any nation then, is the sum of the exchange value of all

---

[1] Cannan correctly observed that Smith did not subscribe to the then popular view that a nation's wealth is its capital (1903, pp. 14-15).

commodities which may be reserved for consumption. The magnitude of that fund may be described in either of two ways. It may be conceived statically, i.e., as a stock or inventory at any particular time. Alternatively, it may be conceived dynamically, i.e., as a flow, as the volume of commodities added to the fund over a specified time, e.g., one year. Smith preferred the latter for reasons he did not state, although convenience of measurement was probably a factor in the decision. Its magnitude might also be described as an aggregate or as an average and if as an average, a number of different variables could be considered relevant. Smith chose to describe the magnitude of the fund as an average using total population as the relevant variable. His reason for that decision appears certainly to have derived from his profound concern over the relative poverty of the majority of citizens (*WN*, p. 79; Hollander 1971, p. 273). The wealth of any nation, then, is the exchange value of the commodities which are annually added to the average person's stock of commodities which may be reserved for immediate consumption.

To have defined the wealth of a nation in this way, however, was not a sufficient analytic basis for an account of the causes of its improvement. In order to show what factors contribute to its increase Smith went on to indicate how annual differences in the magnitude of national wealth are to be measured. For Smith the appropriate measure of wealth is the labor it commands or purchases in the form of the produce of labor. In modern commercial societies commodities, or more precisely their money equivalent, command labor and the use of other factors of production by the purchase of the product of their joint productive venture, the purchase price being divided among the factors of production in the form of wages, profits and rents which others receive from the exchange of their product for it. The value of any commodity sold in an equitable exchange transaction is equal to the revenue of those who purchase it and divide its money equivalent among themselves. Smith was able to use revenue to the factors of production as a measure of the labor command value of the commodity for which their jointly produced product exchanges because he was satisfied that exchange transactions in small local market places were roughly equitable, i.e., that the labor given was roughly equal in value to that received. This strategy for measuring wealth is a reliable procedure, however, only where there is reason to believe that exchange transactions are typically equitable, i.e., are governed by mutually accepted customs, mores, tastes, etc. as indicated in the preceding chapter. Failure to observe this subtlety appears to have led Ricardo and others to the mistaken notion that Smith abandoned the labor command theory of value for a cost of production theory of value (see Chapter V). This same technique of measurement is valid on a national scale, subject to the same qualification.

The whole price or exchangeable value of that annual produce, must resolve itself into the same three parts, and be parcelled out among the different inhabitants of the country, either as the wages of their labour, the profits of their stock, or the rent of their land. (*WN*, p. 270; also see p. 52)

The magnitude of national wealth as defined above may be measured by the annual payments of wages, profits, and rents. Smith observed, however, that not all of these payments may reasonably be included in calculating the magnitude of the exchange value of commodities annually placed in the stock which may be reserved for immediate consumption. Some output never reaches that stock, but is used, among other things, to replenish and otherwise maintain capital at its current rate of productivity, i.e., to cover overhead expenses. Taking this into account Smith declared that the total annual revenue of land, labor and capital after deducting the expense of maintaining the nation's fixed capital and money supply, i.e., net national income, is a reasonably accurate measure of the magnitude of national wealth (*WN*, pp. 270-4). Smith was well aware that taxes are another drain on personal income but preferred to treat tax-policy separately in the last book of the *Wealth of Nations*.

Summarizing briefly, Smith defined the wealth of a nation as the exchange value of the commodities which are annually added to the average person's stock of commodities which may be reserved for immediate consumption. The value of national wealth is computed by deducting the annual expense of maintaining the nation's fixed capital at the current levels of productivity – including the acquired skills and talents of productive laborers (*WN*, pp. 265-6) and the money supply – from the total annual payments to land, labor and capital, which remainder is then divided by the total population of the nation.

Smith's attention to the technique of calculating the magnitude of national wealth lead Cannan and others to conclude that Smith defined wealth as national revenue or national income (1903, pp. 14-15; Taylor 1960, pp. 90-1). Ironically this repeats the very same confusion for which Smith criticized the mercantilists. Here again we find that same type of category mistake which confounds the measure with the measured, the symbol with the symbolized, the expression with the expressed. Apparently Smith's methodological criticism of the merchants and their apologists has fallen upon deaf ears – at least among orthodox western economists since Ricardo. Quite apart from the defensibility of the contention that price and value are identical, it remains altogether improper to prejudice the interpretation of the works of Smith by attempting to reconcile his words with *that* contention.

Having satisfied himself that by wealth Smith meant net national revenue Cannan quickly discovered an inconsistency between wealth so conceived and another of Smith's key doctrines, viz., the distinction between productive and unproductive labor. Cannan's diagnosis of this inconsistency was that Smith was confused (1903, pp. 18-31). Since then others have tried to excuse Smith on the grounds that the use he made of this unfortunate distinction had to do with the knotty problem of acquiring and augmenting growth capital (Moos 1951, pp. 187-201; Bladen 1960, pp. 625-30). This latter suggestion is quite correct, but the confusion relating to the distinction itself rests with Cannan and his mistaken interpretation of Smith's concept of national wealth and not with Smith. This point deserves a word of clarification.

Smith distinguished between two ways in which men employ their energies, two general categories of careers. Those which are devoted to the production of durable and saleable objects he termed productive, e.g., the manufacturing worker. Those which did not were termed unproductive. Among the latter he included such socially beneficial and even necessary careers as physicians, lawyers, the sovereign and military personnel (*WN*, pp. 314-15). His interest was clearly not to demean as had the physiocrats (*WN*, p. 628), but merely to repeat what in his day was a fact, viz., that men typically admired, emulated and deferred to others on the condition that they were possessed of material objects and the rarer the better. Rosenberg correctly observed that the very marked preference of the rich for durable goods as opposed to services was occasioned by the expansion of foreign trade in the Feudal era (1968, pp. 369-72; *WN*, 384-96). The point here, however, is that the preferences of the rich – whatever they happened to be – were decisive for men of all ranks because the rich were possessed of material objects with which they could command whatever labor or produce suited their fancy.

II

The wealth of any nation is the proportion between the exchange value of the commodities annually added to the stock which may be reserved for immediate consumption and the total population of the nation. In the intermediate term, i.e., anywhere from one year to one generation, this ratio is ordinarily governed by two circumstances.[2]

[2] By adopting this time-frame Smith allowed himself to treat other circumstances

But the proportion must in every nation be regulated by two different circumstances; first, by the skill, dexterity, and judgment with which its labour is generally applied; and, secondly, by the proportion between the number of those who are employed in useful labour, and that of those who are not so employed. (*WN*, p. lvii)

Accordingly, any change within a commercial society which either increases the productivity of its labor or decreases the proportion of the population which merely consumes physical output will increase national wealth. Smith held that the crucial phenomenon which simultaneously effects both of these changes is the augmentation of capital. In this he was merely applying the ancient proverb "money makes money" to commercial society as a whole (*WN*, p. 93).

Smith opened the *Wealth of Nations* with a discussion of how the skill, dexterity and judgment with which labor is applied to the production of commodities is ordinarily improved, viz., through a division of labor. As indicated in Chapter IV a division of labor occurs whenever a task which had previously been performed by each member of a group is divided into distinct operations to each of which only one or a few members are assigned. By using the illustration of a pin factory Smith indicated how the introduction of specialization into an already ordered productive operation multiplies the total output many times over. He attributed that increased output to three benefits of job specialization. It allows each man to develop the skill, dexterity and judgment which he brings to bear upon his part of the joint effort well beyond the degree possible where he is held responsible for a wider range of tasks. It minimizes time devoted to re-tooling and change-over. Finally, it encourages

---

relevant to long term growth as constant, e.g., soil, climate, extent of territory and population. He indicated that in the longer term changes in each of these are relevant to the prospects of economic growth. It is generally observed that he believed that in the long term population increases or decreases with the relative availability of the means of subsistence (*WN*, p. 146). This opinion is popularly believed to have been based upon an alleged "propensity to procreate" (Lowe 1954, p. 134). In fact it was based on Smith's observation of a higher mortality rate among the poorer classes (*WN*, p. 79). He also allowed that in the long term the extent to which natural resources are employed could be improved indirectly by relaxing governmental policies which favor manufacturing (*WN*, p. 784; Spengler 1959, p. 3). He acknowledged too, as Nicholson observed (1909), that even the extent of the territory and thereby all other constraints can be changed if the government undertakes to implement a policy of economic imperialism. This prospect has never been lost on mercantile interests but seems to have escaped the attention of recent students of Smith's theory of economic growth. It should also be noted that Smith did not believe that progress in opulence is either inevitable or interminable (Strong, 1932; Forbes 1954). Eventually every nation like China, achieves the "full complement of riches which is consistent with the nature of its laws and institutions" (*WN*, p. 95).

each worker to exercise his ingenuity in developing labor and time saving procedures and devices such as machines (*WN*, pp. 3-10).[3]

The extent to which productivity can be increased by a division of labor is limited on the one hand by the extent of capital and on the other by the extent of the market. A division of labor may be introduced or extended only if and to the extent that a stock of capital sufficient to finance the reorganization is available before revenue from the sale of the increased output is realized (*WN*, pp. 259-60). Furthermore, even if available that capital will be employed to extend the division of labor only if and to the extent that an effective demand for the increased output can be reasonably anticipated (*WN*, pp. 17-21). Smith believed that the extent of effective demand for all goods and services depended upon two factors, one of which is constant, viz., the desire to better our own condition by acquiring fortune. The other, the ability to pay the natural price, is, on a national scale, dependent upon the volume of commerce. Effective demand increases, Smith claimed, only as the volume of commerce increases because with that increase wages and rents increase and this allows more people to become effective demanders for a greater variety of goods and services. That increase in the volume of commerce, however, can result only from an increase in capitalization (*WN*, pp. 69,

---

[3] Smith insisted that this organizational innovation did not originally result from a decision taken for the purpose of increasing the productivity of labor. That this does result from such innovations was unintended and hence cannot have been the consideration which lead to its introduction (*WN*, p. 13). In this the division of labor is like most established practices in society, e.g., the arts (*MS*, pp. 257-8), the sciences and morality (*MS*, pp. 19-25; 269-72), commerce itself (*WN*, pp. 391-2, 422-3) and government (*MS*, pp. 124-30). In each of these cases the primary value of the practice is based on its accord with ancient custom and ritual dimly perceived by even the most reflective. That they are also useful was discovered long after they had become the established practices of the community. This usefulness thereafter served as an additional encouragement to continued support of established practices. Smith, however, was not interested in delving into the ancient origins of the division of labor. He named that origin the "propensity to truck, barter, and exchange one thing for another" and suggested that it probably developed from the "faculties of reason and speech" (*WN*, p. 13). That suggestion appears to have rested upon the parallel patterns of development in language, science and the practical arts ("Lang.," p. 246; see Chapter I). This appears to suggest that the ancient motivation to adopt organizational innovations of the general type illustrated in the pin factory example was the same as the modern motive to better one's own condition, viz., the desire for status and recognition (*MS*, p. 495). In any event the unintended consequences of established social practices, which held such fascination for Hayek (1952, pp. 65, 83) and recent sociologists (Merton 1968, pp. 114-36), were not in Smith's view the primary basis for evaluating the justification of those practices. A careful reading of the relevant texts shows that Smith justified a practice in much the same way as Rawls (1955) and Searle (1964) justify an act, viz., by showing that it satisfied the relevant rules which define social practices – which in Smith's case were the customs and rituals of the society under consideration.

247-8). Thus the augmentation of capital is, in the intermediate term and on a national scale, the sole and controlling factor in determining the extent to which the division of labor can and will be extended and so the extent to which productivity increases.

The accumulation of capital was also, in Smith's view, the controlling factor in determining the ratio between those usefully employed and those who are not. An increase in capitalization improves this ratio in two ways. First, it provides jobs for those who were previously unemployed in either productive or unproductive careers (*WN*, p. 68). Second, it increases the number of employed workers who pursue productive careers through wage competition. Capital is by definition employed to generate a revenue and therefore is used to produce whatever can be sold for a reasonable rate of return. In order to increase produce and as more productive workers are needed, wages for such jobs are bid up thus attracting more workers from non-productive employments (*WN*, pp. 68-9, 316-21).

Thus any increase in national wealth, whether occasioned by increased productivity or an increased proportion of those productively employed, results from an augmentation of capital. The question of what causes increases in national wealth in the intermediate term, therefore, reduces to an inquiry into the factors which occasion increases in a nation's capital. But since all the possessions of a nation fall into either its capital stock or that stock which may be reserved for immediate consumption (*WN*, pp. 261-69), it is clear that capital can be increased only by allocating to capital what could be consumed. "Capitals are increased by parsimony and decreased by prodigality and misconduct" (*WN*, p. 321).

The decisive factor determining the magnitude of a nation's capital and so its prospects for growth is the habitual disposition of the members of the nation. Should they be disposed to prefer present satisfaction above all else even to the extent of encroaching upon their capital, the industry of the people will dwindle as will the division of labor they can support, both of which combine to diminish national wealth. This same effect results from injudicious use of the nation's capital. If on the other hand, the people are disposed to be more prudent and frugal, they will augment the nation's capital and thereby its wealth (*WN*, pp. 322-4).

Smith was keenly aware that there was no lack of examples of prodigal conduct and injudicious use of the nation's capital. The rich, whose principal interest was to parade their equipage before the bedazzled eyes of the great mob of mankind and whose way of life was both "liberal" and "loose," were certainly prodigal (*WN*, pp. 324, 746). Such men, however, were in a distinct minority and that fact dampened the overall impact of their ostentation upon the capital of the nation. Their prodigality was compensated for by "the strict frugality and parsimonious attention" of the great majority of men whose way of life was more "strict or austere." It was the "frugality and good conduct" of "the common people" and not the flamboyant self-indulgence of "people of fashion" which, in most cases, assured augmentation of capital and thereby an increasing national wealth (*WN*, pp. 81, 324, 746).

The only circumstance for which that disposition cannot, or at least cannot always, compensate is the injudicious use of a nation's capital by the public extravagance of its government. Should a government require the nation to support "a numerous and splendid court, a great ecclesiastical establishment, great fleets and armies, who in time of peace produce nothing, and in time of war acquire nothing which can compensate the expense of maintaining them, even while the war lasts;" or should the government require the nation to support a great public debt or a great empire of colonies "which contribute neither revenue nor military force towards support of the empire," that government may well exceed even the compensating effects of the steady and constant parsimony of the common people (*WN*, pp. 325-9, 859-63, 899).

In any event the augmentation of capital, when and to the extent that it occurs, always results from the habitual frugality of the common people. They can be depended upon to increase the nation's capital as quickly as possible even in the face of the prodigality of the rich and the extravagance of governments because they are motivated by the desire to better their own condition by augmenting their fortunes and have the good sense to know that "the most likely way of augmenting their fortune, is to save and accumulate some part of what they acquire, either regularly and annually, or upon some extraordinary occasions" (*WN*, pp. 324-5; also see 81, 379).

The only way a nation's wealth can be increased in the intermediate term is by increasing its capital. Capital is ordinarily accumulated by diverting what may be consumed to investment.[4] This allocation of economic surplus to capital is assured only by the habitual disposition of the common people to attain status and recognition by saving part of what they could consume and employing it for the purpose of revenue. Clearly Smith was not thinking only of the peddler's "principle of turning a penny" when speaking of this disposition, although that principle

[4] The capital of a nation may, of course, be augmented by appropriation. This had occurred in two ways. Capital was first acquired when influential men appropriated to themselves the flocks and herds previously held in common (*LJ*, p. 14-15; *WN*, p. 48). Capital has also been acquired by military conquest (*WN*, pp. 361-4).

would be included under it (*WN*, p. 391). Neither did he intend moral approval of this habit of frugality nor disapproval of liberality (*WN*, p. 332). What he did intend was that the profound desire of ordinary men in many walks of life to achieve recognition by accumulating fortune is the most effective and certain basis of increasing national wealth in the intermediate term. His study of modern European economic history convinced him that it was the steady operation of this disposition and not the grandiose schemes of merchants and kings which had accounted for the increase of national wealth over the centuries since the decline of feudalism (*WN*, p. 238). It was because of the steadiness and persistence of this habit among the common people that national wealth had and continued to increase. This disposition acts in much the same way as Quesnay's *vis medicatrix naturae* stabilizing, restoring and improving the performance of commercial society often in spite of the misconduct and poor judgment of would-be healers and manipulators (*WN*, pp. 326, 638).

III

Smith believed that both his outlook on commerce and his analysis of the causes of increasing national wealth held lessons for those whose main if not sole interest was "to enrich the people and the sovereign," i.e., political economists and legislators (*WN*, p. 397). Certainly the most famous paragraph in the *Wealth of Nations* summarizes most of those lessons. In the first part of that paragraph he alluded to what he termed a "system of natural liberty."

All systems of either of preference or of restraint, therefore, being thus completely taken away, the obvious and simple system of natural liberty establishes itself of its own accord. Every man, as long as he does not violate the laws of justice, is left perfectly free to pursue his own interest his own way, and to bring both his industry and capital into competition with those of any other man, or order of men. (*WN*, p. 651)

In view of clarifications achieved in the course of this volume several features of these sentences take on fresh vitality. First, since Smith regarded ideologically based political discourse to be fanatical (*MS*, p. 343) it appears certain that he did *not* regard this "system of natural liberty" as an ideal to which social reality should be conformed. This expression was no doubt employed to make his arguments more appealing to "men of system" (*MS*, p. 267). The phrase refers rather to the ordered relations of men in actual societies. In such societies actions are typically governed by customary rules of practice which have become a part of the habit structure of mature and normal people and which they have no cause to resent or regard as coercive (see Chapter III). Such societies are systems of natural liberty.

Second, the "rules of justice" which limit the options of individual agents in such societies are shared attitudes relating to the modes of behavior which constitute the proper object of resentment or public outrage. These attitudes may and to some extent are embodied however imperfectly in civil and criminal laws (*MS*, p. 319, 501-2). Still, the individual's options are restricted in the situation of natural liberty not by these laws alone, but by those confirmed attitudes which the law only partially expresses, i.e., by the public morality (see Chapter IV).

Third, within those limits of long established practice, recognized by an exercise of moral sympathy, agents are at liberty to seek recognition and acclaim by seeking to acquire symbols of status. In "civilized" societies this pursuit is a competition because in these societies such symbols are designated by a special type of custom, viz., fashion. Their symbolic value is directly proportional with their rarity. It is only in a community in which it is the custom to accord public esteem according to the rules of fashion that the results of competition can be socially significant. So long as that is the custom, as it always is in plutocratically stratified communities, then every member should be allowed to strive, within the restraints of the public morality, to employ his talents, energies, and property to obtain such symbols of status. This prerogative is what Smith meant by "perfect liberty" (*WN*, pp. 56, 62, 99).

Smith had examined and evaluated the current commercial policies of the British government which, by restraining imports and encouraging exports, were designed to enrich the nation by fostering a favorable balance of trade. With the exception of drawbacks (*WN*, pp. 466-71), he found encouragement of exports objectionable. Except for the protection of industries vital to national security and infant industries, he found restraints on imports to be likewise objectionable (*WN*, pp. 429-37; 712). His fundamental objection was that these measures afforded effective control over the allocation of national wealth to that class whose interest was opposed to its augmentation (*WN*, pp. 249-50). This opposition of the interests of owners of capital to the augmentation of national wealth resulted from what Smith took to be a fact of commercial life, viz., that in any competitive market profit rates decline as capital investment increases (*WN*, p. 87). This is what interests those who live by profits in diminishing the constraints of competition by fostering larger productive and trade units and in seeking the protection of government against the restraints of the customary rules of justice which prevail within the very society they claim to serve – but on their own terms.

Smith was reasonably sure that these tendencies on the part of men who live by profits were, at least for the foreseeable future, intractable. Still, he saw no reason to believe that their a-moral projects could not at least be kept from destroying the integrity of the community. "But the mean rapacity, the monopolizing spirit of merchants and manufacturers, who neither are, nor ought to be, the rulers of mankind, though it cannot perhaps be corrected, may very easily be prevented from disturbing the tranquility of any body but themselves" (*WN*, p. 460).

Smith was intent upon proposing concrete steps which could be taken to assure that the allocation of national wealth be accomplished according to the shared preferences and aversions of the people. Only in this way would the exercise of the power to command labor be legitimate and commercial transactions retain the rudiments of social as opposed to animal relations (*MS*, pp. 124-5). His analysis of the monopoly spirit in particular and institutionalization generally led him to the conviction that no institutional structure, no matter how well contrived, could long maintain its legitimacy (see Chapter IV). Only the people acting from an intimate knowledge of one another's tolerances and responsive to social as well as legal sanctions could assure that commercial relations conform to the confirmed preferences and aversions of the people. But to render commercial affairs subject to that control several changes were necessary, the main one being that the government must begin to withdraw its support of merchants, manufacturers and traders without which they could not remain functionally autonomous (*WN*, pp. 690-712).

The sovereign is completely discharged from a duty, in the attempting to perform which he must always be exposed to innumerable delusions, and for the proper performance of which no human wisdom or knowledge could ever be sufficient; the duty of superintending the industry of private people, and of directing it towards the employments most suitable to the interest of the society. (*WN*, p. 651)

Smith here denied that any government can ever manage the commercial affairs of a nation properly because the knowledge requisite for that task is unattainable in principle.[5] This was the case in Smith's view not merely because sufficiently sophisticated techniques of market research, statistical analysis and forecasting models were not available, but because the only criterion of management available to governments and other

[5] Rosenberg (1960, p. 565) and Freeman (1969, pp. 173-4) noted Smith's observation that governmental policy decisions were frequently based upon poor information and distorted by the bias of interested counsel. They took this and not value displacement (see Chapter IV) to be the basis of his disdain for government and concluded that the *Wealth of Nations* was intended to improve the competence of legislators. This interpretation, especially clear in the case of Freeman, appears to directly contradict the passage cited above.

institutions – utility – of necessity abstracts from the appropriate criteria
of evaluating human relationships, viz., the shared preferences and
aversions of the community (see Chapter IV). By discharging the government from managing the nation's economy Smith was urging the government to rid itself of one of its grandest delusions. But this did not mean
that Smith urged the government to simply ignore commercial affairs.
Smith was not, as Viner established (1927), an advocate of laissez-faire
in that sense. The government still had other duties to perform and each
of these lent support to the method of allocating wealth which Smith believed indispensable.

According to the system of natural liberty, the sovereign has only three duties
to attend to; three duties of great importance, indeed, but plain and intelligible
to common understanding: first, the duty of protecting the society from the violence and invasion of other independent societies; secondly, the duty of protecting,
so far as possible, every member of the society from the injustice or oppression of
every other member of it, or the duty of establishing an exact administration of
justice; and, thirdly, the duty of erecting and maintaining certain public works
and certain public institutions, which it can never be for the interest of any individual, or small member of individuals, to erect and maintain; because the
profit could never repay the expense to any individual or small number of individuals, though it may frequently do much more than repay it to a great society.
(WN, p. 651)

This summary implies a much more active role of government in support of market-place commerce than is readily apparent.[6] The sovereign's
duties extend well beyond providing sentinels on the walls, constables
and magistrates in the towns and highways, parks and lighting for the
public streets. By discharging the government from the management of
the nation's commercial affairs Smith did not discharge it from the responsibility for what he called "police" (LJ, p. 154). In Smith's view
the government has the responsibility to see to it that the nation is well
provided with the "necessaries and conveniencies of life." The legislator
must still be concerned "to provide a plentiful revenue or subsistence
for the people" but is to exercise this responsibility indirectly by enabling
the people "to provide such a revenue or subsistence for themselves"
(WN, p. 397).

The great majority of policy recommendations Smith proposed for
the consideration of Parliament were directed to providing the conditions

[6] Petrella expressed the popular view. "Although Smith recognized a need for
government activity, it was a government with minimal functions, a government
seen as more virtuous and efficient when decentralized, a government which super-
intended and periodically patched minor defects in the institutional superstructure
of the system of natural liberty but which seldom needed to tamper with a sound
foundation." (1970, p. 157).

and support necessary for the effective allocation of goods and services according to the shared preferences of the people. His argument to these men of system was based upon the contention that such measures would assure maximum growth in national wealth by encouraging the common people to act upon their habitual disposition to pursue status and recognition by accumulating fortune. He chose not to emphasize the additional, and for him the decisive point, that they would also allay the injustices currently perpetrated by the system of commerce.

Quesnay erred, in Smith's judgment, when he proclaimed natural liberty to be the sole and sufficient condition for assuring growth in national wealth (*WN*, p. 638-9). Unless the common people, i.e., those of the middle and inferior ranks, can be tolerably sure that they will be able to reap the fruits of their labors they will devote none of their energies or property to the capital stock of the nation. When and where governments have extended that protection which was originally afforded only to the rich (*WN*, p. 674) to the lower ranks of men, e.g., the merchants and traders, those men began to act on the desire to better their condition by accumulating fortune. Thus security in the expectation that one will be able to actually reap the benefits of his labor is a prior condition necessary to interest a man in acting on that habitual disposition which best assures growth in national wealth. What Smith called for was an extension of this protection of the law beyond the rich and the merchants to "every member of society" (*WN*, p. 651).

Still men will not act on this habitual disposition merely because they can be sure that they will be able to reap some benefits. They will do so of their own accord only if they can be tolerably satisfied that the value received is roughly equal to the labor or property exchanged or at the very least that the value received is not flagrantly incommensurate with the prevailing sentiments of justice. This assurance can be attained by the "higgling and bargaining of the market" (*WN*, p. 31) provided the market is sufficiently small to allow a free flow of information and provided that the people who come to it are sufficiently well acquainted to be able to recognize, by an act of sympathy, one another's tolerances and preferences and finally provided that mercantile enterprizes are sufficiently small to be responsive to the discipline of their customers. The duty of government to establish an "exact administration of justice" requires that it insure that commercial transactions remain subject to the effective control of established customs in the factor markets and the established preferences and aversions of customers in commodity markets. This is "the duty of protecting, as far as possible, every member of the society from the injustice or oppression of every other member of it . . ." (*WN*, p. 651)

Smith recommended two general policies to meet this duty as it relates to commercial affairs. First, the government should actively discourage all efforts, whether by merchants or laborers, to further combine themselves into corporate or institutional units of commercial power (*WN*, pp. 60-1; 118-43). Wherever possible support for existing corporate or institutionalized commercial units should be withdrawn (*WN*, pp. 692-712). Smith was confident that without that support such oppressive institutions would founder.[7] These policies would effectively restrict the magnitude and types of projects which could be profitably undertaken by private capital. But, there are projects necessary for the public welfare which require a greater investment than "any individual or small number of individuals" can possibly undertake. It was for this reason that Smith declared that the government has yet another duty, viz., the duty of undertaking these very projects which private capital cannot because they should not be allowed to combine beyond a "small number." (*WN*, p. 651).

The second general policy which Smith proposed to meet the duty of erecting an exact administration of justice as this duty relates to commercial affairs was to prevent merchants, manufacturers and traders from deceiving their customers and from insulating themselves from the effects of the ordinary sanctions which their customers could bring to bear upon them. Clearly Smith realized that these men were scoundrels and that effective policing of their conduct was an immense task. The burden of forcing them to observe the ordinary canons of ethical practice, however, could be quite efficiently accomplished in the small and relatively intimate market places the first policy was designed to preserve.

A dealer is afraid of losing his character and is scrupulous in observing every engagement. When a person makes perhaps twenty contracts a day, he cannot gain so much by endeavoring to impose on his neighbours, as the very appearance of a cheat would make him lose. When people seldom deal with one another, we find that they are somewhat disposed to cheat, because they can gain more by a smart trick than they can lose by the injury which it does their character. (*LJ*, pp. 253-4)

Even so the government should assist consumers wherever conniving merchants engage in practices which surpass the attentive scrutiny or the effective sanctions of the local citizenry. It was for this reason that Smith insisted that governments mint coin and regulate paper currency

[7] Only those types of joint stock companies whose operations were not subject to ruthless manipulation could survive, in Smith's estimate, without the protective policies of government, viz., banks, insurance companies, shipping canal management and water works (*WN*, pp. 713-16).

in order to assure that the value of money is what it is represented as
being (*WN*, pp. 24-7; 40-6; 312-13; 516-22). In an effort to establish an
upper limit on the profits merchants could exact from the sale of commodities in which they have a property interest, Smith supported the
practice of setting an upper limit on the interest rate which could be
charged for loans, i.e., usury laws (*WN*, pp. 88-90; 860). These were an
indirect restraint upon profits because a reasonable rate of profit was
allowed to be a multiple of the current rate of interest. In Smith's day
double interest was regarded as a reasonable profit rate (*WN*, p. 97).

The combined effect of implementing these policies, of exercizing the
three duties which Smith assigned to government in the way he intended
them to be exercised, would be government enforced decentralization of
the power to control the allocation of wealth. This has generally been
acknowledged by even Smith's casual readers. Two features of such an
eventuality are worthy of note. First, Smith advocated a commercial
policy of total decentralization and not merely a shift in the power of
decision from a higher to a lower level of management or from governments to less centralized institutions.[8] He argued for placing the power
to effectively control the allocation of wealth directly and immediately
in the hands of individual people in the market places of the nation.
Indeed, the burden of his critique of all institutions, be they governmental, military, commercial, educational or religious, was that institutions as such cannot long be trusted to administer social affairs
properly. (*WN*, pp. 266, 667-8, 691-2, 718, 744-5).

Second, Smith conceived of wealth as at root the power to command
the labor of others (*WN*, p. 31). In his estimate this had been the decisive
power in western societies since the rise of the ancient Tartar, Arab and
Hebrew tribes. By calling for a total decentralization of control over the
allocation of wealth Smith had called upon Parliament to place the
decisive power of society directly and immediately under the control of
market agents and once more to see to it that they retained that control.
Bonar (1893, p. 161) and Cropsey (1957, p. 64) felt this betrayed a
democratic and equalitarian intent on Smith's part. That surmise is
quite incorrect. Even where the allocation of wealth is effectively con-
trolled by individual market agents in small and responsive market
places the power to exercise that control extends only to those who are
possessed of a surplus of those material objects which are currently

---

[8] Samuels' market-plus framework, although clearly a marked improvement
over earlier readings, does not capture the full thrust of Smith's emphasis on small
markets in which prices are established by a proces of higgling and bargaining
(1966).

admired and sought after. The rich retain decisive control even in the decentralized market both because they possess more of such objects and because of their hold over the imaginations of others. They hold that power, however, because men habitually accord decisive power on precisely that basis. Decentralization would not disturb the plutocratic deference structure of "civilized" society, but only assure that commercial affairs are carried on in conformity with that prevailing custom and thereby be legitimate in the estimate of those who support that custom. Smith's object was legitimacy, not democracy.

Smith's recommendations on commercial policy, however, were not limited to merely advocating total decentralization of the power to allocate wealth through small and responsive markets. He also advocated policies designed to maximize the proportion of national wealth which is allocated through such markets, i.e., in the private sector as it is now called. He did so by calling for policies which would minimize the proportion of a nation's wealth which is allocated by government. It will be recalled that the "public extravagance" of governments is the only circumstance which can, even where economic power is effectively decentralized, thwart the growth effected by the frugal habits of the common people (WN, pp. 325-9). Smith spelled out three ways in which the proportion of national wealth allocated by governments could and should be reduced. First, the extravagance of government should be dramatically reduced. In particular military expense should be kept under stricter control by avoiding, wherever possible, the financing of wars by the acquisition of public debt (WN, pp. 859-82). Furthermore, the ownership of land and capital by the sovereign should be abolished (WN, pp. 769-77). Finally, imperialistic ventures which do not begin to be self-supporting should be abandoned (WN, pp. 898-900).

Second, the functions of government should be decentralized and locally financed wherever possible. Public works such as utilities and transportation if operated in this way would result in both a wiser allocation of capital but also better management and a saving to the public in the cost of their maintenance and operation (WN, pp. 682-9). Third, an enlightened and equitable tax policy should be implemented. Taxes should, wherever possible, be levied on the basis of the value of services received (WN, pp. 767-8). Such a policy would minimize the volume of services required and hence the expense of providing them. This point is especially clear in the case of litigation (WN, p. 680), although it applies equally well to the maintenance of public transportation, and of educational and religious institutions (WN, pp. 682-9, 716-40, 740-66). In these cases where a specific benefit accrues to a few identifiable individuals, they are to bear the burden of the cost. In the case of other governmental functions which do not fall into this category, e.g., national defense, taxes should be levied in proportion to revenue (*WN*, pp. 777-8).

Finally, Smith indicated a strong preference for a fundamental shift in the established pattern of capitalization, in the way the nation's capital or economic surplus was employed. Ever since the Feudal era when towns were granted security and the prerogative of limited self-government which were not afforded the countryside and in particular since the reign of Queen Elizabeth I, the favored employment of capital had been manufacturing and trade (*WN*, pp. 379-80, 393). The expansion of these occasioned a residual expansion of native agriculture and eventually the extension of security and independence to the countryside (*WN*, pp. 384-5). In this way agriculture was extended to meet the expanding requirements of urban commerce. Further expansion of investment in agriculture was frustrated by ancient laws and customs, in particular the law of primogeniture and entails which effectively priced land out of the reach of small investors (*WN*, pp. 360-4, 392-3).

Notwithstanding the fact that this mode of allocating the nation's capital had resulted in economic growth Smith preferred an agriculturally based economy to one founded mainly upon manufacturing and trade. "This order, however, being contrary to the natural course of things, is necessarily both slow and uncertain" (*WN*, p. 392). It is uncertain because capital invested in manufacturing and trade can easily be transferred to a different nation should foreign opportunities appear either more secure or more advantageous. "A merchant, it has been said very properly, is not necessarily the citizen of any particular country. It is in a great measure indifferent to him from what place he carries on his trade; and a very trifling disgust will make him remove his capital, and together with it all the industry which it supports, from one country to another" (*WN*, p. 395). Investment in the cultivation of a nation's natural resources is not subject to such removal. It is slow for two reasons, the one more important than the other. First, all things being equal, men in Smith's day preferred the pastoral and calm life of farming to the turmoil and confusion of the towns. The country life suited their tastes and so would engage their industry more thoroughly than would any pursuit in towns (*WN*, p. 357-8).

The second, and most important consideration which lay behind Smith's conviction that the growth rate of an industrially based commercial society is slower than is that of one which is agriculturally based is that it is, in his terms, "unnatural." This is not simply a reiteration of the pastoral preference mentioned above.

As subsistence is, in the nature of things, prior to conveniency and luxury, so the industry which procures the former, must necessarily be prior to that which ministers to the latter. The cultivation and improvement of the country, therefore, which affords subsistence, must, therefore, necessarily, be prior to the increase of the town, which furnishes only the means of conveniency and luxury (*WN*, p. 357).

Smith here assigned both a temporal and a moral priority to the expansion of agriculture over that of manufacturing and trade. As Rosenberg observed, Smith believed that capital accumulation was historically late in coming because subsistence was the first consideration of early nations (1968, pp. 362-4). Smith approved of this as natural because it was in keeping with the canons of ordinary prudence (*MS*, pp. 310-11). It was only after the rise of the towns and eventually of commercial nations that the capital of nations came to be predominantly allocated to the support of enterprises which supplied the desire of the rich for luxuries. This allowed agriculture, which supplies the necessities of life, to expand only to the extent that it was necessary and convenient for the support of those enterprises. This shift in the pattern of capital allocation was clearly imprudent on two grounds. First, it is unconscionable for a nation to devote any substantial proportion of its capital to satisfying the whims of some until the subsistence of all is assured. Second, more people will be able to devote some of their revenue to capital purposes and so contribute to the increase of a nation's wealth if all are supplied with the necessities of life.

Smith did not feel that the capital of the British nation was being flagrantly misappropriated (*WN*, pp. 393-95). But he did think it proper to realign the priorities for investing her economic surplus. In particular he believed that small, owner-operated farms would be much more efficient than the present system of great landed estates (*WN*, p. 392). Still, he recognized that the latter had become a customary mark of rank and reputation (*WN*, p. 362) and so concluded that significant land reforms were, at least for the time being, out of the question. Thus, he avoided advocating any sweeping policy recommendations which would call for altering the laws of primogeniture and entails and settled for recommending in addition to the several of other policies, tax relief for owner-operated land in the hope that that would be at least a first step in the direction of reversing the priorities which were currently reflected in the distribution of the nation's capital (*WN*, p. 784).

IV

In this and the previous chapter I have tried to present a fair, cogent and accurate statement of Smith's central argument in his *Wealth of Nations*. In addition I have tried to be as brief as possible. The resulting analysis differs sharply from the popular image of the *Wealth of Nations* in many significant respects although it is consistent with the views of informed scholarship more often than may at first be apparent. The most significant difference between it and others which have gone before is not in varying interpretations of particular doctrines but in its entire approach to the *Wealth of Nations*. It has been guided not by the contemporary or even the traditional categories of economic analysis but by what I understand to have been the perspective, interests and strategy of its author. I have tried to interpret this book as a human document rather than as an episode in the development of a set of scientific theorems.

Smith's perspective on the commercial affairs of men in society was much the same as that of Aristotle on the one hand and recent anthropologists on the other. With Aristotle (*Politics* I, 3-13) Smith approached his study of commerce as an aspect of his more general concern with the relation of law to justice, i.e., as a division of what Smith called "jurisprudence." With Polanyi (1957, p. 46) and Nash (1967, p. 9) Smith understood that the commercial affairs of a community are a function of the customs of that community. It was Smith's conviction that the legitimacy of any practice within a community, including commercial practices, is rooted in its conformity with those preferences and aversions which the members of that community regard as sacred (see Chapter IV). One of Smith's signal achievements was to show how that legitimacy could be maintained even in a society in which it was the custom to assign recognition and social standing on the basis of taste and fashion rather than upon more substantial grounds.

This observation occasions two rather troublesome questions. Smith regarded the pursuit of wealth as unfortunate even as one of the principal sources of moral corruption (*MS*, pp. 84-5). He also believed that one of the principal objects of education was the direction of vanity to proper objects (*MS*, p. 380). "Why he should have favored an economic system that fostered money making is one of the questions which every reader of Smith must ask" (Grampp 1965, vol., II, p. 7). Grampp's answer was that Smith favored such a system because he felt that on balance it promoted the good life. There is surely a great deal to be said in favor of this interpretation. Smith did anticipate that the operation of the commercial system as he described it would result in several wholesome consequences. In the course of their pursuit of wealth men of the middle and lower ranks of society develop the habits of inferior prudence, lawfulness, temperance, and fortitude (*MS*, p. 86; Morrow 1923a; Campbell 1967; also see Chap. III). As a result of economic growth it would become possible for those who bore the burdens of society to be better fed, clothed, and housed (*WN*, pp. 78-81; Hollander 1971, pp. 269-82). These are not trivial considerations for a man of "public spirit" (*MS*, p. 342). Still, not all of the consequences of commerce contribute to the good life. The pursuit of fortune promoted anything but the good life among the rich (*MS*, pp. 85-6), the very poor (*MS*, pp. 381-2), and those whose ambition drove them to seek to change their rank or station in life – what is called upward mobility today (*MS*, pp. 259-63).

If the economic system of which Smith spoke is judged in terms of its anticipated consequences, Grampp's answer – that on balance it promoted the good life – appears quite plausible. The difficulty with that answer is that it assumes that Smith subscribed to the utilitarian view that anticipated consequences are the appropriate basis for deciding the justification of an economic system. This assumption, as had been repeatedly shown in the course of this study, is not well taken. The criterion in terms of which Smith measured the justification of commercial institutions was that set of preferences and aversions shared by and viewed as inviolable by the relevant population (see Chap. IV). In view of this conviction on Smith's part it seems appropriate to answer the question posed by Grampp somewhat differently. Smith did not favor a system of commerce which fostered money making, but merely tolerated it and then only on the condition that merchants and traders are placed in a position in which the only way they can pursue the object of their "rapacious greed" is by competing with one another in the observance of the moral sentiments of the larger society – which condition is fulfilled by a completely decentralized pricing procedure. What Smith did favor was a commercial policy on the part of governments which would establish and maintain such a procedure. Under a government which implemented such policies morally sensitive men could rest safe in the knowledge that all men received their money's worth in market places and that unprincipled entrepreneurs could disturb only their own tranquility in their anxious pursuit of personal gain.

When the enterprise of the *Wealth of Nations* is understood in this way it becomes possible to suggest the conditions under which Smith would have again launched a violent attack upon a commercial system. He would surely be sorely critical if economic growth were not to result in a better life for the working poor. He would certainly be outraged if increased economic efficiency were achieved at the expense of the moral character of even the middle ranks of men. But, should commercial institutions become so insulated from and indifferent to the moral sentiments of the larger community as once again to become functionally autonomous of that community, he would most assuredly mount a very violent attack upon the system of commerce.

A second troublesome question is often raised in the form of a set of criticisms leveled against the entire social philosophy upon which the *Wealth of Nations* was, or at least appears to have been based. John Laird condemned that social philosophy because it neglected two considerations of justice, viz., "inequality in the distribution of the means for satisfying human needs and desires" and "that the toilers, so far as it is possible, are able to find dignity and self respect in their labour . . ." (1927, pp. 39-40). While it is clear that Smith was deeply troubled by both the established pattern of distribution and by the debilitating effects of the division of labor upon the specialized worker (see, for example, *LJ*, pp. 162-3; *WN*, pp. 79, 734-5), Laird's complaints have merit.

Smith believed that an expanding market economy would benefit those who bore the burden of society. But he did not foresee nor did he support a distribution of that increased output along egalitarian lines. Smith was convinced that most of the members of his society supported at least passively the plutocratic deference structure (*WN*, pp. 670-74). So long as he believed that to be the case he could not in good conscience support a pattern of distribution which would violate the established constitution of society. Smith was by no means pleased with this state of affairs (*MS*, pp. 84-5), but was too sensible to confuse public spirit with fanaticism (*MS*, pp. 340-43).

In view of all that has been shown in the last two chapters it may appear that Laird's second charge is altogether without merit. That is not the case. Smith was indeed outraged by the oppression of the working poor (*LJ*, pp. 162-3; "Draft of the Wealth of Nations," Scott 1937, pp. 327-8; *WN*, pp. 49, 79), he was also well aware of their vulnerability in contracting for wages (*WN*, p. 66) and few have understood the dehumanizing effects of the division of labor as well as he did (*WN*, pp. 734-5). It is also true that he believed that the real income of the working poor would rise in an expanding economy (*WN*, p. 81) and that he proposed measures which would offset the harmful effects of job specialization, e.g., government support of elementary education (*WN*, pp.

734-40; Hollander 1971, pp. 286-90). Notwithstanding all this there is merit to Laird's second charge. Smith did not address himself squarely and directly to the question of how laborers could find dignity and self-respect in performing the increasingly specialized tasks assigned them in an expanding commercial society, even one in which the size of firms is severely restricted.

In this Laird was correct, but his point is, nonetheless, not well taken. Laird assumed as have others that Smith had set out to lay the foundations of an ideal society, one in which every major social wrong would be remedied. That was not Smith's objective. Indeed, anyone who would propose to "establish the right" by putting forward such utopian schemes must "exact his own judgment into the supreme standard of right and wrong." Smith found the arrogance of such fanatical projects not only foolish but profoundly offensive (*MS*, pp. 342-44).

In his *Wealth of Nations* Smith's objective was not to establish the right but to ameliorate the wrong. He set out only to persuade Parliament to take at least a few steps toward preventing the entire collapse of anything remotely resembling a community among men, even so meager a community as that which was "still upheld by a mercenary exchange of good offices according to an agreed valuation (*MS*, p. 124). Were the *Wealth of Nations* read in this spirit its incompleteness might well be counted among its foremost virtues. This spirit and its justification is perhaps best captured in Smith's own evaluation of the revisions which King George III had recently made in the Corn Laws.

With all its imperfections, however, we may perhaps say of it what was said of the laws of Solon, that, though not the best in itself, it is the best which the interests, prejudices, and temper of the times would admit of. It may perhaps in due time prepare the way for a better (*WN*, p. 510; also see *MS*, p. 342).

CHAPTER VII

RELIGION

Adam Smith was deliberately ambiguous about his religious convictions. This stratagem occasioned two types of debate. On the one hand there is the continuing round of petty gossip relating to the orthodoxy of his religious habits (Rae 1895, pp. 59-60, 295-314, 428-30; Raphael 1969). On the other there is the more serious debate relating to the significance of Smith's religious views for his ethical and economic teachings. Bittermann indicated the basis of this interest in the following way. "Since Adam Smith's theory of morals and his doctrine of natural liberty have often been regarded as corollaries of his natural theology, it is pertinent to inquire what the relation between his theological and his metaphysical views was" (1940, p. 708).

In order to determine the nature and extent of the dependence of Smith's social views upon his religious convictions it is necessary to first formulate a fairly reliable estimate of the character of those convictions. The popular contention today is that while he may have accepted no orthodox creed, he did subscribe to that stoical optimistic deism,[1] or natural religion which was popular among the intellectuals of his age (Rae 1895, pp. 60, 430; Bonar 1926, p. 353; Gray 1961, p. 125; Grampp 1948, pp. 317-21; Taylor 1960, pp. 53-4, 112; Macfie 1967, pp. 102-107; 109-13, 116; Campbell 1971, pp. 60-2, 221-33). This interpretation, first formulated as nearly as I can tell by Hasbach (1891, pp. 129-47) and Leslie (1888, pp. 21-40), was stated most succinctly by Viner: "[T]he essence of Smith's doctrine is that Providence has so fashioned the constitution of external nature as to make its processes favorable to man, and has implanted *ab initio* in human nature such sentiments as would bring about, through their ordinary working, the happiness and welfare of mankind" (1927, p. 202).

Although accompanied by a number of citations allegedly confirming

---

[1] Although most commentators, following Smith, use the word "theism" in this context, I prefer, as did Morrow (1923a, p. 42) and Taylor (1960, p. 54), the term "deism" because it conforms more closely to 18th Century British usage (Mossner 1967).

the validity of the Stoic optimistic deism thesis, these accounts remain unconvincing. The root difficulty with them is that they flatly contradict other features of Smith's position for which independent confirmation is readily available. It is not the case that Smith was particularly optimistic. Of the two evils which most concerned him – the a-moral exercise of institutional power (see Chapter IV) and the unjust distribution of wealth (see Chapter V) – he was, as Bittermann noted (1940, p. 734), largely pessimistic.

The violence and injustice of the rulers of mankind is an ancient evil, for which, I am afraid, the nature of human affairs can scarce admit of a remedy (*WN*, p. 460).

To expect, indeed, that the freedom of trade should ever be entirely restored in Great Britain, is as absurd as to expect that an Oceana or Utopia should ever be established in it (*WN*, p. 437; also see pp. 581-2, 745).

Smith rejected the Stoic religious outlook for two reasons as will be shown below. He objected on the one hand that the argument from design is epistemologically indefensible and on the other that accommodation to evil is unconscionable. Of these objections, the latter was for Smith the more telling. Finally, Smith was equally unsympathetic with the religious outlook of his deistic contemporaries. Quoting the Bishop of Clermont, identified by Eckstein as the renowned French preacher Jean Bapiste Massillon (1926, pp. 300, 305) – whose point he accepted, but whose passionate rhetoric he found somewhat excessive – Smith proclaimed that reverence for the Deity does not warrant accommodation to evil as somehow justified by His inscrutable wisdom. Like the Bishop, Smith had no patience with the God of Job.

Because he is great, should he be weak, or unjust, or barbarous? Because men are little, ought they to be allowed either to be dissolute without punishment, or virtuous without reward? O God! if this is the character of your supreme being; if it is you whom we adore under such dreadful ideas; I can no longer acknowledge you for my father, for my protector, for the comforter of my sorrow, the support of my weakness, the rewarder of my fidelity. You would then be no more than an indolent and fantastical tyrant, who sacrifices mankind to his insolent vanity, and who has brought them out of nothing, only to make them serve for the sport of his leisure and of his caprice. (*MS*, pp. 240-1)

The inaccuracy of the received interpretation of Smith's religious beliefs is no doubt attributable to the scarcity of reliable textual sources. This scarcity of necessity renders every account of these beliefs – including this one – at best probable. Still, relevant texts are not nearly as sparse as is ordinarily supposed. Beside those in the *Moral Sentiments* there are others in the *Wealth of Nations* relating to modern Christian sects and still others in his early essays relating to ancient religions. The purpose of this chapter is to develop a more reliable statement of the nature, content and implications of Smith's religious convictions than is presently available. Drawing upon all relevant texts, Smith's views on the justification of religious convictions will be explored, the nature of his own religious beliefs will be interpreted in the light of those views and the influence of his religious convictions upon other aspects of his social philosophy will be indicated.

I

According to Millar's account, Smith addressed two major concerns in his lectures of Natural Theology, viz., "the proofs of the being and attributes of God and those principles of the human mind upon which religion is founded" (Stewart 1858, p. 12). Analysis of his views on ancient religions and modern Christian sects throws considerable light on the latter of these concerns. In particular it reveals that in Smith's estimate religion is founded upon a particular type of moral rather than cognitive experience. After examining Smith's description of the religious experiences upon which ancient polytheistic and monotheistic religions were based, his criticisms of each will be examined. These in turn will be shown to suggest that Smith looked to neither of these experiences, but to yet another as the authentic foundation of religion generally and Christianity in particular.

The most primitive form of religion mentioned by Smith was that polytheism articulated by the Greek poets and seers before the 5th century B.C., e.g., Hesiod and Pythagoras ("Physics," p. 117). This form of religion "ascribes all the irregular events of nature to the favour or displeasure of intelligent, though invisible beings, to gods, demons, witches, genii, fairies" ("Astron.," p. 49). Smith speculated that men, in the ages before governments had secured peace and order and before philosophers had begun to comprehend the events of nature in ordered systems, were keenly aware of their impotence in the face of a hostile environment. Their inability to forecast the course of nature exacerbated that sense of impotence.

When such men witnessed major natural irregularities they must have found the experience deeply moving. Comets, eclipses and rainbows provoked a profound sense of awe and astonishment. They typically described this experience as a kind of seeing. They apprehended, the poets declared, uncommon power and inscrutable intelligence in the awesome and uncanny spectacle of major natural irregularities. In the presence

of such objects primitive men felt profound fear, as in the case of an
eclipse, or profound gratitude, as in the case of a rainbow. Since these
feelings were excited by those objects they were spontaneously regarded
as their consequence. Furthermore, as these feelings – fear and gratitude
– are of the sort provoked only by moral agents, they were spontaneously regarded as effects intended by that superior power and intelligence.
It was from this kind of experience comprehended in this way that men
came to speak of moral beings making their presence known to them
through special signs and marvels ("Astron.," pp. 47-8).[2]

In the presence of such beings men sought spontaneously to act consistently with their newly formed outlook on the world. The apparent
superiority and majesty of those mysterious beings warranted their
humble subservience, deference, obedience, worship and adoration. This
deference, which ordinarily took the form of ritual sacrifice, was thought
to be the proper posture of so inferior a being as man. Its significance,
however, went beyond that. Deference to the gods was not only the
proper response to the recognized presence of superior beings, but was
also a plea to them for the rectification of nature according to moral
convictions of these men.

These natural hopes and fears and suspicions were propagated by sympathy, and
confirmed by education; and the gods were universally represented and believed
to be the rewarders of humanity and mercy, and the avengers of perfidy and injustice. And thus religion, even in its rudest form, gave a sanction to the rules
of morality long before the age of artificial reasoning and philosophy (MS, p. 233)

The outlook of these early polytheists was profoundly affected, as Ru-
dolph Otto said that of religious men always is (1958, pp. 8-61) by the
apprehension of "the mysterium tremendum." Imbued with a vivid
"creature-consciousness" they tended spontaneously to look to the gods
for vindication of their moral convictions. In particular they drew
strength and inspiration from their religion in advancing the condition
of mankind. They "saw" that the gods intervened in the course of nature
to work their will, and interpreted that as a sign that men may and
perhaps should do the same. In this way they may have regarded themselves as the agents of the divine mission of rectifying nature according
to the demands of morality, as the "vicegerents" of the gods ("Astron.,"
p. 49; MS, p. 234).

Early monotheistic religions first began to take shape, according to
Smith, only after governments had secured peace and order through
law and increased prosperity provided some men with sufficient leisure

---

[2] It seems reasonable to speculate that Smith would place miracles in the same
class with these major natural irregularities.

to ponder the spectacle of nature more deliberately. Plato and Aristotle were among the earliest founders of monotheism mentioned by Smith.[3] Monotheism achieved full stature, however, only later in the work of the Stoics – "the most religious of all the ancient sects of philosophers . . ." ("Physics," p. 120; "Astron.," pp. 49-50). Adherents to this form of religion subscribed to the idea "of an universal mind of a God of all, who originally formed the whole, and who governs the whole by general laws, directed to the conservation and prosperity of the whole, without regard to that of any private individual . . ." ("Physics," p. 117). In a less precarious era men were less inclined to accept the incomplete, strange and often incoherent outlook sponsored by their forebears. Instead they set out to develop a scheme of nature which would render "the universe consistent and of a piece" ("Astron.," p. 50).

Over the centuries the philosophers developed this alternative cosmology until it was so thoroughly consistent, coherent, familiar, and so sublimely beautiful that they became convinced that they had discovered the fundamental dynamic of the universe. All the major and most of the more trifling irregularities were comprehended within a coherent system in which objects and events were ordered according to general laws as means to ends. The magnificent functional efficiency of this spectacle of nature as a whole, and in every detail as well, provoked their profound admiration. They found the spectacle so impressive that they could not but eschew its having resulted from chance and instead perceived it as witness of a supreme intelligence which forms and governs it according to his design. It was in this way that "science gave birth to the first theism . . ." ("Physics," p. 118).[4]

Just as had their predecessors, so the ancient monotheists also believed that their religious experience provided sanction for rules of morality, but in a sharply different way. Earlier polytheists held that their gods were subject to the dynamic of nature and acted only to interdict the ordinary course of events according to standards of moral conviction. The god of monotheism, on the other hand, was regarded as the governor of nature itself, its dynamic proceeds according to his fiat. Furthermore, his governance was held to be determined not by the puny morality of

---

[3] Smith's failure to mention any of the prophets of the Judaic Tradition is understandable in view of the objective of these early essays, viz., to treat "The Principles which Lead and Direct Philosophical Enquiries."

[4] Smith's reference to "the watch-maker" in a parallel context suggests that he viewed the outlook of modern deists to be substantially the same as that of the ancient Stoics (MS, p. 126). He listed the views of Clark. Wollaston and Shaftesbury as modern expositors of basically the same perspective on morality (MS, pp. 428-9).

man – a mere part of the whole system of the universe – but by the inner necessity of his own nature. Worlds are born, develop, are destroyed and reborn again and again according to the pulse of aetherial fire which is Jupiter's essence ("Physics," pp. 120-22).

In the light of this outlook monotheists could not sanction actions intended to interdict the ordinary course of nature. That would be the most presumptuous arrogance imaginable. Conscious of his humble station, a mere part of the great system of nature, a man cannot ought but tremble lest he should even inadvertently disturb the magnificent and delicate organism governed by such transcendent wisdom ("Physics," p. 120). Instead of whining that one's heart's desire is often gravely disappointed, these ancient monotheists – and the Stoics were the prime example – taught that man's proper course lies in accommodation to nature.

A wise man never complains of the destiny of Providence, nor thinks the universe in confusion when he is out of order. He does not look upon himself as a whole, separated and detached from every other part of nature, to be taken care of by itself and for itself; he regards himself in the light in which he imagines the great genius of human nature and of the world regards him: he enters, if I may say so, into the sentiments of that divine Being, and considers himself as an atom, a particle of an immense and infinite system, which must and ought to be disposed of according to the convenience of the whole. Assured of the wisdom which directs all the events of human life, whatever lot befalls him he accepts it with joy, satisfied that, if he had known all the connections and dependencies of the different parts of the universe, it is the very lot which he would have wished for. (*MS*, pp. 405-6).

Stocial monotheism enjoined men to regard what ignorant men call evil as somehow or other a good, a good which they do not comprehend because their understanding is so incomplete and their values so biased. Man's happiness consists "first, in the contemplation of the happiness and perfection of the great system of the universe, of the good government of the great republic of gods and men, of all rational and sensible beings; and, secondly, in discharging his duty, in acting properly in the affairs of this great republic whatever little part that wisdom had assigned him" (*MS*, p. 407). In performing his duty, furthermore, man should select from among the available options according to the value each has "in this natural scale of things" (*MS*, p. 403). Should even his own life appear to be a proper object of rejection, then suicide would be the proper course (*MS*, pp. 410-420). The morality enjoined by this outlook envisions life as a game the rules of which are to be conscientiously observed. "Our only anxious concern ought to be, not about the stake, but about the proper method of playing" (*MS*, p. 410). Virtue consists in superior proficiency in the discharge of one's function in strict accordance with the requirements of one's station (*MS*, p. 426).

The outlook of these ancient monotheists was enlivened by what Einstein called "The cosmic religious experience." Imbued with a pervasive "sense of causal law in all that happens" they spontaneously tended to disdain "the vanity of human desires and aims," praising instead "the nobility and marvelous order which are revealed in nature and in the world of thought." They regarded, as did Einstein, "individual destiny as an imprisonment" and sought instead "to experience the totality of existence as a unity full of significance" (1930, p. 1).

Smith was critical of both the religion of the polytheists and that of the early monotheists, more so of the latter than the former. He brought two main criticisms to bear upon ancient religions – the one epistemological, the other moral. Polytheism was found wanting only on epistemological grounds. Ancient theism was found wanting on that and moral grounds as well, the latter being the most serious defect.

Polytheists proposed that their attitude of deference to invisible but moral beings was proper in view of their feeling of inferiority in the apprehended presence of awesome power and inscrutable intelligence, which presence provoked in them certain moral sentiments. The only objection Smith ever raised to this persuasion was that it was rooted in "the lowest and most pusillanimous superstition . . ." ("Astron.," p. 49). This did not amount to a blanket condemnation for much of this view was later confirmed by reflective analysis (*MS*, p. 233).

Smith was persuaded only that the experience which polytheists described as an apprehension of a singular external object was not in fact what they took it to be. External objects can be apprehended only through the senses, and that of touch is the only one of these which independently and veridically attests the presence of an external object ("Ext. Senses," pp. 185-223). But since polytheists admitted that they did not touch or even see in the physical sense these singular external objects, it must be that they "imagine but do not see" them. Those objects were products of their imaginations (*MS*, p. 232).

This realization neither rendered their behavior silly, nor terminated Smith's analysis of it. If their feeling of inferiority together with the sentiments of fear and gratitude was not excited by the object to which they alluded, then what did occasion them? The key to this problem lies in their antecedent condition of weakness and ignorance ("Astron.," pp. 47-8). Men who are or at least regard themselves as incapable of securing themselves against the natural and moral evils to which they are constantly subject are especially prone to being thunder-struck and astonish-

ed by the major surprises and wonders which confront them. It is because of a man's profound feeling of inadequacy that like a child he
"caresses the fruit that is agreeable to it [and] beats the stone that hurts
it" ("Astron.," p. 48).[5] The tendency of our passion "to suggest to us
opinions which justify them" is surely nothing extraordinary ("Astron.,"
p. 47). Nevertheless, although this tendency to wait "no other proof that
a thing is the proper object of a sentiment, than that it excites it" is
thoroughly understandable, it nevertheless begs the question. In particular it begs the moral question, viz., what is the proper response to a
world which portends evil?

Anyone who has ever pondered that question at first hand can appreciate how tempting it is to "see" helping arms appearing in the
strangest ways. Still, to leap into those arms unreflectively avoids the
challenge of evil by unloading it upon an "other" and that may or may
not be the proper course of action. Before appeal is made to the Deity
as our consolation in times of affliction, the moral question needs to be
asked and answered.

The ancient monotheists proposed that the proper response of man
to the universe is two-fold. First, he should strain to contemplate its
integrity. By an act of aesthetic sympathy he should strive to identify
with the cognitive situation of the author of nature, in particular through
contributing to the science of his handiwork. Second, he should carefully
cultivate the skill of weighing his practical alternatives within the strict
limits of his humble station, and pride himself on always accepting the
actual world as the best that is possible. This proposal was based upon
the monotheist's conviction that the sublimity of his scientific system of
nature is owing to its being a reliable statement of the connecting links
which in fact join together all events into the magnificent spectacle of
the universe.

Although allowing that scientific systems of nature are admirable,
even sublime, Smith nevertheless rejected the claim that the connecting
principles of our knowledge of nature replicate or signify in any way the
manner in which external objects are or may in fact be connected. All
such systems are merely elaborate, sometimes exquisite, inventions of
the imagination ("Astron.," p. 108; see Chapter I). As it turns out, then,
monotheistic religions were as superstitious as polytheistic religions,
except that they were not crude.

[5] The sentimental attachment of the insecure man for objects "which he has
long made use of" appears to be the basis of that claim which, once it is honored
by his fellows, became the "sacred right of private property." (MS, pp. 136-7;
LJ, pp. 107-8; WN, pp. 121-2, 170).

Smith reserved his main attack on monotheism generally and Stoicism in particular for its moral teachings. He agreed that propriety is the proper concern of every morally conscientious man. He further agreed that it is necessary to judge propriety by means of sympathetic identification with a well-informed and unbiased spectator. But he could not abide, as Bittermann rightly indicated, "Stoic ataraxy or apathy, resignation, indifference to practical results, and tendency to minimize emotion . . ." (1940, p. 724). While contemplation of the sublime has a valid place in human life, it is not proper that it should be "the great business and occupation of our lives" (*MS*, p. 427). "Man was made for action, and to promote by the exertion of his faculties such changes in the external circumstances both of himself and others, as may seem most favourable to the happiness of all" (*MS*, p. 154; also see p. 238). The "perfect apathy" prescribed by these monotheists, the deliberate "indifference" to human misery, the lighthearted estimate of the value of human life itself, is so disgusting, so bizarre, as to be beneath contempt. Those so unfortunate as to be prompted to conduct themselves consistently with this "death-song" (*MS*, p. 416) are "the proper objects not of censure but of commiseration" (*MS*, p. 420). Fortunately, the attraction of this outlook, although it may affect the judgment of men to some degree, is seldom so corrosive as to overwhelm their sense of propriety (*MS*, p. 428).

If the polytheists begged the question of what is the proper response to a world which portends evil, the monotheists answered it improperly. The challenge of evil cannot be properly met by aesthetic identification with an indifferent Deity, but only through moral sympathy with the impartial spectator (*MS*, pp. 426-7). Smith allowed, as we shall see, that anyone who persists in the effort of rectifying nature according to the standard of his moral convictions may and often does require the consolation available only through contemplation of divine benevolence (*MS*, p. 427). Still that appeal should never, according to Smith, replace but only supplement the struggle to render the world hospitable to moral beings. Furthermore, the supposed object of that contemplation is believed to be moved by the same moral considerations as move men. That Deity which is the last resort of morally conscientious men is, as the ancient polytheist obscurely recognized, a personal God, not a Jupiter acting from the inner necessity of aetherial fire (Macfie 1971).

Smith's analysis and critique of ancient religions distinctly suggests that he regarded religion as a human response to evil, i.e., to objects or events believed to be both gravely dangerous and intractable to human remedial effort. It further suggests that although a religious response may be elaborated in theoretical terms or by scientific procedures, it cannot be thereby justified. It appears that in Smith's view the justification of a religious response to evil is fundamentally a moral and not a scientific issue. These inferences appear to be confirmed by Smith's remarks on modern Christian sects.

The function of Christian churches, as indeed every institutionalized religion is, Smith held, moral education, but moral education of a particular type.[6] "This is a species of instruction of which the object is not so much to render the people good citizens in this world, as to prepare them for another and a better world in a life to come" (*WN*, p. 740). The articles of faith promulgated by the clergy are represented as certain and indispensable to proper conduct in this life in view of the rewards and punishments which await us in the next.

Leaving aside all else for the moment, consider how the doctrines promulgated by the clergy are and according to Smith ought to be scrutinized. Congregations recognize their clergymen as possessed of exclusive expertise on matters relating to these articles of faith (*WN*, p. 750). They do so because they believe their clergy to be both intelligent and, most important, committed to helping them preserve and deepen the moral bonds of their community. The influence and authority of the clergy depends originally and ultimately upon the maintenance of this latter belief. Smith was at pains to insist that in matters of religion generally and Christianity in particular, laymen accept the doctrines professed by their teachers as true because they believe their teachers to be committed to the same moral convictions which constitute the bonds of their community. Throughout his discussion of religious instruction (*WN*, pp. 740-66) Smith spoke of authority as an internal relation among men who agree upon a right and a wrong way of doing things. For Smith as for Winch, some people are *in* authority because they are thought to speak authoritatively *on* that shared ethic (Winch 1958). This point deserves some elaboration.

Religions take their origin among those who are afflicted by evil and who are or believe themselves to be impotent, i.e., among the common people (*WN*, p. 747). These peoples, because of their moral ties are most endangered, insist upon strict adherence to the established rules of morality. They look with suspicion upon the more liberal conscience of the rich and powerful (*WN*, pp. 746-7). Anyone, even a sovereign, who

---

[6] Smith nowhere stated explicitly that this is the sole valid function of religion. It seems probable, however, that that is what he believed. His epistemological critique of ancient religions, his stated preference for separation of church and state (*WN*, pp. 744-5, 752-7) and his assessment of Christian religions, a discussion of which follows, leave little room for any other function.

overreaches their tolerance for moral latitude discredits himself in their eyes. "His authority and consideration depends very much upon the respect which this society bears to him" (*WN*, p. 747). The same holds for the authority and consideration of clergymen. Should they fall to patronizing the sovereign (*WN*, pp. 752-4) or to imitating the manners of the rich (*WN*, pp. 754-7) the confidence of the greater part of their congregation is shaken and their authority is in imminent danger of usurpation by dissenters who appeal to the moral concerns of the common people (*WN*, p. 741).

This, for example, accounted for the disenchantment of the common people with the Roman Church during the reformation and their attraction to the teaching of the dissenters. "The austerity of their manners gave them authority with the common people, who contrasted the strict regularity of their conduct with the disorderly lives of the greater part of their own clergy" (*WN*, p. 757). The exemplary conduct of the presbyterian clergyman, on the other hand, together with his learning accounted for his authority, influence and appeal among the common people.

The common people look upon him with that kindness with which we naturally regard one who approaches somewhat to our own condition, but who, we think, ought to be in a higher. Their kindness naturally provokes his kindness. He becomes careful to instruct them, and attentive to assist and relieve them (*WN*, p. 762).

Unless people believe that their religious teachers are intent upon preserving and enhancing the moral bonds of their community, they will not support the doctrines which they promulgate. The credibility of religion is assessed not on theoretical, but on moral grounds. Unless the practices urged by a sect are believed to be consistent with and supportive of commitment to the moral convictions which prevail within a community, they are judged improper. Again, religions are not judged mainly by the elegance of their theological doctrines, but by the propriety of practices enjoined by those doctrines. Congregations ordinarily assess this by the conduct of their teacher. In this way the function of religion is effectively restricted to enhancing men's habit of respect for the general rules of morality, to supporting their sense of duty (*MS*, pp. 229-32).

The function of institutionalized religion is, in Smith's estimate, moral education. When qualified by the above clarification that function becomes quite restricted and at the same time more precise. Religious teachers instruct their congregations on how to conduct themselves in this life in order to prepare themselves for the next. But, since clergy may urge only those practices which are consistent with the moral convictions which prevail within the community, they are in fact teaching that it is by acting consistently with the moral conviction which prevails in this life that a man best prepares himself for happiness in the next. Although many if not most religious doctrines are not explicitly entailed by the rules of morality considered independently of the particular outlook of a religious sect, belief in these doctrines can be represented as obligatory only by showing that the practices which they imply are consistent with, indeed that they are in some relevant sense necessary extensions of those rules. By urging such practices religious teachers are in effect urging men to act consistently with those rules of conduct to which they are already committed as morally obligatory. This restriction, however, does not render institutionalized religions superfluous. Men do need to be urged to live according to their moral convictions, especially in the face of evil. By doing so religions perform a valuable moral function.

II

The other of Smith's main concerns in his lectures on Natural Theology was, again according to Millar, "the proofs of the being and attributes of God . . ." (Stewart 1858, p. 12). In view of the clarification of Smith's views on the justification of religious beliefs attained above it seems reasonable to allow not only that he did subscribe to the claim that God exists, that there is an after-life and that remedial justice will be effected by God in that life, but also that he regarded his acceptance of these doctrines to be justified. It appears reasonable, furthermore in the light of Smith's epistemological objections to ancient Stoic monotheism that his assent was, as Macfie stated, a matter of faith and not of proof in any strict rationalistic sense (1967, pp. 102-3, 107, 111). Macfie's suggestion, however, is far from satisfactory for it seems to imply that assent to these doctrines was for Smith at best a matter of taste, at worst arbitrary. This fails to capture the quality of Smith's faith, the force of his convictions. A more complete appreciation of the quality, character and content of Smith's religious convictions can be achieved by considering how they were for him a necessary response to a specific type of evil which was for him particularly troublesome.

That unjust circumstance which is also intractable to human remedy which most grieved Smith was unwarranted ostracization. Good and virtuous men are often blamed and punished either for acts they did not perform or for acting from sentiments which did not influence their conduct. This results from the tendency of men to assess the conduct of their fellows solely in the light of the actual consequences which follow

upon it (*MS*, pp. 133-5). Unjust censure results from this short-sighted-
ness on the part of others. Faced with such censure the victim can and
does seek solace by consulting his own conscience. He thereby confirms
his estimate of his own innocence. But conscience cannot and does not
relieve him of the social isolation which he unjustly suffers at the hands
of others. The impotence of the man-within combines with the short-
sightedness of the men without to render this injustice both practically
inevitable and humanly irremediable (*MS*, pp. 185-7). It was this ap-
praisal which led Smith to the religious doctrines mentioned above.

In such cases, the only effectual consolation of humbled and afflicted man lies in
an appeal to a still higher tribunal, to that of the all-seeing judge of the world,
whose eye can never be deceived and whose judgments can never be perverted. A
firm confidence in the unerring rectitude of this great tribunal, before which his
innocence is in due time to be declared, and his virtue to be finally rewarded, can
alone support him under the weakness and despondence of his own mind ...
Our happiness in this life is thus, upon many occasions, dependent upon the
humble hope and expectation of a life to come, a hope and expectation deeply
rooted in human nature, which can alone support its lofty ideas of its own dignity, can alone illumine the dreary prospects of its continually approaching mortality, and maintain its cheerfulness under all the heaviest calamities to which,
from the disorders of this life, it may sometimes be exposed. That there is a world
to come where exact justice will be done to every man ... is a doctrine in every
respect so venerable, so comfortable to the weakness, so flattering to the grandeur
of human nature, that the virtuous man who has the misfortune to doubt of it
cannot possibly avoid wishing most earnestly and anxiously to believe it (*MS*,
pp. 187-8, also see pp. 239-40).

Smith was convinced that no man who is on the one hand motivated by
"the love of virtue and the abhorrence of evil and injustice" and confronted on the other by circumstances which both contradict his most
deeply held moral convictions and appear to be unalterable by human
effort, can remain faithful to the one and accommodate himself to the
other (*MS*, p. 240). Unless he renounces his moral bearings altogether –
the moral equivalent of absurdity – he must insist that such injustices can
and will be remedied. If that is impossible in this life under the short-
sighted and impotent efforts of men, then there must be another life in
which they will be rectified under the direction of a Being Who is committed to these same moral principles and Who is both all-seeing and
all-powerful. In Smith's judgment the expectation of a final remedy for
the evils of this life, especially unwarranted ostracization, is a necessary
condition for continued commitment to the dignity of man, to the overriding importance of community with one's fellows and to the inviolable
bonds of that community.

  This was the basis of Smith's assent to the doctrines of the existence of

God, of the after-life and of final remedial justice. His discussion of the
necessity of that assent does constitute a proof of these doctrines, although only in the sense of a justification. He did not pretend to have
shown that these doctrines represent what is in fact the case, but only
why it is necessary for a man committed to the moral life in an imperfect
world to hope that they do. "[T]he very suspicion, of a fatherless world,"
he mused on one occasion, "must be the most melancholy of all reflections . . ." (*MS*, p. 345).[7] For Smith, as for Kant (*Critique of Practical
Reason* Bk. II, Ch. 2.), these doctrines are postulates of moral life in an
imperfect world. In assenting to them Smith postulated a final theological
sanction to human morality.

With this postulate we have specified the principal content of what
Macfie termed "the wider context of [Smith's] ultimate faith" (1967,
p. 102). The introduction of this postulate into Smith's overall perspective occasioned redefinition of three important aspects of that perspective. As these are implied by a postulate, they may be characterized
as corollaries.

The first corollary of this postulate was a redefinition of the status of
the inviolable bonds of community. Considered independently of belief
in God they were regarded as the ordinary rules of conduct. A man
observes them because he values the company of his fellows and recognizes that respect for certain of their preferences and aversions is an
essential condition of sustaining that community. In that frame of reference they were observed as the commands of our moral faculties. Considered within this broader frame of reference, their status is enhanced.
Since it is believed that God will ultimately sanction those preferences
and aversions, they take on the stature of "divine commands," the bonds
of community become "sacred" and respect for them "reverence" (*MS*,
pp. 232-3).

The second corollary of this postulate was a redefinition of the status
of man's competence to judge action in point of its propriety and im-
propriety. Considered independently of belief in God men have no
recourse but to decide for themselves which course of action is proper
and which is not. Our "moral faculties" are the original source of the
distinction of right and wrong. Considered within this broader frame of
reference, in which the Deity concurs with our moral judgment, these

---

[7] I would hope that biographers who are persuaded of the universal validity
of psycho-analytic techniques will not connect this remark and Smith's early loss
of his own father and then proceed to expound yet another in the current spate
of pseudo-historical tributes to Freud.

faculties come to be regarded as possessed of "the most evident badges of authority" (*MS*, p. 233).

The third corollary, not stated explicitly but definitely implied by what has gone before, was a redefinition of the status of nature itself. Considered independently of belief in God nature was regarded as the sum of all circumstances within which men act and to which they respond. Considered within this broader frame of reference, in which God will finally order nature according to the principles of human morality, nature came to be regarded as ultimately subject to God's will.

It was at this point, where his religious reflections led him to assert the ultimate dominance of God over nature, that Smith appears to have noted a bit more than a surface similarity between his views and those of the ancient Stoics and modern deists. He noted that what I have called the first and second corollaries which are, like the postulate of final theological sanctions, based upon subjective moral need were "afterwards confirmed by reasoning and philosophy..." (*MS*, p. 232). It appears that he believed that the third corollary was confirmed in the same way, except that in allowing this he treated this corollary as equivalent to the belief that God is the source or as he put it "the author of Nature" (*MS*, p. 109). Continuing along this line of reasoning he was prepared to go so far as to allow that God has already subordinated nature to the requirement of morality to a significant extent. In this, however, he stopped short of a Panglossion vision, even of natural law and natural rights. But he did note instances of natural events which in fact promoted the development of sound moral dispositions and attitudes. These he used as illustrations of the divine interest in finally subjecting nature to the requirements of morality and as such regarded them as so many encouragements to hope for a final theological sanction of human morality.

Not only do man's deliberated actions promote the advance of morals, but so also do many of his undeliberated response patterns. Those reprisals which flow from the sentiment of resentment, for example, serve to prompt men to respect those shared preferences and aversions which form the very basis of community life (*MS*, pp. 109-10; 124-6). Even the great "irregularities" in the constitution of nature – ambition, fortune, utility, and fashion (*MS*, pp. 84ff, 133ff, 255ff, 279ff.) – reinforce this conviction. In spite of their obviously unjust consequences, each also results in the enhancement of man's concern for the preservation and integrity of the moral community. Ambition, which results in the unjust distribution of wealth, and fortune, which results in unwarranted ostracization, both serve to rouse the industry and attention of men in the desires and preferences of others (*MS*, pp. 152-4, 208-9, 239-40, 263-5). Fashion and utility, according to which men incline to grant a higher priority to consistency than to humanity, both prompt concern for the peace and order of society (*MS*, pp. 263-5, 331-2, 337). Smith embellished these and similar illustrations mentioned in the *Moral Sentiments* with phrases such as "Director of Nature," "Nature" and "the Wisdom which contrived this system of Nature." Previous investigators mistakenly regarded Smith's use of such phrases as conclusive evidence of a deistic outlook on his part. Since this interpretation is unacceptable it must be that Smith employed these phrases for the benefit of others. This rhetorical stratagem may have been a part of his effort to enlist the assent of his readers to the main doctrines of the *Moral Sentiments*, or of his apparent design to obscure the unorthodoxy of his religious convictions, or both.

III

The character and content of Smith's religious convictions have been explored for the purpose of providing a reliable basis for discerning the nature and extent of the influence of these convictions upon his social thought. In the light of his views on the proper function of religion it seems evident that one type of influence can be ruled out, viz., doctrinal dependence. Specifically, Smith believed that the rules of conduct which he supported, including both the moral rules relating to justice, benevolence and prudence and policy recommendations in the area of political economy, to be defensible independently of religious beliefs.

The proper function of religion was, in Smith's judgment, quite restricted. He looked to God to reconcile nature to the requirements of morality, but only in the next life (Macfie 1967, pp. 102, 107). Any such reconciliations which can be achieved in this life are men's responsibility. Furthermore, in the execution of that duty a man must look for guidance not to God but to the moral disposition which prevails within his community (see Chapter II). In morals as well as political economy Smith's principal doctrines – both positive and normative – were, as Bittermann contended, altogether independent of his belief in final theological sanctions (1940, pp. 717-18). The postulate of a final theological sanction, together with all corollaries thereto, served but one function according to Smith, viz., the fostering and strengthening of a man's dedication to persevere in his moral commitments. This function was generally acknowledged, Smith observed, in the common practice of placing greater confidence in the moral fiber of men who support religious convictions than in that of those who do not.

It is in this manner that religion enforces the natural sense of duty; and hence it is that mankind are generally disposed to place great confidence in the probity of those who seem deeply impressed with religious sentiments. Such persons, they imagine, act under an additional tie besides those which regulate the conduct of other men. The regard to the propriety of action, as well as to the reputation, the regard to the applause of his own breast, as well as to that of others, are motives which, they suppose, have the same influence over the religious man as over the man of the world. But the former lies under another restraint, and never acts deliberately but as in the presence of that great Superior who is finally to recompense him according to his deeds. A greater trust is reposed, upon that account, in the regularity and exactness of his conduct. And wherever the natural principles of religion are not corrupted by the factions and party zeal of some worthless cabal; whenever the first duty which it requires is to fulfil all the obligations of morality; wherever men are not taught to regard frivolous observances as more immediate duties of religion than acts of justice and benevolence, and to imagine that by sacrifices and ceremonies and vain supplications they can bargain with the Deity for fraud and perfidy and violence, the world undoubtedly judges right in this respect, and justly places a double confidence in the rectitude of the religious man's behavior (*MS*, pp. 241-2).

To have ruled out any doctrinal dependence of Smith's main social views upon his religious beliefs does not entail the denial of all influences. It is possible that scientific and normative hypotheses, which are defensible quite independently of religious experience, be initially suggested to an investigator by that experience. Where this occurs it seems reasonable to acknowledge the presence of an influence of the latter upon the former, for had the investigator not been a religious man there would be some question of whether he would have ever framed such hypotheses at all. It seems likely that Smith's social thought was influenced in this way. At least four and perhaps five key aspects of his overall philosophic position appear to have been suggested to him by his religious experience.

First, he regarded the occasion of social thought to be the same as gives rise to religion, viz., the confrontation by morally conscientious men of evils which results from the established order of society. Just as wonder is occasioned in natural philosophy when the rules which constitute a systematic scheme of objects and events falter in the face of an object or event which those rules cannot accommodate, so in moral philosophy evil events reveal the "gap" which must be bridged. But the parallel between natural and moral philosophy ends there. In the former case the proper procedure is to change the rules to accommodate the recalcitrant event. In the latter case it is the recalcitrant event which requires to be accommodated somehow to the rules. This is the difference between what Aristotle called the theoretical and the practical sciences (*Nic. Ethics* VI, 2. 1139a 26-33). In moral matters for Smith as for Aristotle "the end aimed at is not knowledge but action" (*Nic. Ethics* I, 3. 1095a 4-5).

Second, the principal failing of previous social theorists was regarded by Smith as the same one as he had discovered in the ancient deistic religion of the Stoics. All "men of system" from Zeno, Cicero and Epicurus to Shaftesbury, Hutcheson and Hume gave greater weight to the aesthetic experience of the sublime than to the moral experience of propriety (*MS*, pp. 402-6, 426, 429, 438, 445, 447-8). In doing so they degraded the fundamental dignity of man and chanted a "deathsong" glorifying, as had Spinoza, (Feuer 1958, pp. 217-18), the splendid symmetry, the sublime simplicity of that social system which was slowly but surely fragmenting loci of human fellowship and rendering men insensitive to one another's unhappy and unjust plight. Since, however, Smith viewed the moral bonds of community as inviolable, he regarded this "perfect apathy" of men of system as at the very least "deceptive," often "splenetic," and sometimes "wholly pernicious" (*MS*, pp. 263, 451).

Third, Smith's declarations that God should be trusted to harmonize the established and often authorized assertions of self-interest or narrow class-interests with the preservation and welfare of society (*MS*, pp. 109-10, 124, 152-4, 208-9, 239-40, 263-5, 331-2, 337) are intelligible only within the framework of his firm commitment to the maintenance of those moral principles which are essential to the integrity of the concrete human community. Such pronouncements were made for the consolation of the afflicted. Since they are appropriate only with regard to those evils which are presently intractable to human effort, they constitute a report of what Smith regarded as the limiting circumstances within which morally conscientious men had, at least for the time being, to be satisfied to act. Smith did not believe that God does, but only firmly hoped that He will ultimately establish a satisfactory condition for the morally conscientious – not in this, but in the next life.

Fourth, the act of subordination by which authority is constituted in the case of governmental and commercial institutions was regarded by Smith as the same as the one by which clergy are granted authority in institutionalized religions. Morally conscientious men who feel impotent in the face of evil seek the assistance of others believed to be more capable than they, but devoted to the same moral convictions. They do so by granting the preferences and aversions of their supposed benefactors a higher priority than they would otherwise warrant. In this way the supposed benefactor attains a degree of influence or authority over the conduct of others which far exceeds that of other men. The "principle of authority," upon which the authority of governmental officials is founded, and "commercial ambition," upon which that of the rich is based, are fundamentally the same in this respect as the pattern of subordination upon which the authority of clergymen rests (see Chapters IV and V).

Smith's parallel analysis of governmental, commercial and religious subordination, however, is more than coincidental. He appears to have regarded religious subordination as the paradigm case. This is indicated by his frequent use of religious terms in describing the quality of that respect which inferiors show to their civil and commercial superiors, e.g., deference, reverence, adoration (*MS*, pp. 74, 367). This is particularly clear with respect to the act of subordination which constitutes civilized societies, which establishes the plutocratic mode of social stratification. "The great mob of mankind are admirers and worshippers, and what may seem most extraordinary, most frequently the disinterested admirers and worshippers of wealth and greatness" (*MS*, p. 85). Furthermore, it was this perception which seems to have lead Smith to describe men's duties in civil and commercial society as he did. They show "reverence" to the established rules of conduct (*MS*, pp. 231-2). The conventional civil right to private property was described as a "sacred right" (*WN*, pp. 121-2, 170).

It seems likely that as regards at least these four aspects of his overall philosophic position, Smith drew upon his religious experience. Textual evidence, although far from conclusive, seems to lean in this direction. One final aspect of his position which may have first been suggested to Smith by his religious experience is even more speculative although probably more interesting. It deserves mention for the latter reason.

In the *Wealth of Nations* Smith was concerned to recommend changes in governmental procedures which would render commercial practices more responsive to the moral convictions of the common people. The overall thrust of these changes was to be total decentralization of the power to control the allocation of national wealth. In the midst of his discussion of Christian sects Smith noted with approval that similar procedural changes had rendered the governance of the Presbyterian churches of Holland, Geneva, Switzerland and Scotland more responsive to the moral convictions of the common people (*WN*, pp. 761-2). This similarity suggests that Smith may have drawn his inspiration for the qualified Laissez-Faire policy recommendations which he proposed in the *Wealth of Nations* from the happy experience of the Presbyterians. If these recommendations were regarded as an attempt to uphold the integrity of the moral imperatives of the common people and if he

regarded these in the light of his religious convictions as divine commands, it seems at least plausible that a successful experiment in the
governance of a religious institution with which he was familiar was
used as the model for possible reforms of other institutions which im-
pinge upon the observance of those same commands.[8]

Macfie correctly observed of Smith that "the whole tone of his work
will convince most that he was an essentially pious man" (1967, p. 111).
He also rightly contended that this pious spirit, although more apparent
in the *Moral Sentiments,* also enlivens the *Wealth of Nations,* except
that in the latter "it comes down to earth, indeed to the market place"
(p. 103). This does not suggest that these works are theological tracts.
Quite obviously they are not. But it does suggest, even demand, that
both were authored by a deeply religious man and that, on that score,
neither can be fully and reliably understood unless the fact and the
quality of Smith's religious convictions are kept firmly in mind.

---

[8] It seems reasonable to suppose that Smith's support of decentralized control
of economic power was consistent with the spirit of the Protestant reformers in
that they too were determined to conform the institutional to the moral order
and that they too supported the conviction that the final authority on moral matters
is the conscience of the mature individual (Tawney 1926, pp. 82, 97).

WORKS CITED

The following list includes full particulars of most books and articles mentioned in the text and notes. These are arranged alphabetically by author and by date of publication. Wherever the publication date of the edition used may be a source of confusion I have indicated the date of first publication. The writings of Smith are cited in the text and notes according to the abbreviations listed at the end of the Preface. This list is neither restricted to works on Adam Smith nor does it include all works about him. As of this date there is no complete bibliography of works by and about Adam Smith. The best partial bibliographies are the *Vander-blue Memorial Collection of Smithiana* (Cambridge, Mass: Harvard University Press, 1939) and Franklin and Cordasco's *Adam Smith: A Bibliographical Checklist* (New York: B. Franklin, 1950). This list may be a useful supplement to these sources.

Alexander, S., *Beauty and Other Forms of Value*. London: Macmillan, 1933.

Allport, Gordon W., "The Functional Autonomy of Motives," *American Journal of Psychology*, vol. 50 (1937), pp. 141-56.

—, *Becoming: Basic Considerations for a Psychology of Personality*. New Haven: Yale University Press, 1955.

Arrow, Kenneth J., *Social Choice and Individual Values*. 2nd ed. New Haven: Yale University Press, 1963.

—, "Values and Collective Decision-Making," in *Philosophy, Politics and Society*, P. Laslett and W. G. Runciman, editors. Third Series. Oxford: Blackwell, 1967, pp. 215-32.

Barnard, C. I., *The Functions of the Executive*. Cambridge, Mass: Harvard University Press, 1938.

Barnes, Harry E. and Becker, Howard, *Social Thought from Lore to Science*. 2nd ed., 2 vols. Washington: Harren, 1952.

Becker, James F., "Adam Smith's Theory of Social Science," *Southern Economic Journal*, vol. 28 (1961), pp. 13-21.

—, "The Corporation Spirit and its Liberal Analysis," *Journal of the History of Ideas*, vol. 30 (1969), pp. 69-84.

Bittermann, Henry J., "Adam Smith's Empiricism and the Law of Nature," *Journal of Political Economy*, vol. 48 (1940), pp. 487-520, 703-34.

Bladen, V. W., "Adam Smith on Value," in *Essays in Political Economy in Honor of E. J. Erwick*, H. A. Innis, editor. Toronto: University of Toronto Press, 1938.

—, "Adam Smith on Productive and Non-Productive Labor," *The Canadian Journal of Economics and Political Science*, vol. 26 (1960), pp. 625-30.

Blau, Peter M., *Bureaucracy in Modern Society*. New York: Random House, 1956.

—, *The Dynamics of Bureaucracy*. 2nd ed. rev. Chicago: Univ. of Chicago Press, 1962.

Bonar, James, *Philosophy and Political Economy*. London: Swan, Sonnenschein, 1893.

—, "The Theory of Moral Sentiments, by Adam Smith, 1759," *Journal of Philosophical Studies*, vol. I (1926), pp. 333-53.

Brodbeck, May, "Methodological Individualism: Definition and Reduction," *Philosophy of Science*, vol. 25 (1958) pp. 1-22.

Bryson, Gladys, *Men and Society*. Princeton: Princeton Univ. Press, 1945.

Bury, John B., *The Idea of Progress*. New York: Macmillan, 1932.

Campbell, T. D., *Adam Smith's Science of Morals*. London: Allen and Unwin, 1971.

Campbell, William F., "Adam Smith's Theory of Justice, Prudence, and Benevolence," *American Economic Review*, vol. 57 (1967), pp. 571-77.

Cannan, Edwin, *A History of the Theories of Production and Distribution in English Political Economy from 1776 to 1848*. 2nd ed., London: King and Son, 1903.

—, "Adam Smith as an Economist," *Economica*, vol. 6 (1926), pp. 123-34.

Clark, John M., et al., *Adam Smith, 1776-1926*. Chicago: University of Chicago Press, 1928.

Cobban, Alfred, *In Search of Humanity*. New York: Braziller, 1960.

Cole, Arthur H., "Puzzles of the 'Wealth of Nations,' " *The Canadian Journal of Economics and Political Science*, vol. 24 (1958), pp. 1-8.

Cropsey, Joseph, *Polity and Economy*. The Hague: Nijhoff, 1957.

—, "Adam Smith," in *History of Political Philosophy*. Strauss and Cropsey, editors. Chicago: Rand McNally, 1963, pp. 549-72.

Dahrendorf, Ralf, "On the Origin of Social Inequality," in *Philosophy, Politics and Society*. P. Laslett and W. G. Runciman, editors. Second Series. Oxford: Blackwell, 1962, pp. 88-109.

Davenport, John, "The Ethics of the 'Wealth of Nations,' " *The Philosophical Review*, vol. 34 (1925), pp. 599-609.

Devlin, Patrick, *The Enforcement of Morals*. London: Oxford Univ. Press, 1965.

Douglas, Paul H., "Smith's Theory of Value and Distribution," *University Journal of Business*, vol. 5 (1927), pp. 53-87. Reprinted in Clark 1928.

Eckstein, Walther, (ed.), *Adam Smith, Theorie Der Ethischen Gefühle*. 2 vols. Leipzig: Felix Meiner, 1926.

Einstein, Albert, "Religion and Science," *New York Times*, Nov. 9, 1930, Section 5, p. 1.

Feuer, Lewis, *Spinoza and the Rise of Liberalism*. Boston: Beacon, 1958.

Firth, Roderick, "Ethical Absolutism and the Ideal Observer," *Philosophy and Phenomenological Research*, vol. 12 (1952), pp. 317-45.

Forbes, Duncan, " 'Scientific' Whiggism: Adam Smith and John Millar," *Cambridge Journal*, vol. 7 (1954), pp. 643-70.

Freeman, R. D., "Adam Smith, Education and Laissez Faire," *History of Political Economy*, vol. 1 (1959), pp. 173-86.

Gay, Peter, *The Enlightenment: An Interpretation*, vol. 1. New York: Knopf, 1966.

Gellner, Ernest, "Explanations in History," *Proceedings of the Aristotelian Society*, Supp. vol. 30 (1956), pp. 157-76.

Gide, C. and Rist, C., *A History of Economic Doctrines*. Smart, transl. New York: Heath, n.d.

Ginzberg, Eli, *The House of Adam Smith*, New York: Columbia Univ. Press, 1934.

Goldstein, Leon J., "The Two Theses of Methodological Individualism," *The British Journal for the Philosophy of Science*, vol. 9 (1958), pp. 1-11.

Grampp, William D., "Adam Smith and the Economic Man," *Journal of Political Economy*, vol. 56 (1948), pp. 315-36.

—, *Economic Liberalism*. 2 vols. New York: Random House, 1965.

Gray, Alexander, *The Development of Economic Doctrine*. New York: Wiley, 1931.

—, *Adam Smith*. London: The Historical Association, 1948.

Guthrie, W. K. C., *A History of Greek Philosophy*. vol. 3. Cambridge: Cambridge University Press, 1969.

Hamowy, Ronald, "Adam Smith, Adam Ferguson and the Division of Labour," *Economica*, vol. 35 (1968), pp. 249-59.

Hart, H. L. A., "Are there Any Natural Rights?" *The Philosophical Review*, vol. 64 (1955), pp. 175-91.

—, *Law, Liberty and Morality*. Stanford, Cal.: Stanford University Press, 1963.

Hasbach, Wilhelm, *Untersuchungen über Adam Smith und die Entwicklung der Politischen Oekonomie*. Leipzig: Duncker und Humboldt, 1891.

Hayek, Friedrich, A., *The Road to Serfdom*. Chicago: University of Chicago Press, 1944.

—, *Individualism and Economic Order*. Chicago: Univ. of Chicago Press, 1948.

—, *The Counter-Revolution of Science*. Glencoe, Ill.: Free Press, 1952.

Heilbroner, Robert L., *The Worldly Philosophers*. New York: Simon and Schuster, 1953.

Heimann, Edward, *History of Economic Doctrines*. New York: Oxford University Press, 1945.

Hollander, Samuel, "Adam Smith's Approach to Economic Development," in *The Varied Pattern: Studies in the 18th Century*. P. Hughes and D. Williams, editors. Toronto: Hakkert, 1971, pp. 269-96.

Howell, Wilbur, *Eighteenth-Century British Logic and Rhetoric*. Princeton, N. J.: Princeton University Press, 1971.

Hutchison, T. W., *"Positive" Economics and Policy Objectives*. Cambridge, Mass.: Harvard University Press, 1964.

Ingram, J. K., *A History of Political Economy*. New York: Macmillan 1908.

Katona, George, *Psychological Analysis of Economic Behavior*. New York: McGraw-Hill, 1951.

Kauder, Emil, "Genesis of the Marginal Utility Theory," *The Economic Journal*, vol. 63 (1953), pp. 638-50.

Keynes, John M., *The End of Laissez-Faire*. London: Woolf, 1926.

Kroeber, A. L. and Kluckhohn, C., "Culture: A Critical Review of Concepts and Definitions," *Papers of the Peabody Museum of American Archaeology and Ethnology*, vol. 47 (1952), no. 1.

Kuhn, Thomas, *The Structure of Scientific Revolutions*. Chicago: University of Chicago Press, 1962.

Laird, John, "The Social Philosophy of Smith's 'Wealth of Nations,'" *Journal of Philosophical Studies*, vol. 2 (1927), pp. 39-51.

Leser, E., *Der Begriff des Reichtums bei Adam Smith*. Heidelberg: Damstadt, 1874.

Leslie, C., "The Political Economy of Adam Smith," in *Essays in Political Economy*. London, 1888, pp. 21-40. (First published in 1870).

Lowe, Adolph, "The Classical Theory of Economic Growth," *Social Research*, vol. 21 (1954), pp. 127-58.

Macfie, A. L., *The Individual in Society: Papers on Adam Smith*. London: Allen and Unwin, 1967.

—, "The Invisible Hand of Jupiter," *Journal of the History of Ideas*, vol. 32 (1971), pp. 595-99.

Macpherson, C. B., *The Political Theory of Possessive Individualism*. Oxford: Clarendon Press, 1962.

—, "The Maximization of Democracy," in *Philosophy, Politics and Society*, P. Laslett and W. G. Runciman, editors. Third Series. Oxford: Blackwell, 1967, pp. 83-103.

Mandelbaum, Maurice, "Societal Facts," *The British Journal of Sociology*, vol. 6 (1955), pp. 305-17.

—, "Societal Laws," *The British Journal for the Philosophy of Science*, vol. 8 (1957), pp. 211-24.

Marshall, Alfred, *Principles of Economics*. Eighth Edition. London: Macmillan, 1920.

McClelland, David, et al., *The Achievement Motive*. New York: Appleton-Century-Crofts, 1953.

Meek, Ronald L., *Economics and Ideology and Other Essays*. London: Chapman & Hall, 1967.

—, "Smith, Turgot, and the 'Four Stages' Theory," *History of Political Economy*, vol. 3 (1971), pp. 9-27.

Merton, Robert K., *Social Theory and Social Structure*. Rev. ed., New York: Free Press, 1968.

Mitchell, Wesley C., *Types of Economic Theory*. 2 vols. J. Dorfman, Editor. New York: Kelley, 1967-9.

Moos, S., "Is Adam Smith out of date?" *Oxford Economic Papers*, vol. 3 (1951), pp. 187-201.

Morrow, Glenn R., *The Ethical and Economic Theories of Adam Smith*. New York: Longmans, Green, 1923. (a)

—, "The Significance of the Doctrine of Sympathy in Hume and Adam Smith," *The Philosophical Review*, vol. 32 (1923), pp. 60-78, (b)

—, "The Ethics of the 'Wealth of Nations,' " *The Philosophical Review*, vol. 34 (1925), pp. 609-11.

—, "Adam Smith: Moralist and Philosopher," *Journal of Political Economy*, vol. 35 (1927), pp. 321-42. Reprinted in Clark 1928.

Mossner, E. C., "Deism," *The Encyclopedia of Philosophy*, P. Edwards, Editor-in-Chief. New York: Macmillan and Free Press, 1967, vol. II, pp. 326-36.

Myrdal, Gunnar, *The Political Element in the Development of Economic Theory*. P. Streeten, Transl. Cambridge: Harvard Univ. Press, 1954.

—, *Value in Social Theory*. P. Streeten, Editor. London: Routledge and Kegan Paul, 1958.

—, *Objectivity in Social Research*. New York: Pantheon, 1969.

Nash, Manning, "The Organization of Economic Life," in *Tribal and Peasant Economies*. G. Dalton, Editor. Garden City, New York: Natural History Press, 1967, pp. 3-12.

Nicholson, J. Shield, *A Project of Empire*. London: Macmillan, 1909.

Otto, Rudolf, *The Idea of the Holy*. J. W. Harvey, transl. New York: Oxford Univ. Press, 1961. (First published in 1923).

Petrella, Frank, "Individual, Group, or Government?" *History of Political Economy*, vol. 2 (1970), pp. 152-76.

Polanyi, Karl, *The Great Transformation*. Boston: Beacon, 1957.

Popper, Karl R., *The Open Society and Its Enemies*. London: Routledge and Kegan Paul Ltd., 1945.

—, *The Poverty of Historicism*. London: Routledge and Kegan Paul, 1957.

Rae, John, *Life of Adam Smith*. London: Macmillan, 1895.

Raphael, D. D., "Adam Smith and 'The Infection of David Hume's Society,' " *Journal of the History of Ideas*, vol. 30 (1969), pp. 225-48.

Rawls, John, "Two Concepts of Rules," *The Philosophical Review*, vol. 64 (1955), pp. 3-32.

—, "Justice as Fairness," *The Philosophical Review*, vol. 67 (1958), pp. 164-94.

Robertson, H. M. and Taylor, W. L., "Adam Smith's Approach to the Theory of Value," *The Economic Journal*, vol. 67 (1957), pp. 181-98.

Robinson, Joan, *Economic Philosophy*. Chicago: Aldine, 1962.

Rosenberg, Nathan, "Some Institutional Aspects of the 'Wealth of Nations,' " *The Journal of Political Economy*, vol. 68 (1960), pp. 557-70.

—, "Adam Smith on the Division of Labour: Two Views or One?" *Economica*, vol. 32 (1965), pp. 127-39.

—, "Adam Smith, Consumer Tastes, and Economic Growth," *The Journal of Political Economy*, vol. 76 (1968), pp. 361-74.

Salomon, Albert, "Adam Smith as Sociologist," *Social Research*, vol. 12, (1954), pp. 22-42.

Samuels, Warren J., *The Classical Theory of Economic Policy*. New York: World Publishing Co., 1966.

Schumpeter, Joseph A., *History of Economic Analysis*. E. B. Schumpeter, editor. New York: Oxford Univ. Press, 1954.

Scott, William R., *Adam Smith as Student and Professor*. Glasgow: Jackson, 1937.

Searle, John R., "How to Derive 'Ought' from 'Is,' " *The Philosophical Review*, vol. 73 (1964), pp. 43-58.

Selby-Bigge, L. A., (editor) *British Moralists*. 2 vols. Oxford: Clarendon, 1897.

Seward, John P., "The Structure of Functional Autonomy," *American Psychologist*, vol. 18 (1963), pp. 703-10.

Simon, Herbert A., *Administrative Behavior*. New York: Macmillan, 1947.

Small, Albion W., *Adam Smith and Modern Sociology*. Chicago: University of Chicago Press, 1907.

Spengler, Joseph J., "Adam Smith's Theory of Economic Growth," *The Southern Economic Journal*, vol. 25 (1959), pp. 397-415 and vol. 26 (1959), pp. 1-12.

Stephen, Leslie, *History of English Thought in the Eighteenth Century*. 2 vols. London: Smith, Elder, 1876.

Stewart, Dugald, "Account of the Life and Writings of Adam Smith. LL.D.," *The Collected Works of Dugald Stewart*. Wm. Hamilton, Editor. Edinburgh: Thomas Constable, 1858. Vol. 10, pp. 5-98. (First published in 1793).

Stigler, George J., "The Development of Utility Theory," *The Journal of Political Economy*, vol. 58 (1950), pp. 307-27; 373-96.

—, "The Ricardian Theory of Value and Distribution," *The Journal of Political Economy*, vol. 60 (1952), pp. 187-207.

Strong, G. B., *Adam Smith and the Eighteenth Century Concept of Social Progress*. St. Louis, 1932.

Tawney, R. H., *Religion and the Rise of Capitalism*. New York: Harcourt, Brace, 1926.

Taylor, O. H., *A History of Economic Thought*. New York: McGraw-Hill, 1960.

Thompson, H. F., "Adam Smith's Philosophy of Science," *Quarterly Journal of Economics*, vol. 79 (1965), pp. 212-33.

Tobin, J. and Dolbear, F. T., "Comments on the Relevance of Psychology to Economic Theory and Research," in *Psychology: A Study of a Science*. S. Koch, Editor. New York: McGraw-Hill, 1963, vol. 6, pp. 677-84.

Viner, Jacob, "Adam Smith and Laissez-Faire," *Journal of Political Economy*, vol. 35 (1927), pp. 198-217. Reprinted in Clark 1928.

Watkins, J. W. N., "Historical Explanation in the Social Sciences," *British Journal for the Philosophy of Science*, vol. 8 (1957), pp. 104-17.

Wellman, Carl, "The Ethical Implications of Cultural Relativity," *The Journal of Philosophy*, vol. 60 (1963), pp. 169-84.

West, E. G., "Adam Smith's Two Views on the Division of Labour," *Economica*, vol. 31 (1964), pp. 23-32.

—, *Adam Smith*. New York: Arlington House, 1965.

—, "Adam Smith's Philosophy of Riches," *Philosophy*, vol. 44 (1969), pp. 101-15.

Westermarck, E., *Ethical Relativity*. New York: Harcourt, Brace, 1932.

Winch, Peter, *The Idea of a Social Science*. London: Routledge and Kegan Paul, 1958 (a).

—, "Authority," *Proceedings of the Aristotelian Society*. Supp. vol. 32 (1958), pp. 225-40. (b)

Wolin, Sheldon, *Politics and Vision*. Boston: Little Brown, 1960.

Wollheim, Richard, "A Paradox in the Theory of Democracy," in *Philosophy, Politics and Society*, P. Laslett and W. G. Runciman, editors. Second Series. Oxford: Blackwell, 1962, pp. 71-87.

Zeyss, R., *Adam Smith und der Eigennutz*. Tuebingen, 1889.

INDEX

Admiration, 8, 9, 10, 45, 46, 48, 55, 64, 65, 67, 69, 76, 77, 102, 114, 126, 137, 140, 147, 151.

Aesthetic preference, 12, 13, 14, 15, 16, 57, 81, 95, 108, 110, 140, 150.

Agriculture, 127-8.

Alexander, S., 36.

Allport, Gordon W., 40.

Ambition, 16, 46, 47, 77, 92, 102, 130, 147, 151.

Anthropology, 37, 129.

Aristotle, xi, 11, 49, 129, 137, 149, 150.

Arrow, Kenneth J., 56, 108, 109.

Arts, 7-10, 23, 24, 77, 116; dance, 10, 12; drama, 18, 19, 23; imitative, 8-12, 15, 75, 76; music, 10, 12; painting, 9-12, 76; poetry, 24; productive, 15, 76; 116; statuary, 9, 76.

Association of ideas, 6, 7, 11, 12, 41, 75, 87, 88, 90, 99, 140, 150, 151.

Authority, of clergy, 142-44, 150, 151; *see* political; principle of, 64, 65, 77, 142.

Autonomy, 42, 48, 57.

Balance of trade, 88, 89, 90, 105, 120.

Barnard, C. I., 103.

Barnes, Harry E., 61.

Barter, 87, 88, 95, 96, 98, 99, 106.

Beauty, 9, 10, 17, 42, 47, 49, 74, 75, 76, 79, 104, 106, 141, 150.

Becker, Howard, 61.

Becker, James F., 2, 3, 4, 6, 44, 75, 78.

Bentham, Jeremy, 31, 75.

Bittermann, Henry J., x, 2, 6, 7, 14, 15, 26, 61, 133, 141, 148.

Bladen, V. W., x, xi, 103, 114.

Blau, Peter M., 79.

Bonar, James, x, 26, 61, 73, 107, 125, 133.

Bond of community, 25, 63, 65, 79, 142, 143, 145, 146, 147, 150.

Brodbeck, May, 54, 56, 57.

Bryson, Gladys, 53, 55, 58.

Bury, John B., 73.

Campbell, T. D., ix, 2, 3, 4, 6, 7, 15, 16, 18, 26, 36, 37, 39, 40, 44, 45, 49, 50, 62, 65, 66, 82, 83, 102, 130, 133.

Campbell, William F., 55.

Cannan, Edwin, ix, xvi, 55, 61, 73, 84, 93, 111, 113, 114.

Capital, 89, 94, 96, 100, 111, 113-19, 124, 126-28.

Capitalism, competitive, 84, 100, 106.

Cassini, 4, 6.

Casuistry, 20, 38.

Christian sects, 134, 135, 142, 151.

Cicero, 150.

Clark, Samuel, 137.

Cobban, Alfred, 18.

Coercion, 41, 51, 56, 65, 66, 67, 70.

Cole, Arthur H., 104.

Colonies, 88, 92, 118.

Commercial life, Smith's attitude toward, xiv, 46, 48, 55, 84, 85, 91, 92, 101, 102, 108, 110, 129, 130, 134.

Compassion, 46.

Competition, 106, 107, 117, 119, 120.

Conscience, 48, 64, 145, 152.

Convention, 6, 7, 11, 12, 14, 57, 58, 59, 98, 119, 151.

Copernicus, 4, 5.

Cropsey, Joseph, 1, 39, 61, 63, 65, 125.

Cudworth, Ralph, 79.

Custom, 3, 6, 7, 11, 12, 17, 37, 93, 96-

100, 106-9, 112, 116, 119, 126-9.
Customary norms of performance, 26, 30, 34, 36, 37, 49, 56, 57, 58, 102-5.

Dahrendorf, Ralf, 65.
Davenport, John, 53, 56.
Decentralization, 122, 125, 126, 130, 151, 152.
Deference, 34, 46, 47, 64, 65, 67, 69, 77, 102, 114, 136, 139, 151.
Deference structure, 63-69, 71-74, 78, 79, 81, 93, 106, 126, 131; gerontocratic, 67-69; plutocratic, 67-72, 80, 93, 106, 120, 126, 131, 151.
Deism, 20, 133, 134, 137, 147, 148, 150.
Democracy, 63, 68, 69, 70, 125, 126.
Devlin, Patrick, 66.
Discipline, 41, 42, 44, 107, 123, 124.
Division of labor, 15, 60, 73, 74, 79, 88, 91, 96, 99, 108, 115, 116, 117, 131.
Dolbear, F. T., 103.
Douglas, Paul H., 95, 103.
Drawbacks, 88, 120.

Eckstein, Walther, 134.
Effective demand, 100, 107, 116.
Efficiency, economic, 62, 79, 85, 86, 89, 131.
Einstein, Albert, 139.
Elizabeth, Queen I, 127.
Empathy, 21, 22, 23.
Emulation, 45, 54, 64, 65, 102, 114; life of, 40, 42-48, 54.
Epicurus, 4, 79, 150.
Epistemology, 3, 5-7, 11, 14, 84, 134, 139, 142, 144.
Equality, 65, 125, 131.
Ethic, of common man, 37, 45-48, 54, 58, 110, 118, 119, 123, 126, 130, 143, 151; plutocratic, 55; of rich, 37, 45, 47, 117-19, 142, 143.
Eudoxus, 5.
Exchange, equitable rate of, 87, 95, 96, 98, 99, 106, 112, 123; rules of, 18, 95-99, 100, 101, 106; theory of exchange value, 84, 85, 87, 88, 92-106, 110-14.
Exports, encouragements of, 88, 120.

Fanaticism, 80, 81, 83, 119, 131, 132.
Fashion, 102, 104, 120, 129, 147, 148.
Fellow-feeling, 18, 21.
Feuer, Lewis, 150.
Firth, Roderick, 35, 36.
Forbes, Duncan, 68, 115.
Forcasting, 5, 6, 8, 92-3, 121, 135.
Freeman, R. D., 121.
Freud, Sigmund, 40, 146.
Functional autonomy, 40, 74, 75, 79, 121, 131.

Galileo, 4.
Gay, Peter, 18.
Gellner, Ernest, 54.
George, King III, 132.
Gide, C., 61.
Ginzberg, Eli, x, 83, 84, 107.
Goal displacement, 43, 75, 77, 78.
Goldstein, Leon J., 54.
Government, 8, 52, 60-83, 116, 118-28, 131, 135, 136, 138; commercial policies of, 62, 78, 80, 82, 85, 86, 88-90, 99, 105, 108, 110-32.
Grampp, William D., x, 28, 35, 39, 61, 62, 84, 98, 99, 100, 102, 108, 129, 130, 133.
Gratitude, 32, 47, 52, 136, 139.
Gray, Alexander, x, 1, 35, 55, 61, 84, 103, 107, 133.
Grotius, Hugo, 61.
Growth, economic, xiii, 86, 87, 95, 108, 114, 115, 123, 127, 130, 131.
Guthrie, W. K. C., 35.

Habit, 6, 11, 29, 34, 48-51, 64, 66, 74, 78, 81, 87, 90, 92, 99, 105, 107, 117-20, 123, 126, 130, 133.
Hamowy, Ronald, 73.
Happiness, 20, 50, 59, 101, 133, 138, 141, 144, 145.
Hart, H. L. A., 62, 66.
Hasbach, Wilhelm, 35, 61, 133.
Hayek, Friedrich, A., 53, 59, 99, 107, 108, 116.
Heilbroner, Robert L., 106.
Heimann, Edward, 57.
Hesiod, 135.

Hipparchus, 4.
History, theory of, xiii, 68.
Hobbes, Thomas, 1, 53, 59, 79, 108.
Hollander, Samuel, xv, 62, 112, 130, 132.
Holt, A., 89, 110.
Howell, Wilbur, 83.
Hume, David, ix, xv, 16, 17, 20, 22, 35, 39, 47, 62, 75, 76, 79, 104, 150.
Hutcheson, Francis, xv, 40, 79, 150.
Hutchison, T. W., 61, 83.

Imperialism, 89, 115, 118, 126.
Imports, restraints on, 88, 120.
Individualism, 39, 40, 53-9, 84, 103, 108.
Infant industries, 88, 120.
Ingram, J. K., 61.
Inquiry, criteria of, 4-10, 13, 14, 17, 62, 74, 82, 86, 95, 106, 137, 143; mechanics and, 1, 2, 3, 14, 15, 19, 39, 58; method of, 1-19, 40, 53-9, 64, 75, 76, 84, 85, 92, 108, 109, 113; see outlook; statistical analysis and, 28, 64, 89, 121.
Interest, class, 52, 150; of consumer, 100, 101, 103-05; customary, 17; diversity of, 25, 27; equal, 50; equitable or impartial degree of, 28, 30-33; extent possible, 34; in fortunes of others, 59; of the great society of mankind, 51; rooted in habit or peculiar circumstance, 29; image of, 28; level of, 25, 27-30; in maintaining society, 25; of the nation, 52, 89; opposed, 27; private, 52; of producers, 100-03; of those who live by profits, 89, 120; rate of, 97, 125; reconciliation of disparite, 25; regard to one's own, 55; self, 1, 39, 55, 59, 61, 75, 77, 78, 106, 119, 150; shared, 14, 15, 25; of society, 121; of speaker, 12, 13; unmediated, 27-29; vital, 25, 33.
Invisible hand, 56, 79.
Irregularities, 29, 30, 135, 136, 137, 147.

Jevons, W. Stanley, 103.
Jurisprudence, 21, 63, 88, 129.
Justice, 62, 65, 67, 72, 82, 85-87, 90-92, 99, 108, 110, 123, 129, 134, 145, 147,

149; administration of, 69-71, 78, 122-24; distributive, 70, 91, 102, 112, 128, 130, 131, 134, 147; duties in, 64-66, 123; lawfulness, 52, 130; maintenance of, 60; natural, 67, 92; remedial, 130, 131, 136, 140, 141, 145-48; rules of, 15, 38, 66, 85, 119, 120; sense of, 31, 47, 110, 123; social, 52; virtue of, 20, 21, 50, 51, 54, 148.
Justification, of a belief, 146; of commercial practice, 85, 130; of government, 60, 71, 72; of a practice, 47, 48, 57, 66, 93, 111, 116, 134, 142.

Kant, Immanuel, ix, 146.
Katona, George, 103.
Kauder, Emil, 103.
Kepler, 4, 5, 6.
Keynes, John M., xiii.
Kluckhohn, C., 37.
Kroeber, A., L., 37.
Kuhn, Thomas, xi, 18.

Labor, productive and unproductive, 84, 93, 114, 117; theory of value, 84, 93-98, 113.
Laird, John, 131, 132.
Laissez-faire, 60, 122, 151.
Land, 94, 96-98, 100, 113, 126, 128.
Language, 3, 11, 12, 13, 15, 73, 90, 116; grammar, 13, 14; rules of composition, 10, 73; semantics, 13, 14.
Law, apprenticeships, 91; causal, 5, 6, 53, 56, 139; corn, 132; entails, 127, 128; lawfulness, 52, 139; natural, 1, 2, 61, 147; poor, 91; primogeniture, 127, 128; of society, 44, 51, 59, 66-68, 72, 81, 91, 97, 119, 120, 123, 127, 129, 136.
Leadership, 65.
Legislators, 29, 80, 81, 88, 89, 105, 110, 119, 121, 122, 125, 132.
Legitimacy, 66, 72, 78, 106, 109, 110, 121, 126, 129.
Leser, E., 93.
Leslie, C., 1, 61, 133.
Liberalism, xiii, 62, 84.
Lindgren, J. Ralph, xv, xvi.
Locke, John, 53, 59, 61, 88.

Logic, 11, 14, 90, 113.
Lothian, J. M., xvi.
Love, of country, 52, 80; of pleasure, 41, 44, 45, 101; of praise, 20, 23, 44, 45, 54, 101; of praiseworthiness, 23, 48, 54; self, ix, 33, 34, 54, 101; of system, 17, 74, 78, 79, 109; of virtue, 17, 49, 145.
Lowe, Adolph, 115.

Macfie, A. L., 26, 59, 82, 133, 141, 144, 146, 148, 152.
Machines, 1, 14, 15, 73, 74, 76, 78, 81, 82, 94, 108, 109, 116.
Macpherson, C. B., 108.
Mandelbaum, Maurice, 54, 57.
Mandeville, Bernard de, 43, 55, 59, 79, 107.
Marshall, Alfred, 98, 107.
Marx, Karl, xiv, 58.
Massillon, Jean Bapiste, 134.
McClelland, David, 103.
Meek, Ronald L., 68.
Men of system, 4, 79, 83, 108, 110, 119, 123, 150.
Menger, Karl, 103.
Mercantilism, 87-92, 93, 110, 113.
Merton, Robert K., 79, 116.
Mill, John Stuart, xiii, 31, 53, 58, 59, 75, 85.
Millar, John, 82, 135, 144.
Misery, 45, 47, 52, 81, 91, 141.
Mitchell, Wesley C., xi.
Monarchy, 63, 68, 69, 70.
Money, 87-90, 92, 95, 99, 100, 104-5, 113, 124-5, 130, 131.
Monopoly spirit, 75, 107, 121.
Monotheism, 135-41, 144.
Moos, S., 114.
Moral, education, 41, 43, 44, 47, 129, 136, 142, 143; enforcement of, 60, 63-67, 71, 72, 120; faculties, 30, 40, 48, 146, 147; general rules of, 33, 34, 49, 82, 135-44, 148; judgment, 15, 20-38; judgment, criterion of, 26-30, 34, 36, 48, 49, 52; preferences, 17, 18, 36, 37, 63, 67, 72, 74, 77-79, 81-91, 92, 110, 120, 130, 131, 136, 137, 141-48, 150, 151; see sympathy.
Morrow, Glenn R., 18, 22, 23, 26, 39,

53, 54, 55, 56, 58, 59, 61, 103, 130, 133.
Mossner, E. C., 133.
Mun, Thomas, 88.
Myrdal, Gunnar, 17, 61, 83, 94, 95, 103.

Nash, Manning, 129.
National security, 68, 78, 88, 120, 122, 126.
Nations of hunters, 68-71, 96.
Nations of shepherds, 93.
Natural, see justice; see law; order, 61; rights, 61, 62, 147; see system of natural liberty; theology, 133, 135, 144.
Nature, 4, 8, 9, 10, 44, 51, 76, 137, 138, 139, 147, 148.
Newton, Isaac, 4, 5, 6, 83.
Nicholson, J. Shield, 115.

Object of practical consequence, 17, 23, 24, 25, 27, 28, 29, 33, 74.
Observation, 4, 6, 11, 31.
Ostracization, unwarranted, 144, 145, 147.
Otto, Rudolf, 136.
Outlook, 3, 4, 5, 86-8, 90, 92, 106, 110, 119, 134, 136, 138, 141, 148, 149-50.

Paradox of value, 103-5.
Passions, which take their origin in the body, 29, 108; selfish, 29, 50; social, 29, 51; unsocial, 29, 51.
Petrella, Frank, 122.
Philosophy, ix, 4, 8, 9, 15, 24, 73, 135, 136, 147; moral, 3, 5, 16-20, 29, 149; natural, 2, 3, 10, 15, 17, 18, 149.
Physiocrats, 89, 93, 111, 114.
Plato, 35, 81, 137.
Pleasure, life of, 40-43; love of, 41, 44, 45, 101.
Polanyi, Karl, 108, 129.
Political, authority, 60, 63-66, 70, 71, 72, 78, 80, 142-3, 150; economy, 20, 21, 55, 63, 83, 84-132, 148; obligation, 53, 60, 62, 63, 66, 72, 77.
Polytheism, 135, 136, 139, 140, 141.
Pope, Alexander, ix.

Popper, Karl R., 2, 53.
Population, 113, 114, 115.
Power, 16, 48, 69, 72, 93, 94, 95, 106, 111, 124-26, 135, 139.
Praise, 30, 45, 77; see love of.
Price, market, 92, 93, 98-100; natural, 61, 92, 97-101, 107, 116; real, 92-99, 103.
Private sector, 126.
Profit, 89, 97, 98, 100, 111, 112, 113, 120, 125.
Property, 61, 62, 70, 71, 72, 91, 94, 97, 125, 140, 151.
Propriety, 17, 30, 42, 48, 61, 62, 72, 74, 79, 82, 83, 106, 125, 139, 140, 141, 143, 146, 149, 150.
Protagoras, 35.
Providence, 1, 2, 7, 133, 138, 141.
Psychology, 22, 28, 39-53, 61, 84.
Ptolemy, 4, 5.
Public, debt, 118, 126; education, 78, 131; health, 79; works, 122, 126.
Pufendorf, Samuel, 59, 61.
Punishment, 32, 44, 62, 64, 65, 66, 69, 71, 134, 142.
Pythagoras, 135.

Quesnay, Francois, 119, 123.

Rae, John, 133.
Raphael, D. D., 133.
Rawls, John, 103, 116.
Reality, external, 5-7, 13, 137, 139, 140.
Reid, Thomas, ix.
Relativism, 36, 37.
Religion, function of, 143, 144, 148.
Religious convictions, influence of, 65, 133-35, 148-52; justification of, 135, 141, 142, 144, 146; nature of, 135, 141, 144-48.
Rent, 97, 100, 112, 113, 116.
Resentment, 18, 32, 47, 51, 61, 62, 64, 65, 66, 70, 120, 147.
Respectability, 22, 26, 47, 80, 101, 102, 104.
Reverence, 34, 41, 51, 65, 80, 129, 134, 136, 140, 146, 151.
Reward, 32, 134, 142.

Rheinholdus, 4.
Rhetoric, 20, 82-3, 85, 86, 90, 110, 134, 148.
Ricardo, David, 75, 95, 113.
Rist, C., 61.
Robertson, H. M., 93, 95, 103.
Robinson Crusoe, 42, 108.
Robinson, Joan, 83, 103.
Rosenberg, Nathan, 73, 102, 114, 121, 128.
Rousseau, Jean J., 59.

Salomon, Albert, 57.
Samuels, Warren J., 57, 100, 125.
Scarcity, 105, 114, 120.
Schumpeter, Joseph A., xi, 1, 20, 56, 61, 84, 93, 95, 99, 103.
Science, 2, 4, 8, 9, 17, 23, 24, 57, 116, 137, 140.
Scott, William R., 89, 91, 110, 131.
Searle, John R., 57, 116.
Selby-Bigge, L. A., 53, 55, 58.
Self, command, 41, 42, 47, 50, 52, 54; deceit, 33; see interest; see love.
Sense, of duty, 31, 138, 139, 143, 148, 149; see justice; of merit, 31, 32; of propriety, 17, 31, 32, 37; of remorse, 31.
Seward, John P., 40.
Shaftesbury, Anthony Ashley Cooper, 1st Earl of, 137.
Simon, Herbert A., 103.
Simplicity, 4, 12, 13, 14.
Small, Albion W., 57.
Sociability, 38.
Social, constitution, 52, 67, 68, 69, 71, 80, 81, 131, 150; contract, 61, 62.
Society, civil, 15; moral, 15; natural to man, 25, 38, 44, 59.
Sociology, xii, 57, 63, 75, 79, 86.
Socrates, 83.
Solon, 81, 132.
Sophists, 35.
Sovereignty, citizen, 56; consumer, 107, 123.
Spectator, average, 29, 30, 64; ideal, 35; impartial, 21, 25, 26, 28, 30, 31, 38, 43, 44, 48-51, 54, 56, 66, 141.
Spengler, Joseph J., 102, 115.

...za, Benedict, 150.
...hen, Leslie, 1, 20, 34, 35, 38.
...wart, Dugald, 78, 82, 108, 135, 144.
...tigler, George J., 84, 93, 95, 103.
Stoics, 35, 61, 79, 84, 132, 133, 137, 138, 141, 144, 147, 150.
Strong, G. B., 51, 115.
Surprise, 3, 4, 5, 140.
Sympathy, 10, 21, 22, 40, 45, 52, 54, 58, 64, 101, 102, 107, 123, 136, 141; aesthetic, 23-25, 27, 30, 76, 108, 140, 141; modes of, 25, 30-34; moral, 18, 24, 25, 28, 30, 31, 44, 48, 74, 120, 141; sources of distortion of, 26-30, 33, 108.
System of natural liberty, 61, 119-20, 122.

Taste, 16, 17, 23, 112, 127, 129, 144.
Tawney, R. H., 152.
Taxes, 113, 126-27, 128.
Taylor, O. H., 2, 7, 21, 22, 28, 39, 84, 93, 95, 99, 100, 103, 113, 133.
Taylor, W. L., 93, 95, 103.
Theism, 1, 14, 137, 139.
Thompson, H. F., 2, 6, 11.
Tobin, J., 103.
Tocqueville, Alexis de, 58.
Townsend, Charles, 108.

Unintended consequences, 66, 71, 108, 116, 130, 147; see functional autonomy; see value displacement.
Usuary, 125.
Utilitarianism, 16, 35, 66, 75, 82, 84, 130.
Utility, 16, 17, 35, 47, 49, 62, 66, 72, 74-9, 81, 82, 83, 86, 103, 104, 122, 147, 148.

Value displacement, 16, 47, 72, 74-78, 79, 82, 107, 121.
Vanity, 23, 43, 44, 47, 129, 134, 139.
Veblen, Thorstein, 103, 105.
Viner, Jacob, x, 1, 2, 7, 35, 60, 61, 78, 122, 133.

Virtue, 17, 20, 21, 26, 30, 48-55, 67, 79, 107, 138, 139, 145; benevolence, 38, 49, 51, 52, 54, 69, 80, 148, 149; see justice; life of, 40, 48-53; see love of; modesty, 20; prudence, 34, 38, 47, 49, 52, 54, 97, 108, 128, 130, 148; self-command, 41, 42, 47, 50, 52, 54; veracity, 20.
Vision, rules of perspective, 27; objects of, 26-7, 139.

Wages, 55, 96, 98, 100, 102, 112, 113, 116, 117, 131.
Watkins, J. W. N., 53.
Wealth, care of, 50; causes of improvement of, 86, 88-90, 105, 112, 114-28; desire to better one's condition by the accumulation of, 45, 54, 55, 77, 101, 102, 116, 118, 123; disinterested admiration of, 46, 55, 65, 77, 102, 151; distribution of, 70, 91, 102, 112, 121, 122, 125, 126, 128, 130, 131, 134, 147, 151; measurement of, 91, 94-101, 112-14; nature of, 92-95, 106, 110-14, 125; popular notion of, 88-90; pursuit of, 16, 45, 46, 48, 54, 55, 77, 84, 101-05, 129, 130.
Wealth of Nations, interpretation of, ix-xi, 84, 85, 107, 129; purpose of, xiv, 62, 80, 84, 96, 110, 129; strategy of, 80-83, 85-87, 110.
Wellman, Carl, 37.
West, E. G., 28, 58, 73.
Westermarck, E., 36.
Winch, Peter, 18, 66, 142.
Wisdom, xiii, 47, 48, 51, 52, 54, 58, 66, 67, 80, 89, 121, 134, 138, 148.
Wolin, Sheldon, xiii, xiv, 63, 79, 108.
Wollaston, William, 137.
Wollheim, Richard, 108.
Wonder, 3, 4, 5, 7, 8, 9, 47, 76, 135, 139, 140, 149.

Zeno (of Elea), 150.
Zeyss, R., 61.